JUN. 1 8 1992

LADY BOUNTIFUL REVISITED

D0139521

THE FOUNDATION CENTER
CLEVELAND FIELD OFFICE
1422 EUCLID AVENUE, SUITE 1356
CLEVELAND, OHIO 44115-2001

JUN. 1 8 1992
' 97
$14 00

LADY BOUNTIFUL

REVISITED: Women,

Philanthropy, and

Power

Edited by
KATHLEEN D. McCARTHY

THE FOUNDATION CENTER
CLEVELAND FIELD OFFICE
1422 EUCLID AVENUE, SUITE 1356
CLEVELAND, OHIO 44115-2001

RUTGERS UNIVERSITY PRESS   New Brunswick and London

Ph

Copyright © 1990 by Rutgers, the State University
All rights reserved
Manufactured in the United States

Library of Congress Cataloging-in-Publication Data

Lady bountiful revisited : women, philanthropy, and power / edited by
Kathleen D. McCarthy.
p.   cm.
Includes bibliographical references.
ISBN 0-8135-1598-X (cloth)   ISBN 0-8135-1611-0 (pbk.)
1. Women volunteers in social service—Cross-cultural studies.
2. Women volunteers in social service—United States. 3. Women
philanthropists—Cross-cultural studies. 4. Women philanthropists—
United States. 5. Voluntarism—Cross-cultural studies.
6. Voluntarism—United States. I. McCarthy, Kathleen D.
HV40.42.L33   1990
361.3'7'082—dc20   90-32549
CIP

British Cataloging-in-Publication information available

For
MY PARENTS

CONTENTS

PREFACE

Lady Bountiful is a stock figure in the gallery of feminine stereotypes, yet this image often obscures more than it explains. Women's giving and voluntarism have played a central, albeit unheralded role in women's history, providing access to power outside the masculine realms of government and commerce. Through gifts of time and money, women have built institutions, provided charitable services, secured the vote, challenged racial and ethnic stereotypes, and opened professions to other women. They have also carved out "invisible careers" for themselves, pursuing distinctive forms of female entrepreneurship.[1]

Yet these activities have rarely been studied as philanthropy per se. Instead, scholars have turned to women's voluntary associations to trace the roots of American feminism, familial relations, female "personalism," and specific charitable and social reforms.[2] A few researchers have also recently begun to explore differences among women's groups. Thus, Nancy Hewitt sifted Rochester's reformers into benevolent, evangelical, and radical groups, and Christine Stansell probed the cultural clashes that lay beneath the surface of charitable exchange. In the process, feminist scholars have moved beyond earlier "social control" paradigms to examine the impact of these exchanges within the larger society, and among the participants themselves.[3]

The following essays amplify and refine these discussions. First presented at a 1987 conference on "Women and Philanthropy: Past, Present and Future" convened by the Center for the Study of Philanthropy of the Graduate School and University Center, City University of New York, these essays examine theoretical issues, international comparisons, and the impact of ethnicity and class in shaping women's responses to emerging opportunities and needs. As such, the volume not only illuminates existing knowledge about middle-class and elite Anglo-Saxon women's activities, but also opens up new fields of inquiry by focusing on voluntarism among their immigrant, Afro-American, Mexican, Russian, and French counterparts. These studies demonstrate both the diversity of female voluntary efforts and the ways in which they enabled women to gain access to power.

My introductory essay provides an overview of the relationship between women's public roles and their voluntary sector efforts both in the United States and overseas. The following section focuses on the American scene, beginning with Anne Firor Scott's essay, which provides a chronological framework for studying women's voluntary associations. While Scott adopts a fairly consensual approach, Nancy Hewitt and Darlene Clark Hine stress the impact of class, ethnic, and racial differences in shaping the contours of women's voluntary sector activities. Hewitt's essay examines the shifting fortunes of Anglo and Hispanic women's voluntary associations in Tampa, Florida, while Hine underscores the enduring importance of female voluntarism within the black community. As Hine points out, black women have historically used their organizations to bolster racial self-esteem, mitigate discrimination, and forge essential networks for reform. Kathryn Kish Sklar provides yet another perspective, examining the role of women's networks in providing the financial underpinnings for one of the nation's leading social settlements.

The second section deals with the social and political context of women's philanthropy outside the United States. Edith Couturier's article explores the differing charitable activities of women and men in colonial Mexico, while Brenda Meehan-Waters's underscores the role of female donors and volunteers in empowering, supporting, and ministering to other women in Czarist Russia. Alisa Klaus's essay compares women's participation in the infant welfare movement in France and the United States, examining the links between voluntarism and access to governmental policymaking positions. Ellen Ross's essay shifts the focus to comparable efforts in Victorian England, exploring relations between women volunteers and those they sought to aid, and the ways in which class considerations shaped middle class responses to the needs of the poor.

Several common denominators that typify feminine largesse emerge from these discussions: an abiding interest in helping women and children; a tendency to move into gaps overlooked by government and male donors and volunteers; and a desire to exercise power. Some women created alternative families through their donations of time and money; others forged enduring networks for reform. Many of these activities were heavily tinged with class, ethnic, and racial concerns. More, certainly, needs to be known about the causes and groups that attracted women donors; the class, communal, and gender considerations that shaped their decisions; the differential roles played by women and men; the nature and extent of comparable activities outside the United States; and the impact of feminist gains.

What is clear is that giving and voluntarism have traditionally provided—and continue to provide—the means through which women have grasped, wielded, and maintained public power—not only in America, but overseas as well. As such, philanthropy lies at the heart of women's history.

NOTES

1   On the latter point, see Arlene Kaplan Daniels, *Invisible Careers: Women Civic Leaders from the Volunteer World* (Chicago: University of Chicago Press, 1987).

2   See, for example, Barbara J. Berg, *The Remembered Gate: Origins of American Feminism: The Woman and the City, 1800–1860* (New York: Oxford University Press, 1978); Keith Melder, *Beginnings of Sisterhood: The American Woman's Rights Movement, 1800–1850* (New York: Schocken Books, 1977); Nancy F. Cott, *The Bonds of Womanhood: Woman's Sphere in New England, 1780–1835* (New Haven: Yale University Press, 1977); Carroll Smith-Rosenberg, "Beauty, the Beast, and the Militant Woman: A Case Study in Sex Roles and Social Stress in Jacksonian America," *American Quarterly* 23 (1971), 562–584; Mary P. Ryan, *Cradle of the Middle Class: The Family in Oneida County, New York, 1790–1865* (New York: Cambridge University Press, 1981); Suzanne Lebsock, *The Free Women of Petersburg: Status and Culture in a Southern Town, 1784–1860* (New York: W. W. Norton, 1984); Kathleen D. McCarthy, *Noblesse Oblige: Charity and Cultural Philanthropy in Chicago, 1849–1929* (Chicago: University of Chicago Press, 1982); Carroll Smith-Rosenberg, *Religion and the Rise of the American City: The New York City Mission Movement, 1812–1870* (Ithaca: Cornell University Press, 1971); Ruth Bordin, *Women and Temperance: The Quest for Power and Liberty, 1873–1900* (Philadelphia: Temple University Press, 1981).

3   Nancy A. Hewitt, *Women's Activism and Social Change: Rochester, New York, 1822–1872* (Ithaca: Cornell University Press, 1984); Christine Stansell, *City of Women: Sex and Class in New York, 1789–1860* (New York: Alfred A. Knopf, 1986). See also, Sara M. Evans, *Born for Liberty: A History of Women in America* (New York: The Free Press, 1989), and Anne M. Boylan, "Timid Girls, Venerable Widows and Dignified Matrons: Life Cycle Patterns Among Organized Women in New York and Boston, 1797–1840," *American Quarterly* 38 (1986), 779–797.

ACKNOWLEDGMENTS

Many people have helped to bring this volume to fruition. First, and most important, were the authors and conference participants themselves, all of whom deserve special thanks for their participation, their interest, and their continuing moral support. I am particularly grateful to Nancy Hewitt for her perceptive editorial suggestions. The Ford Foundation underwrote the meeting, and Barry Gaberman and David Arnold have helped the Center immeasurably through their unflagging kindness and enthusiasm. Harold Proshansky, Steven M. Cahn, Solomon Goldstein, Virginia Hodgkinson, Elizabeth Boris, Francis X. Sutton, Nathan Huggins, Robert Payton, Stanley N. Katz, and Diana Newell Rockefeller also played an important part in the Center's development and continuing success. Elsa Ruiz, John Pereira, Glenn Speer, David Briskin, Andrew Wax, Richard Greenwald, Janis Ruden, J. K. Curry, Marcus Wessendorf, Jennifer Ohman, Pearl Fread, and Farhang Mirfakhraei have helped in more ways than they know. To my parents, my sister, Magda Ratajski, Francois Gabriel, Jim and Valerie Smith, Kenneth Arnold, Mauro Calamandrei, Pauline Pinto, Dick and Debby Kotz, Malcolm Richardson, Katherine Little, and all my other good and gentle friends who stood by me these past two years, I owe a far greater debt of gratitude than I can ever repay. The publication of this volume is a tribute to them all.

KATHLEEN D. McCARTHY

Parallel Power Structures:

Women and the Voluntary Sphere

The enduring caricature of Lady Bountiful has served to stigmatize women's philanthropy, often trivializing its presence on the American scene. Nonetheless, the legacy of the women who participated in charitable and philanthropic movements is impressive, ranging from the creation of new institutions and professions to Constitutional reform. Women have traditionally used these activities to wield power in societies intent upon rendering them powerless. Unlike men, who enjoyed a host of political, commercial, and social options in their pursuit of meaningful careers, women most often turned to nonprofit institutions and reform associations as their primary points of access to public roles. In the process, they forged parallel power structures to those used by men, creating a growing array of opportunities for their sisters and themselves.[1]

This essay provides an overview of five distinctive aspects of women's efforts within the voluntary sphere. The first section, on institutional development, examines the efforts of women and men in providing organizational responses to public needs, ranging from charitable to cultural endeavors. The section on social movements focuses on the impact of women's reform initiatives, both among the constituencies they sought to aid and among themselves. The analysis of the ways in which women used nongovernmental organizations to effect political reform considers the ways in which prevailing political ideologies have shaped women's choices and campaigns. The section on donations centers on the ways in which women have used their contributions to leverage new opportunities and careers. The final

1

section seeks to place American trends within the context of comparable practices in selected countries overseas. In each, the common denominator is power, and the ways in which women have used their charitable, social, and political movements to recast the contours of their public sphere.

Institutional Development

In 1797 a band of New York women gathered together to form a new institution. Their mission was well defined, their goal direct. As they explained, because no other charitable resources existed to succor that "large class of sufferers who have peculiar claims on the public beneficence, poor widows with small children," they had elected to do it themselves. Although the Society for the Relief of Poor Widows with Small Children (SRPWC) was one of the first female relief organizations founded in the United States, the members of the newly formed board had a clear idea of what they wanted to do, and how to it. Prospective clients were to be visited in their homes, and women of dubious moral character winnowed from their more deserving counterparts. "Immorality," the board members firmly resolved, "excludes from the patronage of the Society." For those who qualified, relief would be given in the form of "necessaries," rather than cash, except by special dispensation of the board. The funds for these beneficences were to be culled in two ways: through $3 annual subscriptions from members and contributions from solicitous males who, although barred from membership, were assured that their donations would be entered "with peculiar pleasure on the list of Benefactors."[2]

Gifts of "necessaries," would, of course, come heavily interlarded with sisterly advice. The managers vowed to find schools for the children who indirectly came under their care, and work for their impecunious mothers. The board members had particularly strong views about the proper disposition of the children, noting their intention to withhold aid from any applicant "who refuses to put out at service to trades, such of her Children as are fit; and to place the younger ones of a proper age, at a Charity School." Despite the stern tone of their warning, these women envisioned forming personal relationships with those they sought to serve; transferring applicants from one manager to another was roundly discouraged.[3]

As in the case of many early charities, their attitude evokes an ambivalent response. While the board members' notions about other people's children seem unduly intrusive to the modern observer, their courage and commitment were undeniable. New York was an extremely unhealthy place during the society's infancy. In 1798 and 1799, the city was racked by yellow fever epidemics. Those who could, fled to the countryside. Yet several of the society's board members tarried in the city to minister to their wards, "at risk of their lives," proffering consolation, food, advice, and medicine to those in need. Whether the current epidemic was yellow fever, whooping cough, scarlet fever, or smallpox, these women persisted in their rounds, visiting the homes of the widows they had chosen to aid.[4]

In part, their actions were inspired by empathy. "WIDOW is a word of sorrow in the best of circumstances: but a widow, left poor, destitute, friendless, surrounded with a number of small Children shivering with cold, pale with want . . . her situation is neither to be described nor conceived!" In an era of jarringly high death rates, the founders must have readily identified with the fate of the women they sought to aid. But they were not entirely swayed by images of blameless suffering, for—as they pointed out—the artisan class had a bad habit of living "not only plentifully, but luxuriously" and "our poor widows have been partners in the evil, and now sustain the whole of the punishment." The society's task, as they saw it, was to help these hapless women to "learn oeconomy [*sic*] from adversity," and set them on the road to self-support. Toward this end, much of their available cash was invested in fabric—nearly three thousand yards of it were purchased within the first three years—and distributed to the widows as a means of enabling them to sew their way to financial security. Each woman helped off charity was celebrated as a victory, not only for the society, but as a testimonial to the "industry and frugality" of the widows themselves.[5]

Their businesslike approach was echoed in the society's organizational form as well. Lack of previous experience notwithstanding, these women were obviously adept at promoting their cause. Within the first year more than two hundred annual subscribers had been secured, and over $1,000 in donations culled from members and sympathetic men.

They were also extremely clear about their collective prerogatives. Granted in 1802, the society's formal act of incorporation limited participation to women. Subscribers were duly anointed "a Body Corporate" and legally empowered to "have perpetual succession, be in law capable of suing and being sued, defending and being defended, in all courts and places . . . and shall also . . . be capable in law of purchasing, holding, and conveying any estate, real or personal, for the use of the said Corporation, *Provided,* that such estate shall never exceed in value Fifty Thousand Dollars, nor be applied to any other purposes than the charitable one for which this Incorporation is formed." Just in case, however, the state deemed it prudent to add that members' husbands would be exempted for "any loss occasioned by the neglect or malfeasance of his wife." Only if the man himself pilfered the funds would his estate be liable for repayment. Nonetheless, in an era when Married Women's Property Acts were still far in the future, this must have provided a fairly heady measure of responsibility.[6]

The SRPWC highlighted a host of themes that came to typify female philanthropy. It was devised to aid a narrowly defined constituency, women and children, as were the majority of charities founded by women in the nineteenth century. It blended a significant degree of personal commitment and labor by the participants with small-scale fund raising and modest donations. It placed a strong emphasis on securing the means of self-support for other women. "Personalism" was also a factor: the board members identified with their charges and sought to establish ongoing relationships and programs tailored to individual needs. And, in their corporate state, participation expanded the board members' legal options, enabling them to own and alienate property, go to court, and superintend the futures of those they sought to aid. It gave them an enhanced public role, and a toehold in public policymaking processes.[7]

Yet these were only minor gains in comparison to the range of options available to men. Philanthropy was just one of many routes to public stature open to men in the decades after the Revolution. Even within the philanthropic sphere, male alternatives were more varied, and the avenues for participation more complex. During the first half of the nineteenth century, most women entered charitable work via the church. First, the community would define a need, such as sheltering orphans, and then the task of institutional development would be turned over to interdenominational boards of directresses culled from local congregations. Although American religion became "feminized" in the aftermath of the Revolution, men also used their churches as conduits into a welter of social and charitable reforms, including Bible and tract societies and temperance work. Civic obligations played a role in drawing men into the charitable arena. So did affinity groups: history buffs, fledgling connoisseurs, and burgeoning literati coalesced into inward-turning cliques for self-improvement and cultural uplift. Their efforts were often bolstered by civic motives, since cities with cultural amenities had a competitive edge in the rough and tumble game of urban rivalry. Professional considerations were another lure. Doctors, for example, often founded and served in dispensaries and hospitals, which provided opportunities to hone their skills on impoverished patients.[8]

Benevolent Ladies operated in a more constricted sphere. Cultural institutions are a case in point. Organizations for the promotion of the fine arts, such as the American Art-Union or the Pennsylvania Academy of Fine Arts, often traced their origins to subtle webs of masculine relationships that wedded business, professional, and cultural aims in extraordinary ways. Male artists and their patrons often traveled together, they promoted each others' professional wares among their acquaintances and peers, they dined together and occasionally translated these social relationships into more formal men's clubs such as the Century Association. Women were excluded from these social, professional, and institutional roles for a variety of reasons. Many of these early ventures were begun as joint stock companies, relying on heavy infusions of cash from their members to keep them afloat during times of economic duress. Women's organizations tended to subsist on small amounts of cash backed by substantial contributions of personal labor. But while domestic skills could handily run an asylum, they were superfluous in cultural institutions where the standard bill of fare included signing contracts for exhibitions, managing the transportation of valuable consignments, and devising legal mechanisms such as joint stock companies to keep the institution solvent. Denied control of their own funds by the common law doctrine of *femme couverte*, matrons also lacked the requisite business experience to run a cultural venture.

Nor did they have the necessary public sanctions to comfortably promote public cultural ventures. The justification for women's participation in antebellum charities and reform crusades was primarily domestic. Under the banner of religion, the ideology of Republican Motherhood, and the cult of domesticity, women broadened their range of maternal responsibilities beyond the home to encompass the needs of dependents and the dispossessed. When causes strayed toward more secular aims, their claims to moral authority became more tenuous. In many quarters bluestockings were greeted with a degree of public derision that few Benevolent Ladies would have comfortably borne. Conversely, those who stayed within their duly appointed sphere were rewarded with opportunities to carve out "invisible careers" that paralleled the more public roles of their brothers, spouses, and sires.[9]

In the process, Benevolent Ladies formed "an identifiable women's culture" centered on charities, nourished by "a special combination of sisterhood and ambition," and reinforced by a "dense network of relationships with other women . . . based on kinship, neighborhood, and common experience[s]" rooted in "mutual support in times of childbearing, sickness and mourning."[10]

As the American frontier extended toward the Pacific, these networks stretched across the nation. For women shorn of family and friends by the westward exodus, charitable ventures provided new communities, new support networks, and new challenges. By the 1920s, the gender-segregated initiatives that were borne of these relationships had lost much of their appeal. But in the nineteenth century, women's culture and women's charities played a central role in many women's lives.

Anne Firor Scott's essay provides a chronological framework for studying these trends within the broader context of women's activism and highlights other functions that these organizations have served. She also charts their increasingly secular cast, as women diverted their attention to the Charity Organization Society movement and to volunteer programs inspired by women's clubs, social settlements, and similar institutions in the decades after the Civil War. As Scott explains, women's voluntary associations afforded an "early warning system" for targeting emerging social needs, as well as alternative methods for redressing them. Participation in these organizations also honed their members' leadership skills and self-confidence, drawing them into an ever-widening sphere of public responsibilities.[11]

Other essays focus on the factors that separated women's groups. Significant distinctions existed even within the narrow realm of charitable endeavors, a theme eloquently highlighted in the essays by Nancy Hewitt and Darlene Clark Hine. The influx of waves of immigrants intensified the span of organizational diversity, adding a range of new institutions along a continuum ranging from mutual aid to social and political activism. These organizations served a variety of needs neglected by community-wide and predominantly native-born charitable groups, providing essential services and funds in time of need, affording new avenues for sociability, softening the shock of assimilation, and helping to forge a nationalistic sense of identity among the newcomers. Irish, Germans, Italians, Slavs, and a range of other ethnic groups: each in turn devised their own institutional solutions to their special social aspirations and needs.

Irish women grafted their organizations onto the Church. Because cultural barriers prevented many Irish women from approaching non-Catholic institutions for help, they turned instead to religious orders, or like Mary Lunney, founded asylums to aid other Irish women in need. These traditions were carried into the twentieth century by subsequent waves of newcomers. For example, women in Slavic settlements on Chicago's South Side gravitated most readily toward church-related sewing circles, sodalities, and sectarian auxiliaries of national groups such as the Polish Women's Alliance.[12]

Nancy Hewitt's essay on women in Tampa's Latin community surveys the role of ethnicity, class, and political events in generating institutional responses and mutual aid. She illuminates other important themes as well, such as the role of participation in "Anglo" charities in fostering assimilation into the local elite. At the same time, Hewitt notes the role that Cuban women played in reproducing Havana-based organizations in their new homeland, such as a benefit society to coordinate refugee relief efforts in 1896. Future research may reveal under what conditions members of various ethnic groups adopted American models when they founded their institutions, or replicated patterns imported from their host countries.[13]

Darlene Clark Hine emphasizes solidarities rather than fissures. Voluntarism within the black community has a long and venerable history, stretching back to the eighteenth century. Founded in 1778, Philadelphia's Free African Society set the pattern for the innumerable mutual aid groups that would follow. In return for modest donations of twenty-five cents per week, members were assured of the availability of modest sums to tide them over an array of emergencies, ranging from sickness to death. Shortly afterwards, in 1793, the city's minority women entered the mutual aid arena with the Female Benevolent Society of St. Thomas, to be followed in turn by an array of *dorcas* (sewing) societies, benevolent societies, and even literary groups.

Hine traces these organizational activities into the twentieth century, with the founding of Phillis Wheatley homes and black women's clubs, stressing the ideological implications embodied in their campaigns. As she points out, a primary aim of black women's charities and cultural ventures was to rescue black women from social, sexual, and economic exploitation and to combat racial stereotypes, since "as long as the larger society viewed black women as whores and prostitutes, they remained powerless." Like the founders of countless charities before them, women such as Jane Edna Hunter and Nannie H. Burroughs used philanthropy to transform negative public perceptions of black women's character and to raise appreciation and recognition of their contributions to black survival.[14]

Social Reform

Mark Twain once quipped that "nothing so needs reforming as other people's habits," and women proved no more able to resist the lure of social reform than men. Nancy Hewitt's carefully detailed analysis of women's activism and social change in antebellum Rochester delineates the differing venues of women's philanthropic domain. Reform groups, which were often more radical than those devoted to straightforward charitable work, sought to remedy social ills through noninstitutional means. Rooted in an eager faith in human perfectability, these groups ultimately helped to reshape their proponents' lives as well, carving out new interpretations of gender, geography, and class.[15]

The role of Female Moral Reform Societies has been particularly well researched. Antebellum urbanization engendered a panoply of social ills in its wake, not the least of which was a burgeoning trade in prostitution. Sexual misconduct proved to be a particularly compelling cause for women reformers for a number of reasons. Prostitution posed a constant threat to the sanctity of the family, and significant health risks as well, since venereal diseases were still incurable and wayward husbands could easily pass infections picked up in the bordello to their innocent wives. Moreover, the presence of brothels served as a constant reminder of the limits of wifely influence within the home. They also represented a religious affront, since prostitution was clearly a sin, as well as a repudiation of emerging middle-class values and familial norms.

Poverty, immigration, and broken homes swelled the ranks of urban prostitutes in the decades before the Civil War, trends dutifully charted by social observers such as John McDowall, a former divinity student who published two popular exposés of prostitution in New York: The Magdalen Report, and Magdalen Facts, which alleged that a legion of ten thousand "malevolent and cruel" harlots were plying the city's streets. Galvanized by his findings, a group of women formed a Magdalen Society in 1832, which was followed by the Female Moral Reform Society two years later. Unable to contain their enthusiasm, the founders vowed to clone auxiliaries in every city and village in the United States. As of 1836 they had crafted sixty-six new chapters; by 1840, the number had risen to over five hundred. This vast empire was held together not only by sisterly spirit and collective indignation, but also through its national publication entitled *The Advocate for Moral Reform*, which claimed over sixteen thousand readers at its peak.[16]

Begun as a mechanism for combating vice, the society soon evolved into a weapon in women's attack on the double standard. To bolster their campaign, its members began to publish the names of brothel patrons in their columns, storming local bordellos in search of converts as well as erring males. Their research helped to illuminate the causes of feminine poverty as well, giving yet another slant to women's charitable concerns.

The moral reform movement produced a windfall of changes that reached well beyond its stated aims. Although prostitution continued to flourish, the society's efforts helped to reshape Victorian notions about feminine demeanor and sexual mores. Revolutionary theorists justified women's dependent political status with arguments steeped in ill-concealed misogyny. By their reasoning, women were immodest, easily corrupted, and hopelessly vain. They needed the firm hand of patriarchal guidance to keep their passions in check and curb the threat of their presence within the nascent Republic. The moral reform societies' exposés substantially recast these notions by highlighting the themes of female victimization and masculine sexual excess. In the process, they provided a key crucible in which Victorian mores and notions of women's moral superiority were promulgated and cast. To quote Nancy Cott, "the language of moral reform evoked women's power: power to revenge, power to control and reform."[17]

It also helped to alter the social geography of the city. As Christine Stansell notes in her book, *City of Women*, prior to the 1830s, few respectable women dared to venture into New York's business district, much less commercial establishments such as restaurants, unaccompanied by a man. The Moral Reform Society gave them new license to go where they pleased, even into "the most powerfully tabooed spots for women in the entire city," the oblique demimonde of "male sexual terrain."[18]

Antebellum reform associations helped to recast the boundaries of class as well as gender. In Stansell's words, evangelical moral reform groups "served as a nexus of social identity, an impulse toward self-definition, a need to avow publicly one's own class aspirations which led people to seek each other out across a range of incomes and occupations, differentiating themselves from the classes above and below them."[19]

These differences revealed themselves in widely divergent attitudes about hygiene, privacy, and childrearing practices. Benevolent Ladies and social activists alike were often repulsed by the conditions that greeted them on entering the homes of the poor. At a time when middle-class families were becoming increasingly insular and privatized, working-class families were spilling onto the streets. Stansell does a particularly good job of outlining these cultural conflicts, as middle-class reformers sought to "domesticate" the women of the slums. In effect, these encounters embodied a clash of cultures in which volunteers evinced little sympathy for the noisy sociability, the earthy courtship practices, and the lenient childrearing methods of their impoverished peers. Ellen Ross's essay captures the essence of similar clashes in late Victorian England, as child welfare workers of various sorts infiltrated the homes of the poor and sought to revise their maternal roles.[20]

Whether these programs helped their intended charges, or simply evoked new sources of friction between the classes, remains open to debate. Ross outlines not only the psychological dimensions of "the good mother/bad mother" debates, but also some of the results. As she explains, many infant welfare organizations ended by merely harassing the working-class mothers they sought to aid, rather than helping to secure needed clothing and food. In policymaking terms, then, the London-based groups had a decidedly negative effect.

Their legacies are more clearly etched within the lives of the volunteers themselves. Under the rubric of religion and maternal solicitude, women used their reform organizations as they used their charities, to expand the parameters of their influence and reshape public discourse on the content and meaning of their lives.

Political Reform

Voluntary associations played a crucial political role as well. While men exercised the option of effecting social change through partisan politics, "women carried out social policy through voluntary action." The long campaign for women's enfranchisement serves as an ideal laboratory for tracing the political implications of feminine philanthropy in the United States.[21]

Despite their ostensibly nonpolitical status, voluntary associations have historically provided one of the primary mechanisms for that most fundamental and far-reaching aspect of political change, Constitutional reform. Indeed, these institutions draw their legitimacy from the Constitution itself. Under the provisions of the First Amendment, citizens are guaranteed not only freedom of religion, speech, and the press, but also of "the right of the people peaceably to assemble, and to petition the government for a redress of grievances." In effect, voluntary associations play an indispensable political role in this society by providing ongoing mechanisms for peaceful, gradualist change.

Women's participation in more direct forms of political action was far more limited. Ironically, American women were not specifically disfranchised by the architects of the new republic; they were simply ignored. They are neither mentioned specifically in the Constitution, nor in the Federalist Papers that cadenced the nationalist debates.

Indeed, the latter documents contain only one reference to women's role, warning of the dangers posed by the political intrigues of courtesans and the mistresses of public figures. This silence masked a welter of social and political concerns, one of the most important of which was women's subservient status under common law. Under the doctrine of femme couverte, wives (and this was an era in which most women married) forfeited control of their estates, their possessions, and their future wages to their spouses upon marriage. Since the authors of the Constitution believed that political rights stemmed from property ownership, the ability of the majority of the nation's women to make independent political judgments apart from the influence of their spouses was therefore politically suspect. Technically "covered" by their husbands' legal identity, they were doomed to political invisibility as well.[22]

Added to this were philosophical arguments that held that while men were ostensibly rational beings, women were closer to nature, more governed by their emotions, and therefore better suited to nurturing, maternal roles. The upshot of all of this was that while men's public, political roles were justified by their supposed ability to make informed, rational decisions, women's political roles were cast in a more domestic idiom under the guise of Republican Motherhood. Rather than voting, their task was to preserve the Republic by rearing successive generations of responsible, enlightened citizens.

The tension between the egalitarian rhetoric in which the Revolution and the Constitution were forged, and the domestic, maternal justification for women's political role was to have profound implications for the strategies adopted by women's voluntary associations in their quest for political power. While the champions of suffrage rights for black males forwarded their claims under the banner of social and political justice, women adopted a different rationale. Rather than demanding change in the name of simple justice, equity, or egalitarian norms, they made their greatest impact when they cast their arguments in the idiom of hearth and home.

The history of the suffrage movement underscores the difficulties inherent in sustaining this approach. The relationship of feminism and the suffrage campaign to the abolitionist movement is well known. Female abolitionists made significant contributions to the movement's success, garnering contributions, circulating petitions, addressing audiences, and opening their homes as way stations on the underground railroad. In the process, the abolitionist movement served as a training ground for leading feminists, including such pioneers as Elizabeth Cady Stanton and her colleague, Susan B. Anthony. Yet despite their contributions, women were ultimately asked to set aside their feminist agenda, including the demand for equal suffrage, in order to ensure passage of the Fifteenth Amendment giving black males the right to vote.[23]

This in turn raises intriguing questions about how a radical fringe movement within a movement—the feminist quest for feminist gains, including the right to vote—succeeded in becoming a mainstream crusade by the opening decades of the twentieth century. Hewitt's book on women's groups in Rochester, New York, does an especially effective job of underscoring the distinctions that separated the constituents of various types of causes. While the wives of Rochester's social and commercial leaders created charities, evangelical perfectionists turned their attention to moral reform crusades to curb the excesses of liquor and vice. The more radical elements who espoused abolitionism and women's rights stood at the fringes of the local commercial circles, and as such had the least to lose by advocating the sweeping social, legal, and economic reforms and fundamental political changes that their campaigns entailed.[24]

Indeed, the image of the defiantly bloomer-clad feminist of the mid-nineteenth century contrasts sharply with her Progressive-era counterparts, who ran the gamut from committed ideologues chaining themselves to the White House gates, to moderate reformers and settlement workers such as Jane Addams, to socialists and middle-class clubwomen from the hinterland, and sedate society matrons such as Louisine Havemeyer and Mrs. Potter Palmer. The changing rhetoric of the women's movement provides an important clue to the emergence of this complex coalition. Reduced to its simplest terms, it is possible to trace at least three differing, yet increasingly inclusive rationales for promoting the female franchise between 1878, when the suffrage amendment was first introduced in Congress, and 1919 when it was finally passed.

The fiery rhetoric of an Elizabeth Cady Stanton was uncompromisingly egalitarian. Her Declaration at the Seneca Falls Convention of 1848 borrowed liberally from the sentiments of Thomas

Jefferson, declaring that "we hold these truths to be self-evident: that all men and women are created equal." A straightforward approach, but one that was fraught with problems, since it directly challenged the notion of separate spheres embodied in the ideologies of Republican Motherhood and the cult of domesticity, which were used by many women as the basis for their participation in charities and social reform. As a result, early equal rights advocates faced social ostracism for their unladylike behavior, public ridicule for attempting to invade masculine terrain, and censure from other women activists who were working along different ideological lines. None of this was a particularly appealing prospect, and taken together it undoubtedly deterred many Benevolent Ladies and moral reformers from embracing more radical demands for suffrage and equal rights during the antebellum years.[25]

The movement's appeal was broadened during the Gilded Age through the spread of the Women's Christian Temperance Union (WCTU). Under the able stewardship of Frances Willard, the movement blossomed into a national grass-roots crusade. And, by equating temperance, and eventually suffrage as well, with "home protection," Willard broadened the ranks of American feminism by arguing that women needed the vote to protect their families from the evils of liquor. Unfortunately, the temperance movement ultimately proved an insufficient vehicle for rallying national support for suffrage reform. Cautioned by the threat of an antifeminist backlash from the liquor interests, suffrage leaders developed a wary alliance with the WCTU, which faltered with Willard's passing.[26]

Yet by the 1910s a more inclusive rationale had begun to emerge. The notion of "municipal housekeeping" was promoted by a range of women's voluntary associations and clubs, casting the cause of suffrage in more broadly etched, still more democratic terms. As Addams explained, the political system was merely an extension of the home. Women, as mothers, needed the vote to maintain the quality of the educational system, to ensure that their cities were clean, their children's milk unadulterated, and vice curbed, so that their families would have healthy environments in which to live, prosper, and grow.

Municipal housekeeping provided the common denominator that united women of various persuasions. It was a brilliant strategy, because it coupled the demand for equal rights with domestic imagery, countering antifeminist arguments that predicted that female suffrage would undermine the home. It was a special moment in history, one that has not been repeated since. Neither the Equal Rights Amendment, which was first introduced in 1923 (an even longer period of gestation than the suffrage amendment); nor more recent pro-life/pro-choice campaigns have managed to unite both sides of women's political role. As a result, they have failed to build the broadly based coalitions that lie at the heart of Constitutional reform.

Once the vote was secured, women continued to draw upon their voluntary networks to enrich and consolidate their political gains. It was a symbiotic alliance. Participation in settlements and female-centered social reform movements during the Progressive era provided the necessary credentials used by many women to enter governmental careers, particularly in agencies catering to the needs of women and children. It also forged a platform for their campaigns, and provided a continuing source of new ideas. As Susan Ware points out in her study, *Beyond Suffrage: Women in the New Deal,* "women in government turned to their friends in voluntary associations for expert technical help and to obtain broader public support for specific proposals." In the process, voluntary associations continued to exercise political power in a variety of new fields, enabling women to bolster their public presence in new ways.[27]

Contributions and Careers

While women's voluntary associations campaigned for wide-ranging political reforms, women's donations provided yet another arena for the exercise of feminine power. Prior to the passage of married women's property acts in the mid-nineteenth century, women made their greatest contributions through fund-raising campaigns rather than individual gifts. While men raised funds through individual solicitation among their colleagues and friends, antebellum women turned their attention to charity fairs and bazaars.

As in the case of asylum work, these efforts drew upon domestic skills, as women busily painted, baked, knitted, and sewed the articles to be sold. These small-scale efforts generated public recognition and a modicum of power within the larger community. They also helped to bolster women's roles within a variety of institutions. Congregations became increasingly dependent on women's fund-raising skills, which also fueled the fires of revivalism. According to one historian, women's groups "ultimately built the infrastructure and financed the operations of the revival ministry," including Charles Grandison Finney's first sweep through the fertile soil of the Burned Over District in upstate New York. As they became more adept in these roles, a surprising variety of organizations attempted to tap their skills, providing an entree into abolitionist work and even a marginal role in some of country's more haughty cultural institutions.[28]

The importance of women's fund-raising skills has continued down to the present, constituting an enduring element of their "invisible careers" within the voluntary sphere. This in turn gradually opened new arenas for the exercise of feminine talents. In the Gilded Age, for example, some wealthy matrons became cultural impresarios, opening their mansions to theatrical performances and musical events for carefully selected audiences of their friends. Fees were charged, and the proceeds given to charity. At a time when women still played a negligible role in most major urban cultural institutions, wealthy dowagers such as Mrs. George Pullman succeeded in attracting renowned singers, pianists, and other musicians to their homes for private performances under the rubric of charity.

The role of women as individual donors is harder to trace, and raises many intriguing questions. How widespread was female giving prior to the passage of married women's property laws? Who were their favored recipients? For example, only one woman was recorded among the twenty-eight major donors ($5,000 or more) to Harvard University between 1800 and 1850— Mrs. Sarah Jackson, who made a donation to the Divinity School. Similarly, only one gift of $5,000 or more was given by a woman in Chicago before the Civil War. Like Mrs. Jackson, Chicagoan Eliza Garrett donated a valuable parcel of land to help found a theological seminary in her husband's memory. Were most of their donations invested in religious causes, or did women underwrite other areas as well?[29]

Marital status is another interesting consideration. Were the majority of antebellum women donors single, widowed, or were they wives? At this point the findings are fragmentary, but interesting. Suzanne Lebsock found in her study, *The Free Women of Petersburg*, that women were two times as likely as men to bequeath part of their estates to churches, benevolent societies, or poor relief, although admittedly the percentage of women who made these gifts was extremely low (6.7 percent of the wills examined). F. K. Prochaska posits a similar pattern among Victorian Englishwomen, whom he deems "much more likely than men to leave a large portion of their assets to philanthropy." According to Prochaska's book, widows and single women were particularly generous. Basing his study on a sample of wills probated in the 1840s and 1860s, he concludes that women donated "vast sums," particularly to religious causes.[30]

One of the most important contributions of women's giving and voluntarism was their role in opening a growing array of female careers. From the outset, groups such as the SRPWC evinced a keen interest in promoting female self-support. The development of asylums created new employment opportunities for women, as did groups such as the New York Female Moral Reform Society, which hired only female staff as a matter of policy.

Interest in creating new careers for respectable middle-class women accelerated after the Civil War. Wartime casualties deprived many women of suitable mates, generating fresh concerns for their economic well-being. At the same time, the increasing secularization of feminine philanthropy provided a host of novel ideas for new careers. Some of these, such as nursing, were directly linked to wartime exigencies. Others were born of the women's club movement, new charitable techniques, and emerging social needs. Social work, settlement work, and the medical profession were all opened to women in large measure because of the power of feminine philanthropy.

Health proved to be an area of particular interest to women donors. In Chicago, for example, female donors gave over $700,000 in gifts of $5,000 or more to local women's and children's hospitals and nursing schools in the 1870s and 1880s. More traditional charities such as asylums also fared quite well, netting an almost equal amount (although the figure was distorted by Clarissa Peck's $625,000 bequest to the Home for Incurables). Cultural endeavors lagged far behind, recording a scant $18,000 in major gifts during these years.

This in turn underscores the point that although women began to move beyond religious charities in the decades after the Civil War, they continued to concentrate their giving in traditional areas of feminine concern: health, education, and social work. As the figures from Chicago suggest, health was a particularly popular cause. Many women were undoubtedly drawn to the task of educating female doctors after suffering at the hands of male physicians. Institutions such as the New England Hospital for Women and Children (1862) were heavily dependent on feminine support. Designed to provide advanced clinical training for women doctors, the hospital also assured patients that they would have recourse to qualified feminine medical care. The institution was nurtured during its infancy by a flurry of timely bequests from local women, as well as a series of benefits sponsored by women's groups. As Mary Roth Walsh explains, the director's "dependence on the women's movement was total: she needed female supporters to help finance her education, to raise money, to promote the hospital, to help administer it, to serve as patients, and—probably most critically—to proffer their friendship in critical times."[31]

The extent to which women's friendships promoted institutional development has yet to be fully explored. In some instances, however, alliances between prominent feminists and wealthy female supporters were crucial determinants in individual careers. For example, M. Carey Thomas, the strong-minded president of Bryn Mawr, was appointed to that position after her friend and longtime companion, railroad heiress Mary Garrett, offered the college $10,000 per annum to underwrite Thomas's salary. Hull-House, too, had its financial angel in the form of Mary Rozet Smith, a relationship explored in Kathryn Kish Sklar's essay, "Who Funded Hull House?" Although the exact nature of Mary Smith's relationship to Jane Addams may never be fully determined, her role in financially backing Addams's career was undeniably important. As Sklar points out, other wealthy Chicago matrons such as Louise deKoven Bowen also provided financial backing as well as moral support. Interestingly, she finds far lower levels of support from men, including celebrated philanthropists of Julius Rosenwald's ilk. By concentrating on Addams's financial backers, Sklar's essay helps to add a new dimension to our understanding of women's networks and their role in shaping the careers of women who successfully assumed pioneering roles in new fields.[32]

Margaret Rossiter's study, *Women Scientists in America*, addresses this issue in a more general way in her discussion of the impact of "creative philanthropy" in opening scientific careers to women.

The most famous example of this leveraging technique was Mary Garrett's offer to give Johns Hopkins University $60,000 if the institution would require baccalaureate degrees for admission to its medical school and admit women on an equal footing with men. The offer was finally accepted after she considerably upped the ante, donating the $307,000 needed to top off the school's $500,000 fund-raising campaign.[33]

Occasionally, this technique backfired. In 1865, for example, a group of women in Boston and New York raised $50,000 to endow scholarships for women in leading medical schools. When their offers were repeatedly rebuffed, they used the money instead to enlarge Dr. Elizabeth Blackwell's infirmary in New York. Cornell University was induced to open its undergraduate courses to women in return for a $25,000 gift, but the University of Michigan managed to sidestep a similar offer. According to the stipulations surrounding Dr. Elizabeth Bates's $133,000 bequest, the university was to develop professorships of gynecology and pediatrics and to train women medical students on a par with men, including allowing them access to clinical instruction. Instead, the university used the money to bolster its obstetrics department and build a new wing for the children's hospital, ignoring Bates's other injunctions. Despite these lapses, some women were keenly sensitive to the reforming potential of large gifts. In the words of Dr. Mary Putnam Jacobi, "it is astonishing how many invincible objections on the score of feasibility, modesty, propriety, and prejudice melt away before the charmed touch of a few thousand dollars."[34]

It was a dictum that men had followed for a long time. Throughout the nineteenth and early twentieth centuries, women's gifts tended to be smaller and more targeted than men's. There were occasionally differences in form as well. Foundations are a case in point. Although single-purpose charitable trusts trace their genesis into the mists of antiquity, the modern foundation is of fairly recent vintage. Born at the turn of the century, these institutions were highly flexible, funded in perpetuity, rooted in professional expertise, national and international in scope, and designed to centralize individual giving in the same way that the rise of the corporation had systematized the nation's business affairs. Not surprisingly, this form was pioneered by some of the country's richest and most famous (or infamous, depending on one's point of view) entrepreneurs—men such as Andrew Carnegie and John D. Rockefeller.

Women proved far less likely to create major foundations. One exception was the Russell Sage Foundation. Founded by Olivia Sage in 1907, the Sage Foundation was at first heavily staffed by women and played a pioneering role in promoting the professionalization of social work. Later, it increasingly passed to male managers, and the social work programs were gradually supplanted by other kinds of research. By the turn of the century the scale and power of science were rapidly evolving beyond the influence of many women philanthropists, becoming the province of "professionals, millionaires, and soon, the big foundations, which few women ever penetrated." Whether women shied away from foundation development because of an enduring inclination toward "personalism," or whether their financial and legal advisers warned them away remains to be explored. Equally intriguing are questions about the kinds of foundations they did create, and how their impact differed from that of the "big foundations" funded, managed, and staffed by men.[35]

International Comparisons

Gender comparisons are one means of measuring the role of giving and voluntarism in enhancing women's power; cross-cultural comparisons are another. Religion is a key determinant of the degree of autonomy and public influence wielded by women philanthropists both within and outside the United States. The Protestant Reformation, for example, had a profound impact in shaping the charitable responses of both women and men. In Protestant countries such as England and Holland, would-be philanthropists were accorded an increased measure of responsibility in caring for dependents and the dispossessed as the traditional charities associated with the Catholic Church were disbanded. The Anglo-American humanitarian campaigns of the eighteenth century were born of this secular spirit, as were a variety of charitable and educational campaigns.[36]

Three of the essays in this volume, by Edith Couturier, Brenda Meehan-Waters, and Alisa Klaus, explore the often very different range of alternatives available to women in Catholic and Orthodox countries. In Mexico and Russia, women lavished their time and money on church-related institutions, particularly convents and religious communities that served as the wellsprings for a variety of charities and reforms. The situation depicted in Edith Couturier's essay is a far cry from the activism of the SPRWC, or the gender-based funding patterns described by Sklar. Rather than devoting their energies to the solution of social ills through secular or interdenominational voluntary organizations, women in colonial Mexico clung to an almost medieval concern with spiritual gains, funding convents, Masses, and the distribution of alms to the poor. More socially oriented institutions, such as asylums for abused, abandoned, or wayward women generally fell to the province of masculine largesse.[37]

Meehan-Waters traces the transition from contemplative to more socially oriented religious ventures in Czarist Russia. As she explains, Russian Orthodoxy differed markedly from the Catholic and Protestant sects in Western Europe. The tradition of women entering religious communities at midlife, after their children had reached maturity, helped to spur the growth of secular women's religious communities. Added to this was an intense commitment among Russian women to the pursuit of religious and, later, charitable ends within the context of these communal arrangements, which ultimately helped to give Russian women's philanthropy its special slant.[38]

Alisa Klaus examines the continuing impact of religion and government in circumscribing women's roles in more secular fields. Unlike their American counterparts, French women were cast in far narrower policymaking roles, debarred from full access to power by highly centralized, male-dominated religious, professional, and political bureaucracies. Nor did Catholic charities encourage social activism to the same extent as Protestant groups. As she points out, at least in late-nineteenth- and early-twentieth-century France, "Catholic piety was not a vehicle for independent women's political action or social reform."[39]

Jane Rendall's volume, *The Origins of Modern Feminism: Women in Britain, France and the United States, 1780–1860*, further underscores this theme. In Rendall's schema, responsibility for the public weal in France was neatly divided between religious orders and the state, leaving little leeway for more individualistic, secular concerns. While "evangelical religion provided a model for association, and a powerful imagery which embodied and gave strength to the particular qualities of womanhood" in England and the United States, "in France, the absence of such a moralizing force . . . offered relatively less encouragement to spontaneous association among laywomen." As a result, women's initiatives outside the religious sphere were accorded a far narrower policymaking role than comparable activities in the United States. Nor did women's voluntary associations afford the same access to governmental policymaking positions, a theme echoed by Klaus.[40]

Political factors are another important variable. Meehan-Waters's essay is particularly illuminating on this point, emphasizing the contradictory effects of tighter governmental supervision and more lenient property laws in shaping feminine largesse under tsarist rule. As she so rightly points out, philanthropy is an act of power. Because Russian women exercized greater control over their inheritances and dowries, they also enjoyed a wider array of options in determining the uses of their gifts. On the other hand, political vicissitudes served to delimit, then expand, the range of these options, affording a more volatile political backdrop against which charitable and philanthropic decisions were made. Ross and Klaus also examine women's uneven policymaking contributions to maternal and child health debates in England, France, and the United States. In effect, some political cultures afforded far greater scope for women's participation in national policymaking debates through philanthropic activities than others.[41]

Social factors also play a role in allocating activities within the voluntary sector. Some trends appear to be fairly universal, especially women's tendency to focus on the needs of children and other women as a means of legitimizing their efforts in the public sphere. The essays by Couturier, Meehan-Waters, Klaus, and Ross provide insights into the often very different ways these interests achieved tangible form in differing countries and times. An interest in increasing career options also threads through several cultures, as does the emphasis on fostering women's communities. Martha Vicinus's study, *Independent Women*, does a particularly good job of detailing the various ways in which Victorian Englishwomen translated their donations of time and money into gender-segregated institutions that enabled single women to pursue more meaningful careers. Whether in the form of convents, nursing schools, social settlements, or women's colleges, female philanthropists have often gravitated toward the promotion of institutional alternatives to or revisions of the domestic sphere.[42]

Conclusions

Women traditionally used their gifts of time and money within the American context to create parallel power structures outside the domestic, commercial, and political spheres dominated by men. The essays in this volume seek to examine the extent to which these trends have been replicated outside the United States and shaped by racial and ethnic variables within the American scene.

For nonpoliticized American women, giving and voluntarism have provided ongoing sources of recruitment, socialization, training, and advancement into public roles. For disfranchised groups such as women and minorities, philanthropic activities have provided the means for leveraging political and even Constitutional change. In effect, the charities and voluntary associations that women created functioned precisely as the Founding Fathers intended, providing ongoing mechanisms for achieving peaceful, gradualist, and often fundamental political change.

They have also provided the crucibles in which women have reshaped public policies and popular attitudes about gender, class, domesticity, and race. Female philanthropy has served, and continues to serve, as the means through which American women—once legally invisible and without the vote, and still denied Constitutional assurances that their "equal rights under the law will not be denied or abridged on account of sex"—have made a lasting imprint on social and institutional reforms, professionalization, legislation, and even on the Constitution itself. The differing approaches fostered by ethnic and minority groups, doners and volunteers, as well as the ways in which their achievements may have been replicated in other cultures is just beginning to be understood. The following essays constitute a preliminary contribution toward that end.

NOTES

1   Broadly defined, these voluntary sector activities encompass efforts to provide essential services or initiate social reform outside the governmental sector, including everything from traditional charities and reform groups to individual, corporate, and foundation giving,

voluntarism and mutual aid. In terms of definitions, "voluntary sector" is therefore used to denote the entire range of activities pursued through chartered nonprofit organizations: charities, foundations, social reform groups, and institutions for the promotion of social welfare, cultural, educational, and health purposes. Current usage often distinguishes "charity," which seeks to ameliorate individual suffering, from "philanthropy," which addresses the root causes of social problems and needs in ways designed to achieve more lasting change. However, several of the essays in this volume use the term "philanthropy" as defined in the dictionary: a generalized "love of mankind," which is synonymous with the wider range of voluntary sector activities.

2   Society for the Relief of Poor Widows with Small Children, *Annual Report* (1800), 9.

3   Ibid.

4   Ibid., 15.

5   Ibid., 16, 18.

6   Society for the Relief of Poor Widows with Small Children, Act of Incorporation (April 2, 1802), 3–4, 7. Selected sources on other antebellum charities include Susan Porter Benson, "Business Heads and Sympathizing Hearts: The Women of the Providence Employment Society," *Journal of Social History* 11 (1978), 302–313; and Anne M. Boylan, "Women in Groups: An Analysis of Women's Benevolent Organizations in New York and Boston, 1797–1840," *Journal of American History* 71 (1984), 497–524.

7   For an excellent discussion of the role of "personalism" in shaping women's charities, see Suzanne Lebsock, *The Free Women of Petersburg: Status and Culture in a Southern Town, 1784–1860* (New York: W. W. Norton, 1984), Chapter 7.

8   Gender issues are examined in Kathleen D. McCarthy, *Noblesse Oblige: Charity and Cultural Philanthropy in Chicago, 1849–1929* (Chicago: University of Chicago Press, 1982), and Leonore Davidoff and Catherine Hall, *Family Fortunes: Men and Women of the English Middle Class, 1750–1850* (Chicago: University of Chicago Press, 1987). Women's changing role within the church is outlined in Barbara Welter's landmark essay, "The Feminization of American Religion: 1800–1860," in *Clio's Consciousness Raised: New Perspectives on the History of Women* ed. Mary Hartmann and Lois W. Banner (New York: Harper and Row, 1974), 137–157. For a general overview of cultural developments, see Neil Harris, *The Artist and American Society: The Formative Years, 1790–1860* (New York: Simon and Schuster, 1966); Lillian B. Miller, *Patrons and Patriotism: The Encouragement of the Fine Arts in the United States, 1790–1860* (Chicago: University of Chicago Press, 1966); Helen L.

Horowitz, *Culture and the City: Cultural Philanthropy in Chicago from the 1880s to 1917* (Lexington: University of Kentucky Press, 1976); McCarthy, *Noblesse Oblige*; and Thomas Bender, *New York Intellect* (New York: Alfred A. Knopf, 1977). A sample of some of the standard works on the charitable and social reform movements in which men were involved includes: Paul Boyer, *Urban Masses and Moral Order in America, 1820–1920* (Cambridge: Harvard University Press, 1978); Robert H. Bremner, *American Philanthropy* (Chicago: University of Chicago Press, 1960), and his volume *From the Depths: The Discovery of Poverty in the United States* (New York: New York University Press, 1956); Clifford S. Griffin, *Their Brothers' Keepers: Moral Stewardship in the United States, 1800–1865* (New Brunswick: Rutgers University Press, 1960); Nathan I. Huggins, *Protestants Against Poverty: Boston's Charities, 1870–1900* (Westport, Ct.: Greenwood Press, 1971); Paul Johnson, *A Shopkeeper's Millennium: Society and Revivals in Rochester, New York, 1815–1837* (New York: Hill and Wang, 1978); Ronald G. Walters, *American Reformers, 1815–1860* (New York: Hill and Wang, 1978); Roy Lubove, *The Professional Altruist: The Emergence of Social Work as a Career, 1880–1930* (Harvard: Harvard University Press, 1965); Edward Pessen, *Riches, Class and Power Before the Civil War* (Toronto: D. C. Heath, 1973); and Timothy L. Smith, *Revivalism and Social Reform in Mid-Nineteenth Century America* (New York: Abingdon Press, 1957).

9   Kathleen D. McCarthy, "Culture, Gender and Philanthropy in Antebellum America," unpublished paper presented at a conference on "Women and Philanthropy: Past, Present and Future," Center for the Study of Philanthropy, Graduate School, City University of New York, June 1987. For the idea of "invisible careers," see Arlene Kaplan Daniels, *Invisible Careers: Women Civic Leaders from the Volunteer World* (Chicago: University of Chicago Press, 1987).

10   Lebsock, *Free Women of Petersburg*, 210, 209. For the decline of "women's culture" in the twentieth century, see McCarthy, *Noblesse Oblige*; and Martha Vicinus, *Independent Women: Work and Community for Single Women, 1850–1920* (Chicago: University of Chicago Press, 1985). For an analysis of the continuing importance of all-female networks of volunteers in the late nineteenth century in the United States, see Estelle Freedman, "Separatism as Strategy: Female Institution Building and American Feminism, 1870–1930," *Feminist Studies* 5 (1979), 512–529.

11   Anne Firor Scott, "Women's Voluntary Associations: From Charity to Reform," 35–54. For the Charity Organization Society movement, see George M. Fredrickson, *The Inner Civil War: Northern Intellectuals and the Crisis of the Union* (New York: Harper and Row, 1965); and Gareth Stedman Jones's provocative treatment of the cos in England, *Outcast*

London: A Study in the Relationship Between Classes in Victorian Society (London: Oxford University Press, 1971). The history of the women's club movement is outlined in Karen J. Blair, *The Clubwoman as Feminist: True Womanhood Redefined, 1868–1914* (New York: Holmes and Meier, 1980). The best introductions to the voluminous literature on social settlements are Jane Addams, *Twenty Years at Hull-House* (New York: New American Library, 1960): and Allen F. Davis's two volumes, *American Heroine: The Life and Legend of Jane Addams* (New York: Oxford University Press, 1973), and *Spearheads for Reform: The Social Settlements and the Progressive Movement* (New Brunswick: Rutgers University Press [1967], 1985).

12   Hasia Diner, *Erin's Daughters in America: Immigrant Women in the Nineteenth Century* (Baltimore: Johns Hopkins University Press, 1983); Robert A. Slayton, *Back of the Yards: The Making of a Local Democracy* (Chicago: University of Chicago Press, 1986).

13   Nancy A. Hewitt, "Charity or Mutual Aid?: Two Perspectives on Latin Women's Philanthropy in Tampa, Florida," 55–69.

14   Darlene Clark Hine, " 'We Specialize in the Wholly Impossible': The Philanthropic Work of Black Women," 70–93. See also, Benjamin Quarles, *Black Abolitionists* (New York: Oxford University Press, 1969); Leonard P. Curry, *The Free Black in Urban America, 1800–1950* (Chicago: University of Chicago Press, 1981); Kenneth L. Kusmer, *A Ghetto Takes Shape: Black Cleveland, 1870–1930* (Urbana: University of Illinois Press, 1976); and Gerda Lerner, "Community Work of Black Club Women," *The Journal of Negro History* 59 (1974), 158–167.

15   Nancy A. Hewitt, *Women's Activism and Social Change: Rochester, New York, 1822–1872* (Ithaca: Cornell University Press, 1984).

16   For additional information on Female Moral Reform societies, see Mary P. Ryan, "The Power of Women's Networks," in *Sex and Class in Women's History* ed. Judith L. Newton, Mary P. Ryan and Judith L. Walkowitz (London: Routledge & Kegan Paul, 1983), 167–186; Nancy F. Cott, *The Bonds of Womanhood: Woman's Sphere in New England, 1780–1835* (New Haven: Yale University Press, 1977); and Carroll Smith-Rosenberg, "Beauty, the Beast, and the Militant Woman: A Case Study in Sex Roles and Social Stress in Jacksonian America," in her volume of essays, *Disorderly Conduct: Visions of Gender in Victorian America* (New York: Oxford University Press, 1985), 109–128. Another important women's organization, the maternal association, is described in Mary P. Ryan, *Cradle of the Middle Class: The Family in Oneida County, New York, 1790–1865* (New York: Cambridge University Press, 1981).

17   Christine Stansell, *City of Women: Sex and Class in New York, 1789–1860*

(New York: Alfred A. Knopf, 1986), 21; Cott, *The Bonds of Womanhood*, 153.

18   Stansell, *City of Women*, 69.

19   Ibid., 67–68. See also, Boyer, *Urban Masses and Moral Order*; Johnson, *A Shopkeeper's Millennium*; Roy Rosenzweig, *Eight Hours for What We Will: Workers and Leisure in an Industrial City, 1870–1920* (New York: Cambridge University Press, 1983); and Kathy Peiss, *Cheap Amusements: Working Women and Leisure in Turn-of-the-Century New York* (Philadelphia: Temple University Press, 1983).

20   Ellen Ross, "Good and Bad Mothers: Lady Philanthropists and London Housewives before the First World War," 174–198.

21   Paula Baker, "The Domestication of Politics: Women and American Political Society, 1780–1920," *American Historical Review* 89 (1984), 647. The relationship between women's early voluntary associations and later feminist campaigns has occasioned lively debates. See, for example, Barbara J. Berg, *The Remembered Gate: Origins of American Feminism: The Woman and the City, 1800–1860* (New York: Oxford University Press, 1978); Keith Melder, *Beginnings of Sisterhood: The American Women's Rights Movement, 1800–1850* (New York: Schocken Books, 1977); and Hewitt, *Women's Activism and Social Change*. For the history of the suffrage movement and postsuffrage developments, see Ellen C. DuBois, *Feminism and Suffrage: The Emergence of an Independent Woman's Movement in America, 1848–1869* (Ithaca: Cornell University Press, 1978); Aileen Kraditor, *The Ideas of the Woman Suffrage Movement, 1890–1920* (New York: Columbia University Press, 1965); Mary Berry, *Why the ERA Failed: Women's Rights and the Amending Process of the Constitution* (Bloomington: Indiana University Press, 1986); and Nancy F. Cott, *The Grounding of Modern Feminism* (New Haven: Yale University Press, 1987).

22   This discussion is based on Linda Kerber, *Women of the Republic: Intellect and Ideology in Revolutionary America* (Chapel Hill: University of North Carolina Press, 1980), 105, 120–121 and *passim*; and Mary Beth Norton, *Liberty's Daughters: The Revolutionary Experience of American Women, 1750–1800* (Boston: Little, Brown, 1980).

23   Women's role in the abolitionist movement is detailed in Blanche Glassman Hersh, *The Slavery of Sex: Feminist-Abolitionists in America* (Urbana: University of Illinois Press, 1978), and Gerda Lerner, "The Political Activities of Antislavery Women," in *The Majority Finds Its Past: Placing Women in History* (New York: Oxford University Press, 1979), 112–128.

24   Hewitt, *Women's Activism and Social Change*.

25   "Declaration of Sentiments and Resolutions" (New York: Seneca Falls Convention, 1848), in *Up From the Pedestal: Selected Writings in the History of American Feminism*, ed. Aileen Kraditor (New York: Quadrangle, 1968), 184.

26   For the history of women's temperance work, see Ruth Bordin, *Women and Temperance: The Quest for Power and Liberty, 1873–1900* (Philadelphia: Temple University Press, 1981); and Barbara Lee Epstein, *The Politics of Domesticity: Women, Evangelism and Temperance in Nineteenth Century America* (Middletown, Ct.: Wesleyan University Press, 1981).

27   Susan Ware, *Beyond Suffrage: Women in the New Deal* (Cambridge: Harvard University Press, 1981). On the other hand, Alisa Klaus's essay reveals that political territory gained by women's groups could occasionally be reclaimed by men when professional interests were at stake.

28   Ryan, *Cradle of the Middle Class*, 102.

29   Ronald Story, *Harvard and the Boston Upper Class: The Forging of an Aristocracy, 1800–1870* (Middletown, Ct.: Wesleyan University Press, 1980), 28; McCarthy, *Noblesse Oblige*, 44–45. For women's roles in promoting missionary work, see Patricia R. Hill, *The World Their Household: The American Woman's Foreign Mission Movement and Cultural Transformation, 1870–1920* (Ann Arbor: University of Michigan Press, 1985).

30   Lebsock, *Free Women of Petersburg*, 224; F. K. Prochaska, *Women and Philanthropy in Nineteenth-Century England* (Oxford: Clarendon Press, 1980), 35, 33.

31   Mary Roth Walsh, *"Doctors Wanted: No Women Need Apply": Sexual Barriers in the Medical Profession, 1835–1975* (New Haven: Yale University Press, 1977), 396–397.

32   Helen Lefkowitz Horowitz, *Alma Mater: Design and Experience in Women's Colleges from their Nineteenth Century Beginnings to the 1930s* (Boston: Beacon Press, 1984); Kathryn Kish Sklar, "Who Funded Hull House?," 94–115.

33   Margaret W. Rossiter, *Women Scientists in America: Struggles and Strategies to 1940* (Baltimore: Johns Hopkins University Press, 1982).

34   Ibid.; Mary Jacobi, "Social Aspects of the Readmission of Women Into the Medical Profession," Papers and Letters Presented at the First Women's Congress of the Association for the Advancement of Women (1873), 177; quoted in Walsh, *"Doctors Wanted,"* 169.

35   Rossiter, *Women Scientists*, p. 88. For the role of foundations in American life, see Barry D. Karl and Stanley N. Katz, "The American Philanthropic Foundation and the Public Sphere," *Minerva* 19 (1981), 236–270, and their essay on "Foundations and Ruling Class Elites," *Daedalus* 116 (1987), 1–40; Francis X. Sutton, "The Ford Foundation: The Early Years,"

Daedalus 116 (1987), 41–91; John Ettling, *The Germ of Laziness: Rockefeller Philanthropy and Public Health in the New South* (Cambridge: Harvard University Press, 1981); Martin and Joan Bulmer, "Philanthropy and Social Science in the 1920s: Beardsley Ruml and the Laura Spelman Rockefeller Memorial, 1922–1929," *Minerva* 19 (1981), 347–407; Robert E. Kohler, "A Policy for the Advancement of Science: The Rockefeller Foundation, 1924–29," *Minerva* 16 (1978), 480–515, and his essay on "The Management of Sciences: The Experience of Warren Weaver and the Rockefeller Foundation Programme in Molecular Biology," *Minerva* 14 (1976), 279–306; Ellen Condliffe Lagemann, *Private Power for the Public Good: A History of the Carnegie Foundation for the Advancement of Teaching* (Middletown, Ct.: Wesleyan University Press, 1983); Guy Alchon, *The Invisible Hand of Planning: Capitalism, Social Science, and the State in the 1920s* (Princeton: Princeton University Press, 1985); Robert F. Arnove, ed., *Philanthropy and Cultural Imperialism: The Foundations at Home and Abroad* (Boston: G. K. Hall, 1980); and Waldemar Nielsen's two volumes, *The Big Foundations* (New York: Columbia University Press, 1972), and *The Golden Donors: A New Anatomy of the Great Foundations* (New York: E. P. Dutton, 1985). For changes in the Russell Sage Foundation, see Carol Brown, "Sexism and the Russell Sage Foundation," *Signs* 1 (1972), 25–44.

36   See, for example, Sheila D. Muller, *Charity in the Dutch Republic: Pictures of Rich and Poor for Charitable Institutions* (Ann Arbor: UMI Research Press, 1985); Wilbur K. Jordan, *Philanthropy in England, 1480–1660: A Study of the Changing Pattern of English Social Aspirations* (London: George Allen & Unwin, 1959); David Owen, *English Philanthropy, 1660–1960* (Cambridge: Belknap Press of Harvard University Press, 1964).

37   Edith Couturier, "'For the Greater Service of God': Opulent Foundations and Women's Philanthropy in Colonial Mexico," 119–141. Later developments in Mexico are briefly detailed in Silvia Maria Arrom, *The Women of Mexico City, 1790–1857* (Stanford: Stanford University Press, 1985).

38   Brenda Meehan-Waters, "From Contemplative Practice to Charitable Activity: Russian Women's Religious Communities and the Development of Charitable Work, 1861–1917," 142–156.

39   Alisa Klaus, "Women's Organizations and the Infant Health Movement in France and the United States, 1890–1920," 157–173.

40   Jane Rendall, *The Origins of Modern Feminism: Women in Britain, France and the United States, 1780–1860* (London: Macmillan, 1985), 322–323; Klaus, "Women's Organizations and the Infant Health Movement."

41   Meehan-Waters, "From Contemplative Practice to Charitable Activity";
     for a very different role played by women in Moscow's mercantile fam-
     ilies, see Jo Ann Ruckman, *The Moscow Business Elite: A Social and Cul-
     tural Portrait of Two Generations, 1840–1905* (DeKalb: Northern Illinois
     University Press, 1984).

     Less well understood, but no less intriguing, are the ways in which
     the wives of political figures have used their philanthropic activities to
     consolidate their own political roles, or those of their husbands. This is a
     particularly interesting question in places such as Latin America, where
     giving is often embedded in patron-client relationships. The Eva Peron
     Foundation provides a classic example of the use of ostensibly phil-
     anthropic activities to bolster political ends. Where have there been in-
     stances in which well placed women used their gifts of time and money
     to achieve political returns, and what social or cultural factors permitted
     them to do so? The best treatment of the Eva Peron Foundation (albeit
     one that mutes its political overtones) is in Nicholas Fraser and Marysa
     Navarro, *Eva Peron* (New York: W. W. Norton, 1985). For earlier develop-
     ments in Argentina, see Cynthia J. Little, "Education, Philanthropy, and
     Feminism: Components of Argentine Womanhood, 1860–1926," in *Latin
     American Women: Historical Perspectives* ed. Asuncion Lavrin (Westport,
     Ct.: Greenwood Press, 1978).

     Grass-roots organizations can also assume a strongly political cast.
     The recent upsurge of women's groups in developing nations has served
     to translate a variety of feminist concerns into concrete programs. In
     many instances, these self-help campaigns for better employment op-
     portunities or improved maternal and child health have influenced
     broader policymaking processes, giving women a voice in governmen-
     tal affairs and national legislation through their voluntary efforts. For a
     general overview of the voluntary sector in eight developing nations, see
     Kathleen D. McCarthy, "The Voluntary Sector Overseas: Notes from the
     Field" (New York: Center for the Study of Philanthropy, 1988).

42   Vicinus, *Independent Women.* Englishwomen's charities are also de-
     tailed in Prochaska, *Women and Philanthropy*; and Leonore Davidoff
     and Catherine Hall, *Family Fortunes: Men and Women of the English
     Middle Class, 1750–1850* (Chicago: University of Chicago Press, 1987).
     Gareth Stedman Jones provides a provocative overview of the history of
     London's Charity Organization Society in *Outcast London.*

     Many of the institutions Vicinus describes were replicated in the
     United States as well, comparisons that have yet to be fully explored.
     Asylums provided "total institutions" for the shelter and rehabilitation of
     children, "friendless" (but virtuous) women, reformed prostitutes, bat-

tered and abandoned wives, and the aged poor. Created in the image of an extended household, these institutions afforded their directresses a public role, a modicum of power, and an opportunity to mold the manners and mores of the inmates entrusted to their care. Nursing schools, on the other hand, stood at the midpoint on the continuum between the highly controlled milieu of the asylum and the more collegial setting of the social settlement. Differences and similarities between such quasi-domestic institutions as convents, asylums, nursing schools, women's colleges, and social settlements in different countries await further study.

ONE

The American Scene

ANNE FIROR SCOTT

Women's Voluntary Associations:

From Charity to Reform

Sociologists since Alexis de Toqueville have understood that voluntary associations constitute one of the primary social institutions in this country. Yet until historians of women began to examine such associations, their history had received very little sustained attention.[1] In 1944 Arthur Schlesinger, Sr. tried to bring the subject forcefully to the attention of his fellow historians and offered a general statement that can hardly be improved upon:

> The trend toward collective activity began slowly in American history, but it gathered impetus as the years revealed new opportunities and men perceived the advantages to be gained. Broadly speaking, the rise of associations paralleled the development of democratic self-confidence and the greater complexity of social and economic life. Each fresh application of the principle opened the way for further ones and at the same time afforded the experience needed for more extensive undertakings. In the end no department of human existence remained unaffected.[2]

Arthur Schlesinger pointed the way, but almost no one followed, and despite an enormous amount of attention to the contemporary situation of voluntary work, there is as yet no comprehensive historical analysis of the role voluntary associations have played in shaping American society. As for *women's* voluntary associations, although we now have an impressive body of work about particular associations and individual communities, we lack a conceptual framework that might allow us to see how these studies are related to each other and to some broader pattern. This essay suggests such a framework.

Three questions (under which many smaller questions could be grouped) provide guidelines for formulating a more theoretical approach to studying women's voluntary associations. First, what functions have these organizations performed? It stands to reason that, since literally thousands of these groups were founded over the past two centuries, they must be serving vital functions within American society. Second, what were the social, political, and economic consequences of women's work in these associations? Third, how has associational activity affected the status of American women and the social definition of woman's sphere?

Phase One: Benevolence

In order to assess these questions, it is necessary to sketch the history of women's voluntary associations as they have evolved since the Revolution. The story begins in the eighteenth century. In the 1790s, women could neither vote nor hold office, and they were customarily excluded from most public institutions. Although women formed a majority of the communicants in most churches, they were not allowed to fill positions of leadership. Yet some of them saw human needs that were not being met and felt themselves to be the proper people to begin to address those needs. Following the example of the men who had developed the use of voluntary associations for public purposes, and responding to the changing sense of moral responsibility inherent in the rise of humanitarianism, women in all the seaboard cities began to organize benevolent societies.[3]

One of the first such organizations, the Society for the Relief of Poor Widows with Small Children, appeared in New York City in 1797.[4] The Widow's Society, as it was called, came into existence at a time when New York City was growing rapidly, when the gap between rich and poor was visibly widening, and when the number of widows was increasing. The founder, a bold, skillful, and pious leader named Isabella Graham—herself a self-supporting widow—understood that charity solved no long-run problems. As she and several friends went to work, they quickly realized that there were very few ways for a woman on her own to earn a living in New York City, and if she had small children it was almost impossible. The Widow's Society experimented with various kinds of work relief, especially with schools that permitted the widows to support themselves by providing education for the orphans. This effort to break the cycle of poverty has sometimes been described as a harbinger of the city's public school system. Certainly it foreshadowed the steady interest in education that would characterize women's voluntary associations throughout the nineteenth century. During its first winter the society helped ninety-eight widows with more than two hundred small children; the numbers rose in succeeding years.

The Widow's Society soon had counterparts in Boston and Philadelphia and the other seaboard cities, and after 1800, benevolent, missionary, and "cent" societies appeared in almost every town and village as well. This was the beginning of an evolutionary sequence that can be divided into several phases. Although there is a certain amount of overlap, these categories provide a means of relating broader social trends to changes in women's associations.

The first phase ran from 1793 to about 1820. During these years benevolent societies, broadly defined, were the principal type of women's association.[5] Sometimes church related, sometimes ecumenical, their goals were formulated in religious terms and focused on people who for one reason or another were unable to take care of themselves, especially women and children. Benevolent women sought to save souls as well as bodies, their own as well as those of their clients. Women's societies also raised money to support missionaries who were going to the frontier or to foreign countries. The archetypal benevolent woman visited poor women, bearing food and clothing in one hand and a Bible in the other.

Each society was carefully organized with a constitution, bylaws, and strict rules about accounting for the money and goods that passed through its hands. Men were called upon to open meetings with prayers and to give money, but the essential work of visiting poor people and supplying their needs was done by the women, who were forced thereby to begin to think about poverty and its causes.

In the beginning, as women tried to seek out the "worthy" poor, they tended to blame poverty on vice, especially the vice of intemperance. But as individuals began to emerge from the abstraction of "the poor," the women began to trace vice to ignorance rather than to some inborn defect; thus it was that founding and conducting schools became a major part of benevolent activity. The women of the Raleigh, North Carolina Female Benevolent Society, for example, recorded their belief that children whom they educated might go on to become "shining lights in the world both for talents and for piety."[6] The idea that education could provide a cure for social ills has a long history, one that benevolent societies helped to embed in American culture.

Phase Two: Making the World Over

American society has always been in process of change, but certain decades have been notable for changes that affected fundamental institutional arrangements. In the 1820s and 1830s, everything from transportation to religion was in a state of upheaval, and it is not surprising, therefore, to find the nature and function of women's organizations changing as well. Benevolent societies continued to multiply, and provided a basic welfare structure in almost every community, but now, in addition, some women were organizing not simply to do good but to bring about social reform: temperance, moral reform, and antislavery were the three most common causes to which women were dedicated. Some reformers were "graduates" of benevolent societies, but most benevolent women stayed safely in traditional groups.

Nancy Hewitt's study of women's associations in Rochester, New York, before the Civil War suggests that membership in particular kinds of groups was a function of social and cultural status. Belonging to an antislavery society, for example, put one almost at the outer limit of female respectability, and the women who joined were often Quakers who were somewhat outside the local status system. At the other end of the spectrum, membership in a benevolent society or a church-related sewing circle raised few eyebrows. Members of such groups tended to be wives of the mercantile and political elite who enjoyed community approval and were not at all inclined to rock the boat.[7] It would be dangerous to generalize from Rochester alone, however, as is evident from Amy Swerdlow's evidence that a majority of the leaders of two New York City antislavery societies were wives of leading merchants.[8] It is also interesting to speculate about the effect of generational change: the daughters of the "Republican Mothers" were coming to maturity, and a good many of them felt a patriotic need to save the Republican dream from the destruction with which it seemed to be threatened by growing prosperity and urbanization.[9]

The first sign of a new kind of activism among women was the appearance of a Female Moral Reform Society in New York City, which was soon followed by the establishment of similar groups throughout New England and the western reserve.[10] Setting out to reform prostitutes and enforce a single standard of morality, the moral reformers wound up learning a good deal about human nature as well—and about politics.

Women organized to promote temperance at about the same time. The early temperance movement had been the work of elite men, and at first women simply joined the existing societies. In the 1830s, however, all-female temperance societies began to appear, and as the movement went through various permutations, leading up to the vigorous support of legal prohibition in the 1840s, societies made up entirely of women developed *pari passu.*[11]

The change in style, behavior, and degree of defiance of traditional norms of female behavior was nowhere more evident than in the antislavery movement. In this case, women not only joined with men in both local and national antislavery societies, but also created their own. By 1836, 10 percent of the more than 500 antislavery societies were all female; a year later when the total had reached 1,006, 77 were women's groups. The spirit of the female antislavery societies is well expressed in the Annual Report of the Boston Society for 1836: "They found for their encouragement abundance of 'abstract principles.' They also found a strong opposition to [their] *acting* in *accordance* with those principles."[12]

As early as the 1820s, male-dominated antislavery societies had begun to admit women, but with the implicit understanding that they would be seen and not heard. Women's efforts to speak in meetings aroused vigorous controversy and gave impetus to a growing women's rights movement, which was formally launched in 1848 at the famous convention at Seneca Falls, New York. Other conventions followed in quick succession. If the well-established pattern of reform movements had prevailed, the next step would have been the formation of a permanent organization, and indeed the 1852 call to convention signed by Elizabeth Cady Stanton, Pauline Wright Davis, and Lucy Stone suggested that the time had come for a "thorough and efficient" organization. When the convention met, however, some of these same women made stirring speeches arguing that a permanent organization was undesirable. Lucy Stone was quoted as saying that they had all *been* in permanent organizations, and therefore dreaded them. No association was formed, though local, state, and national conventions continued to be held until the Civil War, when the advocates of women's rights agreed to suspend agitation in favor of war work. Such unusual behavior is difficult to explain—unless these strong-minded women had had as much of sitting on committees as human nature could stand.[13]

Phase Three: The Civil War

The Civil War ushered in the next phase of voluntary association activity, as women brought to bear all that they had learned in benevolent and reform organizations over the preceding fifty years. While the guns were still booming in Charleston harbor, women all over the country began to organize what would become literally thousands of soldier's aid societies. They gave every evidence of knowing exactly what they wanted to do and how to go about it. Many of these groups in time would be brought under the umbrella of the giant United States Sanitary Commission, an enterprise run by a group of men who had been much influenced by the experience of the British in the Crimean War and by the work of Florence Nightingale. Their self-imposed task was to care for the health and welfare of soldiers, which they did very well.[14]

Their success was, in part, made possible by the supplies gathered, organized, and delivered to depots by women's associations. In one place after another the regional work of the commission, initially placed in the hands of local male leaders, was taken over by women. In Boston, for example, the men who had been appointed as regional associates "transferred their work, at an early day, to the New England Women's Auxiliary Association, an organization conspicuous during the whole war for its vigor and energy." In New York the Women's Central Relief Association coordinated the efforts of aid societies all over the country. In the area covered by Pennsylvania, Delaware, and western New Jersey the men delegated their responsibility for collecting supplies to "a number of ladies who afterwards took the name of the 'Women's Pennsylvania Branch.'"[15] In Chicago two women, Mary Livermore and Jane Hoge, ran the Northwestern Sanitary Commission with outstanding success.[16]

Southern women, too, responded quickly to the outbreak of war. In Alabama alone by January 1862 there were over a hundred organizations hard at work spinning, weaving, sewing, and knitting military apparel, and gathering other supplies for the army.[17] Across the Confederate states, women's societies began to organize and staff hospitals, to raise money for gunboats, to establish wayside rest stations for wounded soldiers, and to care for widows and orphans as well as dependents of soldiers.[18] Over and over, male observers, North and South, expressed astonishment at the administrative capacity and business acumen of the women, which suggests that they had hardly noticed what had been going on for many decades in the prewar women's voluntary associations.

Phase Four: The Great Expansion

The war ended, and many Americans felt a letdown. There is something morale building about sharing work in a great cause, even one that brings pain, suffering, death, and destruction. In both the North and South, some women—no matter how strenuous the war years had been for them—missed the feeling of importance, the opportunities to shape events, which had been theirs in wartime. This feeling, coming in the context of the far-reaching social and economic changes that followed the war (the rapid urbanization and industrialization of the country, the increase in immigration, and the growing number of wage-earning women, for example) gave rise to a new stage of associational life. The characteristics of this new phase were a very rapid expansion and differentiation among women's associations. A new style of organizing also began to appear as associations grew larger and as the whole society began to experience what Robert Wiebe termed "the search for order."[19]

From 1865 onward, women's associations were formed along two separate, though related, tracks. In the years before 1865 almost all women's collective endeavors had a religious basis; even during the war, soldier's aid societies opened with prayer and were often simply transformed benevolent societies. Women's societies for secular purposes were not entirely unknown (the Ladies Physiological Society in Boston or the black women's mutual aid groups in Philadelphia, for example), but they were few and local.

In the last thirty years of the century, religious organizations grew with astonishing speed, and three groups in particular became large and extremely influential, encompassing significant numbers of women: the home and foreign missionary societies of the Protestant churches, the Woman's Christian Temperance Union, and the Young Women's Christian Association.[20] There is no way to determine how many millions of women were included, one way and other, in these three groups, and certainly a majority of them were as conservative in religious matters as they were in politics. An articulate minority, however, argued forcefully that social justice was as much a part of a Christian's responsibility as was individual salvation and began to formulate what would later be called the Social Gospel. Many women got their first leadership experience in religious organizations. Some went on to join secular groups; others remained to become part of an impressive array of leaders whose primary work was carried out in a Christian (and usually Protestant) context. Religious organizations trained women for public life, educated some of them about social problems, and taught a few how to shape public policy. A good number became feminists as a consequence of battles for women's laity rights within the Protestant churches.

Paralleling the increasingly intense and widespread involvement of women in religious organizations was a new phenomenon, the secular woman's club or association. This movement got underway in the late 1860s with the almost simultaneous formation of a small literary club in Quincy, Illinois, and two large multipurpose associations: Sorosis, in New York and the New England Woman's Club in Boston. At the same time, women's rights advocates decided they did, after all, need a national organization and established two organizations: the National Woman Suffrage Association, which was all female, and the American Woman Suffrage Association, which admitted men.[21]

Over the next two decades literary clubs, self-help clubs, ladies' library associations, women's education associations, political equality societies, and dozens of other forms of club sprang up in every town and hamlet. A town of any size might have too many to count. By 1890, to take one example, there were at least fifty women's clubs in Portland, Maine.[22]

In an extraordinary development, which is only beginning to be studied, black women in Southern cities organized mutual aid societies, cooperative medical programs, and other kinds of groups to meet the needs of poor freedpeople.[23] Somewhat later in the century, middle-class black women formed a variety of associations, sometimes modeled on the white women's clubs from which they were almost universally excluded. Despite meager resources, these groups became vital centers for community development in black neighborhoods.[24]

Socialist women organized. Wage-earning women began to form all-female trade unions, and middle-class women tried to help them. By the 1880s perhaps a majority of women's organizations in the northeast spent some part of their time working to meet the needs of working-class women, whom they often labeled "working girls." The YWCA and the WCTU, along with the Woman's Trade Union League and the Women's Educational and Industrial Unions made serious efforts to cross class boundaries.[25]

Settlement houses such as Hull-House in Chicago and Denison House in Boston brought middle-class women, often graduates of the new women's colleges, into close association with immigrant women. It is worth noting that these same settlement houses were also one of the incubators of the new social science that was soon to take shape in the universities. The whole landscape, in short, was covered with women's societies of many kinds.

By 1893—when the great Chicago World's Fair, celebrating four hundred years since Columbus, opened with its Board of Lady Managers representing every state in the Union, its Women's Building filled with exhibits, its Congress of Representative Women from around the world, its women participants in every one of the more than two hundred cultural and scientific "congresses"—it was clear to any observer that women's organizations had become a major part of American society. Women in many communities had established "Columbian associations" to raise money for the Women's Building and to prepare for the fair, some of which continued to exist long after it had ended. There were speeches by women every day in the Women's Building, and nearly every national women's group held a conference in conjunction with the fair. The Chicago Woman's Club, one of the most active and wide ranging in the country at that time, held an open house every Wednesday afternoon so that women from other places might meet and exchange ideas. The effect of the World's Fair experience on many of the women participants was electric. The North Carolina lady manager—to take a representative example—returned home from Chicago so invigorated that she spent the next twenty-five years building a network of women's clubs in her home state.[26]

The creation at about the same time of the General Federation of Women's Clubs and the National Association of Colored Women—along with numbers of state, regional, and city federations—vastly stimulated the growth of local associations. In the General Federation alone, the number of clubs and number of members doubled in the last half of the 1890s, and numerous other kinds of groups, including patriotic societies, began to take shape as well.[27]

The most striking characteristic of this rapidly growing phenomenon of women organizing in the context of the Progressive era was their strong tendency, no matter what their original purpose, to move toward community activism. Local curricula, well-built schoolhouses, the school lunch program, hospitals, libraries, symphony orchestras, community standards for the quality of milk and water, day-care centers and public kindergartens, juvenile courts, parks, playgrounds, and public baths—these are only a few of the long list of things created by some woman's group. Black women's clubs ran through roughly the same agenda as the white women's groups, but with a special focus on the black community.[28] When Galveston, Texas, experienced one of the major natural disasters of the century—a tidal wave and flood that killed six thousand people and inundated the town—a Woman's Health Protective Association took the lead in beginning to put the town back together.[29] In 1914 the National Municipal League commissioned a young historian, Mary Ritter Beard, to find out just what women's associations were doing in the area of municipal reform. Her report filled more than three hundred pages and detailed an immense variety of activities.[30]

Meantime, the national federations were busy developing a national political agenda. Conservation of resources, for example, had come to be a concern of women's clubs in many places; their work, undertaken in the nineties, preceded what is generally called "the conservation movement" by about a decade. The California red-woods, the Kings Canyon National Park, Mesa Verde, and the palisades of the Hudson were preserved from almost certain destruction by the efforts of the clubwomen. The General Federation was given credit for the passage of the Pure Food and Drug Act of 1906, and increasingly its leaders saw themselves as responsible for representing women's views to Congress and the Administration. Women's associations, including the missionary societies, the WCTU and the YWCA, as well as numerous secular groups, took part in shaping the social justice agenda of the Progressive movement. Such things as factory inspection laws, the regulation of child labor, minimum wage and maximum hours legislation, the creation of a federal Children's Bureau were promoted by a coalition of social workers and political reformers, men as well as women. Many of the planks in the Progressive party platform of 1912 came originally from women's organizations or the settlement houses.[31]

One of the significant social changes that contributed to this growth of women's political involvement was the rapid opening of higher education for women. Women's voluntary associations in many places had worked to create women's colleges (Pembroke and Goucher, for example) or to open universities to women. By 1900, women were graduating with the bachelor's degree at the rate of five thousand a year; some were going on to graduate and professional study. The numbers of women doctors and lawyers—who often took a leading part in voluntary associations—were multiplying. College women, moving into positions of leadership, gradually changed the nature of women's associations, which grew in complexity and demonstrated a growing capacity for the organized, systematic pursuit of social and political goals based on the findings of the new social science.[32]

From about 1910 onward, the new style of women's organizational behavior was particularly visible in the suffrage movement. State and national suffrage clubs, working in tandem, organized on the basis of congressional districts, kept detailed files on each member of the legislature and each congressman (such things as information about his friends, his wife, and his views on a wide variety of subjects). A grass-roots network was created, which could fill the Senate or House office buildings in Washington, or the state capitals, with well-informed women at appropriate moments.[33] As a result of this intense effort at organization and a great deal of hard work, one state after another moved into the suffrage column; newly elected congressmen increasingly were suffragists, and by 1920 the long battle finally ended when the Congress passed and the state legislatures ratified the Nineteenth Amendment.

Conclusions

Clearly, there will be no single answer to questions about the functions served by women's voluntary associations either in terms of their participants or the broader society. Yet it is possible to argue that since the late eighteenth century, women's organizations have provided a kind of early warning system, identifying emergent social needs and trying to deal with them, first on their own and then by persuading some governmental body to undertake responsibility. Take four widely separated examples: in 1800, when urban poverty began to outrun the capacity of traditional structures, women organized benevolent societies and began to establish the principle of community responsibility for people who for whatever reason could not take care of themselves. Step by step, over more than a century, what began as philanthropy led to the organization of state and national welfare programs.

In the 1830s, when the transition to urban life and factory production made drinking a great social problem, women undertook to promote temperance, first as a matter of individual conversion, then as a matter of law. The rapid population growth of the late nineteenth century gave rise to a whole series of community needs in areas that had hitherto been handled by individual families. In response, women's clubs developed the concept of "municipal housekeeping" and went to work to make the environment cleaner and more conducive to good health.

This in turn had important social, political, and economic consequences. Women were constantly forced to ask themselves: why does poverty exist and can it be prevented? Poor health was often as important corollary of poverty. In the early years of this century, when it became apparent that infant mortality in the United States was higher than in most other industrial countries, women first persuaded the Congress to establish a Children's Bureau, and ten years later brought about the passage of the Sheppard-Towner Act for maternal and child health. The infant mortality rate declined.

Moreover, the issues first addressed by women—education, health, housing, sanitation, unequal wages, the environment—are now seen as major issues of urban politics. Similarly, some of the international issues women espoused, such as arms control, which they began to address during the First World War, and international trade, which they took up during the Second, are now vital parts of our national political agenda.

In the process of identifying emergent needs, women also began to develop some elements of an alternative ideology. Basing their arguments on traditional themes, particularly the theme of the responsibility of mothers, women began to argue for a society whose values were not centered solely on competition and material success. The dominant ideology in this country has usually been so powerful that it has simply absorbed most dissent, but to the extent that we have moved away from Social Darwinism as a fundamental belief, and toward what Jane Addams called democracy and social ethics, women's organizations have played a central role. In the beginning, women had seen themselves as doing God's work; by the twentieth century they argued that they were doing women's work. But in both cases they tried to bring an element of humanity and compassion into the public policymaking process.[34]

Other aspects of women's philanthropic activities remain to be explored. For example, although women were not alone in identifying social problems, they often tended to approach these problems differently from the ways in which men did. Nor have their efforts necessarily resulted in uniform success. Women organize, develop a capacity for leadership, observe social problems, devise proposals for solutions, or at least for amelioration, learn to lobby, achieve legislation. Communities are improved, the national agenda is humanized, the alternative ideology is available. But even when a women's group identified a key problem—as, for example, the needs of Native Americans in the late nineteenth century—and set out to do something about it, their efforts sometimes caused more harm than good.

Furthermore, American women were as much a part of the larger culture as men were, and while their outsider status may have made them sensitive to some human needs, they shared the unexamined assumptions of their own time about race, class, and ethnicity, a fact that is vividly demonstrated in the records of the General Federation of Women's Clubs and the National American Woman Suffrage Association.[35]

It must also be noted that women's clubs were sometimes a road to social status, that patriotic organizations exacerbated racial and ethnic conflict, that having developed as an effective tool, the voluntary association became available to any point of view. In our own day, we have the American Friends Service Committee—and the Ku Klux Klan; we have NOW and the Right to Life groups; Americans for Democratic Action and the John Birch Society. A full picture of the social reality of the past should include them all.

Inside their associations women, like men, sometimes jockeyed for position, sought power and status, quarreled with their colleagues, threatened to quit if they were crossed, and took impassioned stands based on meager information. Yet on the whole, women appeared more persistent in the face of discouragement than men in similar associations, and, at least in the nineteenth century, were far more inclined to get their hands dirty doing the actual work before them.

How has associational experience affected the status of women and the social definition of women's sphere? One of the most visible consequences of associational activity for individual women was the rapid development of leadership skills and self-confidence. Some psychologists have emphasized the importance of expectation in human development. As the community at large, and men in particular, began to see women working effectively in the public sphere, expectations of what women *could* do rose, with the result that they were asked to do more. This interactive process had dramatic consequences for individuals, as well as broadening the definition of what constituted appropriate activities for women. "The new woman" was no mere catch phrase; it described a significant social development.

Was Arthur Schlesinger's analysis an apt description of the work of women's voluntary associations? It is certainly true that among women the trend to collective activity began slowly, gathering momentum as new opportunities presented themselves. The development of self-confidence and the greater needs of social and economic life increased the reach of such organizations and each new experience opened the way for further ones. In the end, as he so presciently noted, almost no department of American life remained unaffected.

NOTES

1   Since it is impossible to study women's history without encountering the pervasive influence of voluntary associations perhaps it is not surprising that historians of women are responsible for important work in this field, but the mystery of almost a century of neglect on the part of male historians of what has also been a significant male enterprise remains.

   The handful of studies of men's voluntary associations includes two books about the so-called benevolent empire: Clifford S. Griffin, *Their Brothers' Keepers: Moral Stewardship in the United States, 1800–1805* (New Brunswick: Rutgers University Press, 1960), and C. I. Foster, *An Errand of Mercy: The Evangelical United Front 1790–1837* (Chapel Hill: University of North Carolina Press, 1960). Don Harrison Doyle, *The Social Order of a Frontier Community: Jacksonville, Il., 1825–1870* (Champaign: University of Illinois Press, 1978) is excellent on men's associations in a new community, but pays no attention to women's groups. Oscar and Mary Handlin, in *The Dimensions of Liberty* (Cambridge: Belknap Press of Harvard University Press, 1961) discuss the general theory of voluntary action.

2   "Biography of a Nation of Joiners," *American Historical Review* 50 (1944–1945), 1–25.

3   Frank Warren Crow, "The Age of Promise: Societies for Social and Economic Improvement in the United States 1783–1815" (Ph.D. diss., University of Wisconsin, 1952) is the best available study of eighteenth-century associations. Two recent works by Richard D. Brown are more limited, since they deal only with Massachusetts, but are illuminating: "The Emergence of Voluntary Associations in Massachusetts, 1760–1830," *Journal of Voluntary Action Research* 2 (1973), 64–73, and "The Emergence of Urban Society in Rural Massachusetts, 1760–1820," *Journal of American History* 61 (1974), 29–51.

4   Joanna Bethune, ed., *The Power of Faith Exemplified in the Life and Writings of the Late Mrs. Isabella Graham of New York* (New York, 1816).

5   The term "benevolent society" was also applied to the national, non-denominational societies set up to awaken an interest in Christianity

beyond the church. The principal groups were the American Board of Commissioners for Foreign Missionaries (1810), the American Bible Society (1816), the American Sunday School Union (1824), and the American Home Mission Society (1826). Women formed part of the labor force for all these groups, but always in a subordinate or auxiliary relationship. I am not, therefore, including them in this analysis, which is focused on organizations organized and run by women. The standard works on this so-called "benevolent empire" are Foster, *Errand of Mercy*, and Griffin, *Their Brothers's Keepers*. Both these books are myopic with respect to benevolent women.

6   *Revised constitution and by-laws of the Raleigh Female Benevolent Society with Reports of the Society From Its Commencement* (Raleigh, N.C., 1823).

7   Nancy A. Hewitt, *Women's Activism and Social Change: Rochester, New York, 1822–1872* (Ithaca: Cornell University Press, 1984).

8   "Abolition's Conservative Sisters: The Ladies' New York Anti-Slavery Societies 1834–1840." Paper delivered at the 1976 meeting of the Berkshire Conference on Women's History. The conservatism to which Sweerdlow refers in her title has to do with these women's views on women's rights, not on their antislavery views.

9   See Linda K. Kerber, *Women of the Republic: Intellect and Ideology in Revolutionary America* (Chapel Hill: University of North Carolina Press, 1980) for a fine discussion of the ideology of the republican mother. Of course, the idea was that women should raise their sons to be good republicans, but daughters learned from their mothers as well.

10   Caroll Smith-Rosenberg, *Religion and the Rise of the American City: The New York City Mission Movement, 1812–1870* (Ithaca: Cornell University Press, 1971), and Barbara J. Berg, *The Remembered Gate: Origins of American Feminism: The Woman and the City, 1800–1860* (New York: Oxford University Press, 1978), taken together, provide a picture of the early days of moral reform. Mary P. Ryan, *Cradle of the Middle Class: The Family in Oneida County, New York, 1790–1865* (New York: Cambridge University Press, 1981), looks at moral reform in Utica, and Hewitt, *Women's Activism and Social Change*, writes about moral reform in Rochester.

11   Jed Dannenbaum, "The Origins of Temperance Activism and Militancy Among Women," *Journal of Social History* (15), 235–247.

12   Figures are found in the third and fourth annual reports of the American Anti-Slavery Society (New York 1836 and 1837). The quotation is from the annual report of the Boston Female Anti-Slavery Society, *Right and Wrong in Boston* (Boston, 1836).

13   Mari Jo and Paul Buhle, *The Concise History of Woman Suffrage* (Urbana: University of Illinois Press, 1976), 198.

14   For the official view of what the Sanitary Commission aimed for and
      what it accomplished, see Charles J. Stille, *History of the United States
      Sanitary Commission* (Philadelphia, 1866). The modern history is
      William Quentin Maxwell, *Lincoln's Fifth Wheel* (New York: Longman's,
      Green, 1957), and a fascinating ironical view of what the leaders had in
      mind may be found in George Fredrickson, *The Inner Civil War* (New
      York: Harper and Row, 1965). None of these historians understood the
      fundamental part played by the soldier's aid societies.

15   Stille, *U.S. Sanitary Commission,* 180–184.

16   The written history of this enterprise has tended to focus on the national
      male leadership and to ignore the regional and local base, which was
      largely run by women. A recent dissertation has begun to redress the
      balance. Lori Ginzburg, "Women and the Work of Benevolence: Morality
      and Politics in the Northeastern United States 1820–1905" (Ph.D. diss.,
      Yale University, 1985). See also Jeanie Attie, "Forging a Liberal Political
      Culture: the ussc, Northern Women and the Care of the Union Army,"
      paper delivered at the April 1986 meeting of the Organization of Ameri-
      can Historians, based on a dissertation in progress.

17   "List of Ladies' Aid Associations in Alabama Jan. 1, 1862," Executive Pa-
      pers, Alabama Department of Archives and History, cited in H. E. Sterkx,
      Partners in Rebellion: Alabama Women in the Civil War (New Brunswick:
      Rutgers University Press, 1970), 94.

18   I am indebted to Kim Fayssoux who made a study in 1983 of women's
      work in the Civil War based on seventeen manuscript collections in the
      William R. Perkins Library of Duke University. Fayssoux's research, as
      well as that of H. E. Sterkx, suggests that there were many more women's
      benevolent societies in the South than is usually understood, since they
      were available to be rapidly transformed into soldier's aid societies.

19   Robert Wiebe, *The Search for Order* (New York: Hill and Wang, 1967).

20   Ruth Bordin, *Woman and Temperance: The Quest for Power and Liberty,
      1873–1900* (Philadelphia: Temple University Press, 1981) and Bordin,
      Frances Willard (Chapel Hill: University of North Carolina Press, 1985);
      Barbara Lee Epstein, *The Politics of Domesticity: Women, Evangelism
      and Temperance in Nineteenth Century America* (Middletown, Ct.:
      Wesleyan University Press, 1981); Jack S. Blocker, *"Give to the Winds Thy
      Fears": The Woman's Temperance Crusade 1873–1874* (Westport, Ct.:
      Greenwood, 1985); Susan Dye Lee, " 'Evangelical Domesticity': The Ori-
      gin of the Woman's National Temperance Union Under Frances E.
      Willard" (Ph.D. diss., Northwestern University, 1980) are among the best
      recent works on the wctu. Historical work on the home and foreign mis-
      sionary societies is still largely to be found in in-house church histories,
      in R. Pierce Beaver, *All Loves Excelling* (Grand Rapids, Mich.: W. B.

Eerdmans, 1968) and in Rosemary Keller et al., eds., *Women in New Worlds* (Nashville: Abingdon, 1981). The YWCA has yet to find its historian. The best thing so far available is Mary S. Sims, *The Natural History of an Institution: the YWCA* (New York: The Woman's Press, 1936). There is a great deal of interest in the history of the Y just now, so we may hope for a efflorescence of scholarship on the subject soon.

21   Ellen C. DuBois, *Feminism and Suffrage: The Emergence of an Independent Woman's Movement in America, 1848–1869* (Ithaca: Cornell University Press, 1978) is the best study of the early history of these groups. See also Anne F. and Andrew M. Scott, *One Half the People: The Fight for Women Suffrage* (Philadelphia: Lippincott, 1975).

22   Karen J. Blair, *The Clubwoman as Feminist: True Womanhood Redefined, 1868–1914* (New York: Holmes and Meier, 1980), the only monograph so far which deals with the whole club movement, has an excellent bibliography.

23   Kathleen C. Berkeley, "'Colored Ladies Also Contributed': Black Women's Activities from Benevolence to Social Welfare" in Walter J. Fraser et al., eds., *The Web of Southern Social Relations* (Athens: University of Georgia Press, 1985), 181–203. For other kinds of associations see, for example, Nancy Schrom Dye, *As Equals and As Sisters: Feminism, the Labor Movement, and the Women's Trade Union League of New York* (Columbia: University of Missouri Press, 1980); Allen Davis, *Spearheads of Reform: The Social Settlements and the Progressive Movement* (New Brunswick: Rutgers University Press, 1985); Abbie Graham, *Grace H. Dodge: Merchant of Dreams* (New York: The Woman's Press, 1926).

24   See Gerda Lerner, "Community Work of Black Club Women" in *The Majority Finds Its Past* (New York: Oxford University Press, 1979), and Susan Lynn Smith, "The Black Women's Club Movement: Self-Improvement and Sisterhood, 1890–1915" (M.A. Thesis, University of Wisconsin–Madison, 1986).

25   See Carroll Wright, ed., *Bulletin of the Department of Labor* No. 23, July 1899, which reports on a questionnaire sent to women's clubs. On the basis of more than a thousand returns, about a fourth of the clubs replying reported that they had "working women" as members. Some had set up auxiliaries, which met in the evening for the benefit of workers, of which The New Century Guild in Philadelphia with nearly a thousand members was perhaps the most impressive. It is not altogether clear whether these "working women" were blue-collar workers or clerical workers, but doubtless they included both. The clubs are often characterized as bastions of middle-class exclusion; this evidence might suggest that the judgment is too simple.

26   Sources for a study of women and the Columbian Exposition are volu-

minous. Values, attitudes, and events of the worldwide woman's movement are exhibited in three large volumes of speeches: Mary K. O. Eagle,
ed., *The Congress of Women* (Chicago: International Publishing, 1984), 2
vols., and May Wright Sewall, ed., *The World's Congress of Representative
Women* (Chicago, 1894). Jean M. Weimann, *The Fair Women* (Chicago:
Academy, 1981) is weak on context, but contains useful information. See
also Gayle Gullett, "The Political Use of Public Space: The Woman's
Movement and Women's Participation at the Chicago Columbian Exposition, 1893," paper delivered at the 1987 Berkshire Conference on the
History of Women.

27   Mary I. Wood, *History of the General Federation of Women's Clubs* (New
York: Norwood, 1912); Tullia Kay Brown Hamilton, "The National Association of Colored Women" (Ph.D. diss., Emory University, 1979); Bev-
erly Jones, "Mary Church Terrell and the National Association of
Colored Women," *Journal of Negro History* 67 (1982, 248).

28   There is a vast amount of data in state federation histories, in *The American Clubwoman, The National Municipal Review,* and in manuscripts
around the country.

29   Elizabeth H. Turner, "From Benevolent Ladies to Civic Women: Galveston's Female Voluntary Associations, 1880–1910," paper delivered at
the 1986 meeting of the Southern Historical Association. Turner's dissertation will be a major addition to the growing literature on women's associations in particular communities.

30   Mary R. Beard, *Women's Work in the Municipalities* (New York: D. Ap-
pleton, 1915).

31   When Jane Addams was criticized for seconding Theodore Roosevelt's
nomination on that platform, she rejoined that she could hardly fail to
support a party that had committed itself to the things she had worked
for all her life.

32   The phenomenon of the woman college graduate in the voluntary association would be worth careful study. Gertrude Weil, for example, was
the first woman in North Carolina to attend Smith College, where she
was taught the techniques of systematic study and exposed to a great
deal of discussion of social justice. When her family persuaded her
against a career, she returned to spend the rest of her life in Goldsboro,
North Carolina, and in time became one of the most significant political
figures in the state. Her vehicles were the Goldsboro Woman's Club, the
North Carolina Federation of Women's Clubs, the Political Equality Club
of North Carolina and, after 1920, the League of Women Voters. Gertrude
Weil Papers, North Carolina Department of Archives and History,
Raleigh, N.C.

33   The level of organizational acumen and administrative skill that could

exist in a single state—and one in which suffrage was far from a popular cause—is beautifully illustrated in the records of the Virginia Suffrage Organization in the Virginia State Library, Richmond. Doubtless there are many similarly revealing records in manuscript depositories across the country. Contrary to what is often asserted, important aspects of the history of suffrage remain to be examined.

34   The willingness of well-to-do women club leaders to call businesses to account for what they perceived as the human cost of industrialization is striking, and a challenge to some historian to analyze. See, for example, Bertha Honore Palmer, welcoming women to the Columbian Exposition with the following words: "The few forward steps which have been taken during our boasted nineteenth century—the so-called age of invention—have promoted the general use of machinery . . . with the result of cheapening manufactured articles, but have not afforded the relief to the masses, which was expected. The struggle for bread is as fierce as of old. We find everywhere the same picture presented— overcrowded industrial centers, factories surrounded by dense popula- tions of operatives, keen competition, many individuals forced to use such strenuous effort that vitality is drained, in the struggle to maintain life under conditions so uninviting and discouraging that it scarcely seems worth living. It is a grave reproach to modern enlightenment that we seem no nearer the solution of many of these problems than during feudal days" (Weimann, *The Fair Women*, 249). Palmer's husband was one of the merchant princes of Chicago.

35   My wise friend and mentor, Caroline F. Ware, whose long life included outstanding contributions to voluntary associations here and in Latin America, wrote to me on February 1, 1987: "It should not be too difficult for someone who has not thought about it to recognize that men who have or are presumed to have full access to the dominant functional or- ganizations of the society are likely to use voluntary associations, if at all, for relatively frivolous or insignificant or esoteric purposes. Women, who are engaged in voluntary activity as their norm and who have been ignored or shut out by the dominant established organizations would use an extension of their voluntary functions as the first line of expan- sion and offense and should therefore use these associations as their in- struments of social change. Yes?"

NANCY A. HEWITT

Charity or Mutual Aid?: Two Perspectives on

Latin Women's Philanthropy in Tampa, Florida

In his autobiographical novel, *The Truth About Them*, Jose Yglesias describes his Uncle Candido, an Americanized immigrant living in Tampa's Cuban community in the 1920s. "He did not say Old Folks Home with the sad, pitying accent of Latins who believed only Americans are so callous as to rid themselves of the old. That worried me."[1] From a more positive perspective, Cuban émigré Emilio Del Rio noted the generosity of female neighbors in the early years of settlement in Tampa: "When a woman gave birth, immediately the surrounding families came to offer help and brought the mama and baby, chicken and chocolate."[2] Acclaim for the informal care provided by neighbors and skepticism regarding organized charity abound in the memoirs of immigrant Cubans and Hispanics. Yet Latin women, like their native-born American counterparts, did form associations through which they provided essential social services to their communities. Also like native-born women, Latin women differed with each other over the proper forms of social assistance and the preferred direction of social change, differences shaped by distinctions of class, ethnicity, and race within the immigrant community. Though these differences were sometimes transcended, they were as often sharpened in the first decades of residence in the United States.[3]

By examining the Latin community of Tampa, we can begin to sort out the various meanings of philanthropy and the ways that gender, ethnicity, and class shaped the contents of one's philanthropic efforts. Though the Spanish term *filantropia* was rarely heard in Tampa, the involvement of Latin women in particular "charitable actions or institutions" on the one hand, and their more general "effort to increase the well-being of mankind" on the other, suggest the importance they placed on the deed if not the word.[4] These immigrant women were also objects of philanthropy, and the distinctive responses of working-class and more affluent Latins to Anglo offers of aid help clarify both the degree to which gender served as a conduit for and class served as a barrier to the flow of philanthropy across ethnic boundaries.

This essay, then, explores the range of voluntary activities that Latin women initiated or in which they participated in turn-of-the-century Tampa, Florida. Like the "early warning system" described by Anne Scott in her summary of native-born women's efforts, the associations founded by Florida's immigrant women also presaged emergent social needs and provided alternative means of meeting them. Indeed, it was often the failure of Tampa's native-born philanthropists to include immigrants among their coworkers or clients that helped nurture a separate network of ethnically based mutual aid societies. The resulting network of émigré organizations—cutting across class, race, nationality, and gender boundaries within immigrant enclaves—encompassed all five dimensions of female voluntarism outlined by Kathleen McCarthy in her essay in this volume. Creating clubs, labor organizations, and health facilities; promoting educational reform or prohibition; supporting political revolution in Cuba and working-class rights in Tampa; raising funds for rebel forces, hospital beds, and civic beautification; and melding Cuban-based models of mutual aid with North American patterns of social welfare, Tampa's Latin women formed a power structure parallel not only to that of men in their own community but also to women in the Anglo community.[5]

It was the arrival of immigrants that first sparked Anglo women's entrance into the realm of public welfare work in Tampa. In the immediate post–Civil War years, Tampa was inhabited by ex-slaves and ex-owners, free blacks, fishermen, cattle barons, soldiers, and a few women. In 1886, the construction of a company town, built by Spanish entrepreneurs and peopled by highly skilled Afro-Cuban and white Cuban laborers, turned Tampa into an industrial city. Anglo women's first recorded public efforts were begun the following year with the formation of a local branch of the Women' Christian Temperance

Union (WCTU). By 1910, the immigrant population—including large numbers of Italians as well as Spaniards and Cubans—numbered over 12,000 of the Tampa area's 56,000 residents. The cigar centers of Ybor City and later West Tampa were incorporated into the city proper, but they remained distinctly working class and Latin.

Native-born Tampa women pursued a broad spectrum of voluntary projects in these pioneer years, projects that sometimes embraced but more often excluded the efforts of their immigrant neighbors. Still, during the 1890s, the battle for Cuba's independence from Spain, culminating in the Spanish-Cuban-American War, promoted alliances among Cuban, Spanish, and Anglo women and between wealthy and poor Latins in Tampa. In the decade following the war's conclusion, however, two major and several minor strikes by laboring Latins heightened class antagonisms and created a complicated patchwork of conflicts and coalitions within the Latin community and between Latin and Anglo women activists.

In general we can trace Latin women's voluntarism along two spectrums: one, concerning the form of activity, ranges from charity to mutual aid; the other, concerning the background of activists, ranges from affluent to working class. These two sets of categories, of course, overlapped. The affluent wives of factory owners and merchants were more likely to undertake charitable projects to aid their less fortunate countrywomen and countrymen, while less fortunate Latins were more likely to depend on mutual aid societies and trade unions to sustain themselves and their families. The former allied more often with their Anglo counterparts—in pursuing prohibition or providing for orphans or the elderly—while the latter joined forces more often with Italian coworkers—in seeking higher wages and better working and living conditions.[6]

This portrait, despite its general accuracy, requires qualification, however, to capture the complex development of Latin women's philanthropic efforts, particularly among the middle class and affluent. In the years after the Spanish-Cuban-American War, these women participated in two primary arenas of voluntary labor. Anglo women's organizations sometimes invited Latin women to serve on their boards, while mutual aid societies and social clubs founded by Latin men encouraged contributions from women's auxiliaries. Although some Latin women also labored within church-based societies, local religious organizations were surprisingly limited in their scope and significance in the cigar cities.[7] It is by focusing on these parameters and permutations of women's activism among Cuban and Spanish women across all classes and in both Anglo women's organizations and Latin mutual aid societies that we can best test the influences of ethnicity and class on the particular forms of women's participation in philanthropic endeavors.

Prior to the 1890s, Latin women's contact with organized voluntarism was primarily through the local WCTU. The Anglo leaders of the organization established an Ybor City branch in 1887, though only two Latin women were among the first dozen officers, and they were listed, literally, at the bottom of the club's roster.[8] It was international politics that expanded Latin women's autonomous activities and organizations. Cubans had been actively seeking independence from Spain since the Ten Years War of 1868–1878. In 1895, the Cuban War for Independence was launched with the full economic and political support of émigré communities in New York City, Key West, and Tampa. Sympathetic Spanish factory owners and their wives, some of whom were born of Spanish parents in Cuba and all of whom depended on Cuban labor for their success, offered their support. So, too, did Anglo men and women swept up by the romantic rhetoric of national self-determination and the interventionist demands of United States capitalists and politicians.

Cuban women had begun forming revolutionary clubs as early as 1892; their numbers multiplied after war was declared. In 1895, for example, sisters Maria Luise and Fredisvinda Sánchez, daughters of revolutionary leader General Federico Sánchez, founded the Discípulas de Martí so that "the young señoritas of Tampa" might "work together" to "help conquer our independence."[9] Inspired by female heroes of earlier rebellions in Cuba, some of whom emigrated to Florida in the 1880s, the Discípulas along with Cuba Libre, 24 de Febrero, Estrella Solitaria, Hijas del Consejo de Martí, Club Patria, and other women's clubs contributed to Tampa's reputation as the "civilian camp of the revolution."[10]

The chief responsibility of the women's clubs was fundraising. Initially, most money raised for Cuban independence came from subscriptions among cigar workers, both male and female, who donated as much as one day's wages per week to the cause. The other impor-

tant sources of funds—evening entertainments, fiestas, picnics, bazaars, and door-to-door solicitations—were organized primarily by
the women's clubs. At least one such event was held almost weekly
between 1895 and 1898, raising from under $100 to over $1,000 each.[11]

Neither class nor race differences limited the commitment of
Cubans to the cause. From unskilled tobacco stemmers to wives and
daughters of Cuban capitalists, the residents of the "cigar cities" supported Cuba Libre. Inspired by the egalitarian vision of José Martí and
the military heroism of Afro-Cuban Antonio Maceo, Afro-Cubans contributed funds as well as soldiers. Paulina Pedroso, one of the leading
Afro-Cuban patriots, hosted Martí whenever he visited Tampa.[12]

Differences did emerge, however, in the forms of assistance that
various classes of Cubans could provide. While the wives and daughters of Cuban politicians and professionals, like America Herrera, donated silver table services, elegant parlor sets, and other luxury items
to be auctioned for the cause, working-class patriots sold their most
valuable resources (for Paulina and Rupert Pedroso this included their
home) to raise money.[13]

The war was not the only project that required women's services.
By April 1898, nearly three thousand Cuban refugees "were 'in great
destitution in and around Tampa' and a continuous flow of new ar-
rivals augmented that number."[14] The refugees were initially taken
into existing households and given food and housing until work could
be found. In 1896, more affluent Cuban women formed the Sociedad
de Beneficencias, modeled on a society in Havana, to coordinate relief
efforts. By 1898, no longer able to fund both the war in Cuba and relief
efforts at home, they sought additional support in the city at large. It
was then that they joined forces with Anglo and Spanish women in the
formation of a new association. The Central Relief Committee received donations from and distributed goods with the assistance of the
wives of Spanish factory owners, such as Mrs. Vicente Ybor, and Anglo
benevolent leaders, such as the president of the local Children's Home
Association, Mrs. William B. Henderson.[15]

While Anglo, Spanish, and Cuban women all worked in support of
Cuba Libre, the forms of their effort differed. In general, Anglo and
Spanish women specialized in providing charity to needy refugees,
while their Cuban counterparts collected food, clothing, and medical
supplies as well as arms and ammunition for military expeditions.

Even among Cuban women, differences emerged between the efforts of the more well-to-do wives of émigré leaders and the wives of cigar makers. The former largely directed their efforts toward aiding others, while the latter saw their husbands join insurgent forces and were left behind to sustain both armies abroad and their own families at home.

In the war's aftermath, Spanish women briefly retreated to domesticity; many well-to-do émigré leaders and their families returned to Cuba; and cigar workers, male and female, launched lengthy strikes to assert workers' control over the production process and to gain union recognition. Increasingly in Tampa, wealthy Latins were Spaniards and working-class Latins were Cubans. A five-month strike in 1901 unified both workers and manufacturers and heightened tensions between classes and ethnic groups. Factory owners expanded the activities of the Cigar Manufacturers Association formed two years earlier, while workers recruited hundreds of new members into the Sociedad de Torcedores de Tampa, popularly known as La Resistencia. A shorter strike in 1899 had provided the initial incentive for Anglo political and business leaders to integrate their Latin counterparts into such institutions as the Tampa Board of Trade and the Citizen's Committee, an anti-union vigilance (and vigilante) group. Solidified and expanded during the 1901 upheaval, these coalitions among male leaders foreshadowed the further integration of affluent Latin women into Anglo women's voluntary organizations.

The Children's Home Association was particularly receptive to Latin women. The president of the home had served alongside Spanish and Cuban women on the Central Relief Committee, and in the midst of the independence struggle, cigar manufacturers had donated funds for repairs to the institution.[16] A Day Nursery Association formed in 1902 by Anglo women also sought the support of their Latin counterparts, claiming that it was "the earnest desire of its promoters that all good ladies, without regard to creed or language, may . . . contribut[e] to the success of the work in hand." Still, the project's Anglo developers assured supporters that their work was "necessary if the foreigners who come to our shores are ever to understand American ideals."[17] Such nativist sentiments may explain why another ten years would pass before Latin women began to occupy leadership positions within such associations.

The developments over the next decade are captured in Tampa's first *Blue Book*, published in 1913, which provides a portrait of Latins' acceptance into Tampa's most prestigious charitable and social organizations. By then, middle-class Latin women—the wives, widows, and daughters of cigar factory foremen, for instance—served as WCTU officers, joined neighborhood civic clubs and local religious societies, and worked with the Ladies' Memorial Society to care for local cemeteries. Thus, Mrs. Alfredo Diaz, a cigar maker's wife, served as recording secretary of the local WCTU, while Miss Julia Figueredo, daughter of a cigar maker, was among the leaders of a Methodist society for young women. More elite Latin women—the wives and daughters of professionals and the owners of cigar factories—found one or two places open for them on the Children's Home Board and on the less important committees of the Tampa Woman's Club, and a few more in its artistic stepchild, the Friday Morning Musicale. These latter families were also listed among the small number of Latins invited to join Tampa's most exclusive social organization, the Tampa Yacht and Country Club. The vast majority of the Latin women listed in the *Blue Book* were of Spanish descent; a few with Latin surnames were Anglos who had married into Spanish wealth.

Neither middle-class nor affluent Cuban or Spanish women simply waited, however, upon invitations from their Anglo counterparts to advance the welfare of their communities. Rather, they secured for themselves critical roles in the maintenance of the city's ethnic clubs—the Centro Español, Centro Asturiano, Circulo Cubano (for white Cubans), the Union Martí-Maceo (for Afro-Cubans), and the Unione Italiana. These institutions were both social clubs and mutual aid societies. For a very small monthly fee, they provided health care, prescription insurance, and burial benefits to members who came from across the economic spectrum. Because the fees were small, clubs organized numerous social events, the admission to which added to the club's treasury. Women cigar workers and Latin housewives as well as the wives and daughters of factory foremen and owners served informally as fund-raisers, social organizers, hostesses, and on decorating committees at the turn of the century.

As early as 1901, two women, daughters respectively of a cigar maker and a minister, were listed among the officers of El Club Nacional Cubano. When this society became El Circulo Cubano in 1902, however, women were eliminated from the ranks of official board members.[18] It was a decade later that the affluent ladies of Centro Español first formalized women's role in club management through the formation of an auxiliary. In 1913, the wives of club leaders formed La Sección de Damas de Protección y Auxilio. Under the direction of Mrs. Julia Lopez, wife of a factory owner and a Centro Español leader, the ladies organized theatrical performances, festivals, *verbenas*, picnics, and other benefits. With the funds raised, they soon paid for the construction of a wall around the Centro Español cemetery and bought dozens of modern beds for surgical patients and a new operating table for the club's hospital.[19]

The members and activities of the women's auxiliaries quickly multiplied to include organizations within each of the ethnic clubs, associations of girls, young ladies, and *damas*, with separate organizations to direct recreational, health, and fund-raising projects. Within Centro Español, such activities continued to be monopolized by the most affluent women, as the club itself maintained its reputation as the cigar city's most elite institution. Its very elitism, however, was one factor that led more socially minded Spaniards to form a second club in 1902, Centro Asturiano. Here, women from less affluent families, some of whom were themselves employed as cigar makers, salesladies, or secretaries, formed a women's auxiliary with the primary purpose of improving the club's clinic and hospital facilities.

Women activists in the Circulo Cubano and Union Martí-Maceo, who were also likely to be employed themselves or to have husbands in cigar factory jobs, focused nearly all their efforts in the early years of the clubs' existence on practical benefits to aid the clubs' constituency. By the 1910s, however, recreational and cultural events vied with medical care as primary concerns of Circulo Cubano members, whose exquisitely decorated new clubhouse was described as a "cathedral for workers."[20] As in the struggle for Cuba Libre, then, all Latin women participated in mutual aid associations, yet the forms and the goals of their participation varied with their ethnic and class identity.

As Latin women increased their role in the activities of ethnic clubs, the clubs themselves increased Latins' standing in the city at large. In 1920, the editor of the *Tampa Morning Tribune* noted that when it came "to sociability, and open house hospitality, there are no people in the world who are ahead of the Latin social, and benefit, clubs and societies." Having constructed "magnificent modern club houses," Latins then opened the doors to "their American friends. Honorary and complimentary memberships are enjoyed by a large number of Tampa's best American men and women," the editor concluded.[21]

At the same time, the wealthiest members of the ladies' auxiliaries established themselves more securely in the ranks of Anglo women's associations. In 1921 Mrs. Andres Diaz, wife of a cigar manufacturer and member of the Centro Español's Sección de Damas, was appointed first vice-president of the Children's Home. The following year, during a prolonged illness of the home's leader, she served as acting president. She was the first Latin to hold such lofty positions in an organization founded by native-born women. One of her co-workers on the home's board of managers was Mrs. Celestino Vega, who was both the wife and daughter of cigar factory owners. This association's board may have been more receptive to a Latin leader since, following a devastating fire the year before, the home had been located in a renovated factory in West Tampa donated by the A. J. Mugge Cigar Company. At the time, two cigar factory owners served on the male board of trustees, and both owners and workers contributed funds to assist needy children during this critical period.

Other Anglo women's organizations were less receptive to Latin officers than the Children's Home, but by 1925 most of Tampa's charitable and reform organizations counted at least one Latin among their male trustees and female officers. Women's social and literary clubs lagged further behind, though those devoted to music continued to create some openings for Latin women in this area. Stereotypes regarding Latins' musical and theatrical abilities may account as well for the appointments of Mrs. Vega and Mrs. Diaz to the entertainment committee of the Tampa League of Women's Clubs in the 1920s. They were the only two Latin women to hold committee offices of any kind.

Indeed, in 1920, the ethnocentric biases of local clubwomen became more visible as the league launched an Americanization program in West Tampa. By 1922, a West Tampa Americanization and Charity League had been established; no Latin women were among its officers. In addition, the Young Women's Christian Association, despite its direct concern with assisting working girls and women,

appointed no Latin women to its board and had little success attracting working-class Latins to its programs. National leaders of the YWCA
claimed the local was too evangelical and old-fashioned to appeal to
the large population of female cigar workers.[22]

The potential for tension between Anglo and Latin women leaders,
reflected in aggressive Americanization programs and a disinterested
YWCA, was exacerbated by a prolonged strike in 1920–1921 that
aroused nativist and racist rhetoric against Latin laborers and resulted in vigilante actions by the husbands of Tampa's leading philanthropic ladies. As in 1901, militant union activity brought to the
surface subtle racial, ethnic, and class tensions that were obscured or
muted in more peaceful times. Local newspaper editors declaimed
against "hot-blooded Latins" who were "easily led to ruin by bol-
sheviki agitators" and declared for the deportation of "alien
troublemakers."[23]

Latin factory owners and their wives must have wondered at the
underlying beliefs of their anti-union allies. Yet the majority were able
to distance themselves from charges against Latin laborers who were
predominantly Cuban by emphasizing their own Hispanic heritage
and their readier assimilation into Anglo organizations and institutions. Class, if not ethnic, distinctions were reinforced by Anglo elites,
who proclaimed that the "American citizens of Tampa have long admired the manner in which the better element of the Latin members
of the city have gone ahead and made themselves an honored and distinctive place in the city's life." Noting that "especially along lines of
social welfare and intercourse, is this true," Tampa's affluent Latin
women may have found consolation in such accolades.[24]

Class consciousness was also central to the attitudes and self-
perceptions of workers, who responded vehemently to their class en-
emies, regardless of ethnicity. Robert Lovett, a native-born American
and secretary of the Florida State Board of Trade, captured the sentiments of Latin strikers in a report to the *Tampa Citizen* in July 1920. "I
cannot understand," he wrote, "how men who will take the grand-
stand part in any campaign to raise funds for a children's home, an old
folks' home, or any other move where there is unlimited chance for
publicity, will turn the other hand and assist in pinching the life out of
poor workmen." A few weeks earlier Mayor D. B. McKay had offered
the Children's Home as a refuge for the children of Cuban and Italian

strikers, and "was met with a firm refusal." By July, McKay was leading the fight against the striking cigar makers. Mr. Lovett concluded, "One can only admire the foresight of those starving Latin families. I would regret to have to leave my children to the tender mercy of men, who will try to squeeze the life blood out of me while living."[25] Of course, neither the strikers nor the charity workers were all male. Indeed, it was Latin women, workers and wives of workers, who most likely made the decision not to leave their children in the care of Anglo and Latin women voluntarists.

At the same time, one of the factors that allowed laboring families to survive during prolonged strikes was the medical benefits and other social services provided by mutual aid societies in which both wealthy and working-class, Spanish and Cuban women, voluntarily labored. During strikes, mutual aid took on a new and more radical form among workers as the unemployed pooled and then redistributed everything from food to housing on the basis of need. The rejection of more conventional charitable assistance necessitated this more democratic brand of philanthropy if laborers were to survive. That they did survive then led working-class Cubans to view the offers of charity from affluent neighbors, whether Anglo or Hispanic, with even greater skepticism.

The philanthropic activities of women in Tampa illustrate the complex and fluid character of ethnic and economic alliances among Latin and Anglo women and men. Clearly by the mid-1920s, Latin women's involvement in both charity and mutual aid projects had become widely accepted, indeed was essential to the provision of social services in Ybor City and West Tampa. Though Latin women continued to be outnumbered by Anglos in Tampa's mainstream benevolent organizations and remained auxiliary to men within Latin mutual aid societies, they were not the subservient and domesticated lot suggested by the paternalism of Anglos or the Latin legacy of machismo. Mrs. Dolores Rio, a cigar maker who was active in Centro Asturiano, recalled that the clubs "had men's and women's [sections], but they were the ones to tell us what to do." Nevertheless, when the women wanted to have a dance in 1925 to raise money for hurricane victims, and one of the male directors opposed it, Rio said, "We had it anyway, and it was a success."[26]

Not until the 1970s, however, did women gain official status alongside men on the boards of the Latin Clubs. In that year, Marie Fontaniello led a one-woman campaign for representation on the Centro Español Hospital Board. Yet, she assured her male colleagues that she was "no 'women's libber.'" "I'm a fighter for people, not just one group of people," she said.[27]

It is important to note that even among ethnic minorities, factors such as class and race channeled women into distinct and sometimes competing associations and movements. Affluent Spanish women, for instance, often defined their voluntary labor as charity, while their working-class Cuban "sisters" involved themselves in various forms of mutual aid and collective action. Middle-class Latin women found themselves pulled in both directions, their efforts at any particular moment being shaped by political struggles, labor conditions, and nativist sentiments, and by the needs of their own families.

Still, Latin women shared an ethnic identity that did provide grounds for establishing a distinctive form of philanthropy that crossed class boundaries. Those grounds were exclusion from the Anglo community, the continued prejudices of that community, the recreational and health needs within the Latin communities, and the collective residential segregation of Spaniards, white Cubans, and Afro-Cubans. Latin women of all classes shared a commitment to the programs of mutual aid societies. In pursuit of mutual aid, certain tasks, most notably fund raising, consistently fell to women, regardless of ethnic or racial heritage; and women's auxiliaries often extended their fund-raising efforts to aid the victims of storms, epidemics, or wars, whether or not the victims were members of their club. The health benefits provided by these societies were particularly attractive to women, and oral histories testify to women's greater concern with the medical services related to childcare, maternity, and occupational health risks, and men's greater concern with the social benefits of club membership.[28] Health services were often central as well to women's efforts to assist nonclub members.

Finally, it is clear that the choice of particular forms of action and of allies were complex and changeable. They were shaped in part by relations with Latin men and Anglo women, in part by ethnic antagonisms and international politics, and in part by Latin solidarity in the face of Anglo nativism. Still, the fundamental divide was between those who chose to aid and improve (and often thereby control) others and those who sought—through mutual aid—to lift even as they climbed. That some Latin women participated in both forms of philanthropy demonstrates the intricate interdependency of individuals' class, ethnic, and gender identities and experiences.

The study of Latin women in Tampa suggests the critical need for studies of immigrant women in other sections of the country before we can draw a complete portrait of ethnic women's activism and therefore of women's activism in the United States. These studies will do more than simply expand the spectrum of women activists, for as the study of Tampa's Latin women reveals, we will be forced to examine more fully that which Kathryn Kish Sklar argues is essential—the social and political context in which women forged alliances and formed associations.

By focusing on these different contexts and the different forms of activism they nurtured, we can make visible the multifaceted components of philanthropy and return to the term its original richness. No longer confined to simple charity, philanthropy will once again refer to the diverse expressions of women's and men's "love of mankind."[29] Having thus expanded the field of inquiry, scholars can then more accurately assess the ways that gender, racial, ethnic, and class relations rooted in structures of social, political, and economic power shaped the forms and consequences of particular philanthropic ventures.

NOTES

1   Jose Yglesias, *The Truth About Them* (New York: World, 1971), 80.
2   Emilio del Rio, *Yo Fui Uno de los Fundadores de Ybor City* (Tampa: By Author, 1972), 74. Quote translated from the original Spanish by the author.
3   It is necessary to say a few words about terminology here. In Tampa, the word "Latin" has been used historically to designate Spaniards and Cubans collectively. The word "Hispanic," meaning literally of Spain, was used only in its original and narrowest meaning. Since the first Cuban immigrants were seeking to overthrow Spanish imperialism in their homeland, they did not wish to be confused with their oppressors. Latins used the word "Anglo" to refer to their native-born neighbors. I will use this term as well because some of the Latin women I will be

discussing were American citizens and because it distinguishes white from black Americans. Racial distinctions are also important when discussing Cubans whose activities became more racially distinct the longer they lived in the segregated South.

4   Definitions from the *Concise American Heritage Dictionary* (Boston: Houghton, Mifflin, 1980), 531.

5   See Anne Firor Scott, "Women's Voluntary Associations: From Charity to Reform," and Kathleen D. McCarthy, "Parallel Power Structures: Women and the Voluntary Sphere," both in this volume.

6   These patterns are discussed in detail in Nancy A. Hewitt, "Varieties of Voluntarism: Class, Ethnicity and Women's Activism in Tampa, Florida" in *Women, Politics, and Change*, ed. Patricia Gurin and Louise Tilly (New York: Russell Sage Foundation, 1990).

7   For a discussion of the reasons for the anticlericalism of Tampa Latins, see Gary Mormino and George Pozzetta, *The Immigrant World of Ybor City: Italians and Their Latin Neighbors, 1885–1985* (Urbana: University of Illinois Press, 1987), Chapter 7.

8   *Tampa Journal*, May 21, 1887.

9   *Juventud Rebelde* (Havana), August 23, 1982, p. 2, describes Anita Merchan's role in the founding of this club. For the role of the Sanchez sisters, see Wen Galvez, *Tampa: Impresiones de un Emigrado* (Havana: Tipográfico de Cuba, 1897).

10   José Martí, father of Cuban Independence, quoted in Joan Marie Steffy, "The Cuban Immigrants of Tampa, Florida, 1886–1898" (M.A. Thesis, University of South Florida, 1975), 52.

11   Ibid., 72, 96.

12   See, José Muñiz, *The Ybor City Story* (Tampa: Tampa Tribune Press, 1969), 91–92.

13   *Tampa Morning Tribune*, April 7, 1895, p. 1; and Muñiz, *Ybor City Story*, 91–92.

14   Steffy, "Cuban Immigrants of Tampa," 97.

15   Ibid., 124–125.

16   *Tampa Morning Tribune*, November 24, 1898.

17   Ibid., November 23, 1902, and December 6, 1903.

18   Tampa City Directory, 1901. At the same time, Afro-Cubans were excluded from club membership, and they founded their own mutual aid society, Union Martí-Maceo.

19   History of Centro Español, *Memorial Book, Fiftieth Anniversary 1891–1941* (Tampa Tribune Press, 1941), 98–99.

20   Quoted in Mormino and Pozzetta, *Immigrant World*, 185.

21   *Tampa Morning Tribune*, October 22, 1920.

22   Mrs. George Wittick, Report (November 1923) and Eleanor Coperhaver, Report (March 1928), Local Files, Reel 169: Florida and Georgia, Papers of the Young Women's Christian Association, YWCA Archives, New York, New York.

23   From an editorial in the *Tampa Morning Tribune*, January 2, 1921. This was typical of editorials in the local newspapers and in tobacco trade journals during the strikes of 1910, 1919, 1920–1921, and 1931.

24   *Tampa Morning Tribune*, October 22, 1920.

25   Robert Lovett to L. P. Dickie, July 20, 1920, published in the *Tampa Citizen.*

26   Interview by author with Mrs. Dolores Rio, September 4, 1985.

27   See the article on Marie Fontaniello's fight to get women on the Centro Español Hospital Board in the *Tampa Tribune*, September 14, 1977.

28   Del Rio, *Fundadores*, 59. Interviews by the author with Mrs. Dolores Rio, September 4, 1985, Mrs. Angie Garcia, December 18, 1984, and Mrs. Carmela Cammaratta, April 27, 1987.

29   *Concise American Heritage Dictionary*, 531.

DARLENE CLARK HINE

"We Specialize in the Wholly Impossible":

The Philanthropic Work of Black Women

The philanthropic work of nineteenth- and early-twentieth-century Afro-American women ensured the survival of many of the most vulnerable members of the black population. To date, this important dimension of the black self-help tradition has received scant scholarly attention. In part, to correct the historical oversight, but also to probe the ways in which black women's perceptions of and involvement in philanthropy changed over time, this essay will examine the life and philanthropic work of Jane Edna Hunter, founder of the Phillis Wheatley Association in Cleveland, Ohio. Hunter's life is best understood when examined as interrelated sequences; migration to the urban Midwest, establishment of an institution to serve and to save black girls from poverty and prostitution, and the sharing of her private life with a significant female friend, Nannie H. Burroughs.

For centuries, black women, during slavery and in freedom, played a significant role in the creation of social, cultural, educational, religious, and economic institutions designed to improve the material conditions and to raise the self-esteem of Afro-Americans. The records detailing black women's involvement in mutual aid societies, literary and social clubs, churches, antislavery and temperance organizations, as founders of primary schools, orphanages, clinics, and old folks' homes are only now being discovered and interpreted.[1]

To comprehend fully the origins and nature of the modern institutional infrastructure of Black America requires a sustained analysis of the motives and deeds of the generations of black women active between the collapse of Reconstruction and the outbreak of World War II.

This rich and turbulent period encompassed the domestic feminism of the Progressive era and the economic crises of the Great Depression. Through it all, the vulnerable black community—especially its aged and sick, its orphaned children, and abandoned wives and mothers, its unskilled and illiterate workers—suffered a plethora of social ills. In many communities black women proved especially resourceful, either through the agency of their clubs or as the bedrock of the black church, to redress the harsh consequences of black economic discrimination, political subordination, and white supremacy.[2]

At the turn of the century, Midwestern urban black women had become much more professional in providing assistance to blacks in need. Spurred by the exigencies of the massive migration of black Southerners and their concentration in key cities such as Chicago, Cleveland, Detroit, Milwaukee, and Indianapolis, black clubwomen embarked upon a veritable crusade of philanthropic or beneficient work. By 1920 determined black women had established in every representative community, homes for the aged, hospitals and sanitariums, nursing schools and colleges, orphanages, libraries, gymnasiums, and shelters for young migrants, especially those who were, as historian Joanne J. Meyerowitz contends, "women adrift."[3]

The black leaders of the women's clubs and organizations, which spearheaded so much institution building and race-reclamation work, never possessed the resources distributed by white philanthropists, such as John D. Rockefeller, Julius Rosenwald, or Andrew Carnegie. Yet in many ways their giving of time and effort and commitment to racial uplift work—including providing protection for young black womanhood—and their endless struggle to create living space for segregated, often illiterate, unskilled, and impoverished blacks were as valuable as were the two-room Rosenwald schools built throughout the South, the libraries funded by Carnegie, and the Rockefeller-supported black medical schools—Meharry in Nashville, Tennessee, and Howard in Washington, D.C.[4]

Unlike the impersonal institutional forms promoted by wealthy whites, such as the General Educational Board or the Rosenwald Fund, black philanthropy and charitable giving usually assumed the form of small-scale, personal assistance and involvement. In most cases the women knew well the individuals, families, or groups whom they assisted. They emphasized the importance of volunteer service as preferable to simply making financial donations to worthy causes. Black women's philanthropy, in short, attempted to help blacks to survive and to improve their lot by developing themselves. The goal was social change and individual improvement not social control.[5]

The life and work of educator Ada Harris of Indianapolis, Indiana, illustrates one of the special forms of individual giving and self-help leadership provided by a local community. A 1909 *Indianapolis Star* article heralded Harris as the leader of the reclamation of Norwood, a small impoverished, all-black settlement situated on the outskirts of Indianapolis. According to the *Star*, Norwood was "a moral blot on the map of Marion County." The settlement acquired its bad reputation from the crap games and the prostitution rings that allegedly flourished in the area. Harris, well aware of Norwood's shortcomings, nevertheless moved into the community. She had taught school in the area since the late 1880s. By 1909 Harris was not only a resident of Norwood but principal of the local school. She insisted that her "greatest ambition" was to serve her race: "I want to see my people succeed. I want them to have an equal chance."[6]

To ensure that her students would have that "equal chance," Harris gave a great deal of herself, foregoing a private life in service to her race. At one point she reasoned that hunger, illness, fear, and hopelessness impaired her students' academic performance. Drawing upon the people's desire to improve their own lives and surroundings, especially the women in the community, Harris launched a drive to raise funds for the development of a Boys' Club, which she proclaimed would allow the adults to "teach right living in addition to the 3R's," to the young boys. The initial fund-raising campaign for the establishment of a Boys' Gymnasium and Clubhouse netted only $35.00, which Harris used as down payment on property valued at $1,500. In defending her decision to place so much emphasis on erecting a gymnasium, Harris declared, "if it only teaches the colored boy to fight with his first, and not to pull a knife or a gun on the slightest provocation it will have been worthwhile." She insisted that a gymnasium would allow the young boys to master important work skills and develop appropriate habits. Moreover, she asserted that "The class-work and the drills will strengthen our boys up and give them lungs that fight the tuberculosis that reaps such a harvest in the race."[7]

Although the *Star* article only hinted at the problems of prostitution in the Norwood area, no mention was made of the uninvestigated assaults on black women. Harris's focus on establishing a boys' gymnasium may well have reflected her concern with the ill-treatment and low status of black women in the community. She, as did other women, deplored the molestations of black females in the area and, for that matter, in other parts of the state. Harris, however, believed that to protect black women effectively from criminal abuse and sexual assaults, it was necessary to eradicate the negative stereotypes of their sexuality. Protecting black women also depended upon the success of efforts to teach black boys and men to respect black women more. Developing pride, providing creative outlets for juvenile exuberance, and challenging negative assessments of the moral fiber of black women were the driving motivations of many black women who engaged in social service and reform work during the opening decades of the twentieth century. In assessing her life work, Harris declared, "My field has been small in Norwood, but it has been plenty large enough for my abilities. At least I shall have spent my life for my race."[8]

The schools and colleges they founded, the old folks' homes, orphanages, and sanitariums, settlement houses, and clinics built to ameliorate the disorder of emancipation followed by the trauma of Southern violence, migration, and urbanization became monuments representing black women's racial uplift and philanthropic work.[9] There is yet another dimension to black women's philanthropic work, one that is not reflected in structures of brick and mortar. It is what they gave in order to reclaim black women's pride, dignity, and self-esteem. Only black women had the responsibility to fight the larger society's best efforts to define them as inferior, immoral, and therefore as undeserving of respect and equal educational and employment opportunities. Before black women could move into the larger arena of civic reform work, they had first to establish that their sexual natures were above reproach. Only when the larger society accepted them as virtuous women would it be possible to press their broad demands for social reform.[10]

One of the more revealing and successful sets of institutions created by early-twentieth-century black clubwomen and community women were the training schools and industrial institutes. Often these vocational high schools were reserved for black girls, but on occasion they were coeducational. The founders of the most noteworthy and long-lived industrial-vocational training schools and institutes were indomitable black women who deserve considerably more scholarly attention than they have heretofore received. Among the most significant activist founders were Mary McLeod Bethune (1875–1955), Charlotte Hawkins Brown (1883–1961), Jane Edna Harris Hunter (1882–1959), and Nannie H. Burroughs (1879–1961).

Mary McLeod Bethune was born on July 10, 1875, at Mayesville, South Carolina, the fifteenth child of former slaves, Samuel and Patsy McLeod. Following completion of her education at Scotia Seminary (now Barber-Scotia College) at Concord, North Carolina, she attended the Moody Bible Institute in Chicago and was graduated in 1895. Bethune founded at Daytona, Florida, on October 4, 1904, the Daytona Literary and Industrial School for Training Negro Girls. In 1923 the school merged with an all-boys' school named Cookman Institute to become Bethune Cookman College. Asked why she founded the training school and its significance, Bethune remarked, "Many homeless girls have been sheltered there and trained physically, mentally and spiritually. They have been helped and sent out to serve, to pass their blessings on to other needy children."[11] Bethune served a two-term stint as president of the National Association of Colored Women's Clubs (1924–1928).

Charlotte Hawkins Brown was born in Henderson, North Carolina, on June 11, 1882, and was educated at the Cambridge English High School in Cambridge, Massachusetts. She attended the Salem Normal School, receiving her diploma in 1901. In 1902, Brown founded the Palmer Memorial Institute, at Sedalia, North Carolina, and served as its principal until 1952. In subsequent years she would launch a fund-raising drive to establish an Industrial Home for delinquent black girls. Brown once lamented, "Until somebody can express confidence enough in a Negro women to give her the chance to do something big for her people, she will always be looked upon as a maid or as a servant."[12] In 1909 Brown helped to organize the North Carolina State Federation of Negro Women's Clubs. She became the president of the federation in 1915 and occupied that position until 1936. Under her guidance the federation purchased and maintained the Efland Home for Wayward Girls located in Orange County, North Carolina. She was also instrumental in founding the Colored Orphanage at Oxford, North Carolina.[13]

It is ironic that Nannie H. Burroughs and Jane Edna Hunter established institutions precisely to make available to black women training that would enable them to be better maids. Burroughs was born in Orange, Virginia, on May 2, 1879. Her parents, John and Jennie (Poindexter) Burroughs had been slaves. She was graduated from the Washington High School in Washington, D.C., and secured a post as bookkeeper and associate editor of the *Christain Banner* in Philadelphia. Her interest in the affairs of the Baptist Church brought her into contact with the officers of the National Baptist Convention. Upon moving to Louisville, Kentucky, she worked for several years as the private secretary of Dr. L. G. Jordan, secretary of the Foreign Mission Board of the National Baptist Convention. She also lectured and wrote denominational papers. In one year, 1908, Burroughs raised more than $13,000 from black women alone to finance the missionary and educational work for the Women's Convention Auxiliary.[14]

Burroughs's talents and passion for religious and missionary work soon catapulted her into the higher echelons of the convention's bureaucracy. She served as the corresponding secretary of the Women's Auxiliary of the National Baptist Convention from 1900 to 1947 and as its president from 1949 until 1961. An anonymously written description of Burroughs exulted,

> She lives a simple life, and is free from vanity and affection. She has a head full of common sense, and that head is well pinned on. Success does not turn it. Women in all walks of life admire her. She is not affected by praise. Here is a story of a young woman who is just beyond thirty and has come from the bottom of the round to the position of President of the only school of national character over which a Negro woman presides.[15]

Burroughs acquired national renown for establishing the National Training School for Women and Girls in Washington, D.C., which she opened on October 19, 1909, with thirty-one pupils. The building that housed the school was a dilapidated eight-room farmhouse located "in a community called Lincolnville, of less than a dozen houses and without streets, water, telephone or electric lights." Welcoming women and girls of all denominations, Burroughs commented on the purpose of the combination boarding school and training school. "Two thirds of the colored women must work with their hands for a living, and it is indeed an oversight not to prepare this army of bread-winners to do their work well." In 1934 the school was renamed the National Trades and Professional School for Women.

Burroughs raised almost all of the money for the maintenance of the school from blacks. Indeed, the black woman banker of Richmond, Virginia, Maggie L. Walker, donated $500 to the school while it was still in the planning stage. Burroughs sometimes referred to the institution as the school of the three "B's"—the Bible, the Bath, and the Broom. As one writer described it, "The Institution, then, started as a school, Christian in its teaching, character building in its ideals, cultural in its atmosphere, standardized in its academic work, practical in its vocational courses." The school provided instruction at the secondary and teacher-training levels, and offered vocational courses in "housekeeping, domestic science and art, household administration, management for matrons and directors of school dining rooms and dormitories, interior decorating, laundering, home nursing, and printing."[16]

Although the early circumstances of their lives differed greatly, Jane Edna Hunter's work on behalf of black women can be viewed as the Midwestern counterpart to that of the eastern-based Nannie H. Burroughs. Jane Edna Harris Hunter was born on December 13, 1882, in a two-room tenant house on Woodburn Farm, near Pendleton, Anderson County, South Carolina. Her sharecropping parents, Harriet and Edward Harris, moved four times before she was ten, and with each move their standard of living deteriorated. The death of her father in 1892 left her mother no alternative but to place each of her four children into the employ of white families as domestic servants. Throughout this turbulent period, poor, rural black women had virtually no hope of securing employment outside of domestic service or agriculture. Although many sex-segregated jobs in offices and department stores were opening for women, racism proved inimical to black women's advance even in the cities.[17] The most accessible occupation or profession for black women of Hunter's working-poor background was nursing.

While still a teenager, Jane was compelled to marry a man forty years her senior. Her mother deemed it the best protection for her daughter. The marriage, however, was a disaster, lasting only fifteen months. At the age of seventeen, Jane went to Charleston, South

Carolina, to work as a domestic servant and child nurse for a prominent white family. While there she learned from Ella Hunt, Chairwoman of the Ladies' Auxiliary of the recently opened black hospital, of the opportunity to pursue nursing training.[18]

The Charleston Hospital and Training School for nurses was founded in 1896 by a group of black physicians led by Alonzo McClennan. Rigid adherence to racial exclusion and the denial of attending privileges at the white hospitals had motivated black physicians across the country to found a network of hospitals and nursing schools in the last decade of the twentieth century. Hunter entered the Charleston Hospital, and after completing the eighteen-month course, she worked as a private duty nurse in the city. In 1904, feeling the need for more training, she entered the Dixie Hospital and School for Nurses at Hampton Institute in Hampton, Virginia. Immediately upon the completion of this second training program, Hunter, like so many other blacks, joined the great migration north in search of better employment opportunities.[19]

Hunter arrived in Cleveland, Ohio, on May 10, 1905, with $1.75 in her pocket. During the first frustrating week of searching for a job, she met with contempt, slammed doors, and outright hostility. One white physician allegedly admonished her "Go back South; white doctors don't employ nigger nurses." Fortunately, with only $.25 left, Hunter persuaded the white county coroner, L. E. Seigelstein, to give her a job. Through his intercession she subsequently secured work providing massages for well-to-do white women. She eventually established a good reputation and became a highly desired bedside nurse. Nursing among Cleveland's prominent white elites allowed Hunter to make important contacts and to win the confidence of people who controlled sizable resources.[20]

Up to 1905, Hunter's life was characterized by the same trials and tribulations experienced by most poor, barely educated, young, single black women who grew up in the impoverished South and who believed that nursing or domestic service, coupled with migration, was the key to a better life in the North. The details of Hunter's migration experience, her struggles to find a job, a decent, affordable place to live, and the process through which she became part of a community of women mirrored the processes of migration, immigration, and adaptation of ethnic European and American native-born farm

women.[21] The powerful impact of racism, however, severely restricted Hunter's chance for economic advance. Unlike the white farm
girls who went to the cities, or the European immigrants who crossed
the ocean, Hunter could not aspire to jobs in most factories, department stores, offices, or industrial plants. In describing the conditions
of black women workers in Chicago, historian Meyerowitz observed,
"Almost no black women held jobs in offices and stores in Chicago in
the late nineteenth and early twentieth centuries. . . . Employers also
excluded black women from many manufacturing jobs. The growing
number of black women who found work in industry frequently found
themselves with the work that white women refused to accept."[22]

The vast majority of black women worked only in agriculture or in
domestic service, while others performed only the meanest, the
lowest paid, and the most undesirable jobs—and were always the last
hired and first fired. For most black women, dreams of acquiring
higher education and better jobs were little more than delusions. After
World War I, urban black women tended to form a servant and laun-
dress class. In three major Midwestern cities, Chicago, Cleveland, and
Detroit, "black women were 4 percent of all women, yet comprised
from 23 to 30 percent of servants and from 43 to 54 percent of laun-
dresses." Similarly, historian Alice Kessler-Harris points out that "Agricultural labor, domestic service, and laundry work accounted for 75
percent of all black women who worked in 1920." In some cities, she
noted, "the proportion of wage-earning black women in domestic service rose to 84 percent."[23]

Hunter's early childhood and young adult encounters with hard-
ships could have induced bitterness and a sense of resignation to a life
of poverty and despair. Instead, drawing upon the values instilled in
her youth, and a deep religious faith, Hunter eschewed thoughts of
giving up or returning to the South. Fully cognizant of the even more
restricted opportunities and the sexual dangers inherent in being an
unattached and therefore vulnerable black woman in that region,
Hunter realized that going home was simply out of the question.

After years of observing the underside of black life in Cleveland,
Hunter took action. She mused in her autobiography, "Sometimes I
feel I've just been living my life for the moment when I can start things
moving toward a home for poor Negro working girls in the city." She
resolved to consolidate the negligible resources of the other similarly

excluded and oppressed black women with whom she interacted and labored to create an agency to assist young black females in their adjustment to urban life. On November 11, 1911, she called a meeting of a group of young black servant girls whom she had met while nursing in private white homes. She persuaded the girls to pool their resources, and in 1912 they established the Phillis Wheatley Association. A year later they opened a boarding house.[24]

At the initial planning meeting for the Phillis Wheatley Association, one young woman had exclaimed, "Poor people like us can't do anything." Undaunted, Hunter rejoined, "It's only poor people like you and me who can do anything." She allayed their doubts and misgivings, declaring, "We've all of us been poor motherless children, and the Lord is going to help us build a home for all the other poor daughters of our race."[25] This agency thus became both a "home for friendless negro (*sic*) girls," and a "training-school for the industrious," and ambitious. As one writer put it: "Her aim was to rescue and to assist young negro (*sic*) girls alone and friendless in a great city, without employment, reduced to squalor in disreputable tenements, and well-nigh helpless against mental, physical and moral degradation; and to lift the standards of negro-working women by adequate training for efficient and self-respecting service."[26]

The "moral degradation" obliquely referred to was the prostitution trap awaiting so many naive, impoverished, black country women who, like Hunter, had migrated to Northern cities in search of better lives. Of course, some had fled not only poverty, but domestic violence and sexual abuse. Historian Ruth Rosen argues that poverty directly affected women's choice to enter prostitution. She maintains that "the low wages paid to women workers, the sudden changes in family income status, and the desire for upward mobility were some of the most important economic factors influencing women's decision to practice prostitution. For black girls and women, the effects of racism and poverty made for a powerful push towards prostitution."[27]

It did not take Hunter long to observe the process whereby country women found themselves trapped in prostitution. She observed:

> The few months on Central Avenue made me sharply aware of the great temptations that beset a young woman in a large city. At home on the plantation, I knew that some girls had been seduced.

Their families had felt the disgrace keenly. The fallen ones had been wept and prayed over. In Charleston I was sent by the hospital to give emergency treatment to prostitutes, but they were white women. Until my arrival in Cleveland I was ignorant of the wholesale organized traffic in black flesh.[28]

Hunter's home, named after the eighteenth-century black poetess, Phillis Wheatley, eventually became a pivotal center around which Cleveland's working-class black women residents mobilized and directed their charitable work for girls and young women, many of whom could very well have been their own sisters and daughters. These community women raised funds, and those who had no money to give rolled up their sleeves and "washed the dirty windows, scrubbed the dirty floors, and scraped off twenty layers of old paper from the walls." Through well-orchestrated annual fund-raising drives, and an exhausting speaking schedule, Hunter developed and honed her public relations skills; and as the decades wore on, she secured substantial contributions from prominent whites in Cleveland, some of whom she had met while practicing private duty nursing in their homes. Undoubtedly, many whites were motivated to donate money in order to preserve the racial exclusiveness of the local Young Women's Christian Association. Other whites, especially middle-class women who frequently bemoaned the inadequacies of their hired help, supported the association out of a desire to promote the production of better trained domestic servants.[29]

Indisputably, the volunteer services and donations of working-class black community women sustained the institution, especially throughout the early years. To be sure, not all blacks in Cleveland supported the home. Some, on ideological grounds, objected to it because, as they argued, the home represented an accommodation to, and indeed fostered, racial segregation. Hunter appeased this group of dissenters by inviting a number of the most distinguished white men and women in the city to serve on the association's board of directors. It was a wise tactical move, but one done with some ambivalence, for the result was that the management and control of the institution had to be shared with, as historian Kenneth Kusmer put it, "a group of upper-class white women who knew little about the needs and interests of recent southern migrants."[30]

By the advent of the Great Depression, the Phillis Wheatley Home had amply demonstrated its value and had become a model and an inspiration to other communities throughout the Middle West. An average of 150 girls were being housed yearly in the home, and many more were using its facilities. As word of Hunter's work spread, she was soon elected to a prominent position within the National Association of Colored Women's Clubs, and oversaw the development of Phillis Wheatley Homes across the country. By 1934 the following cities had homes patterned after Hunter's Phillis Wheatley Home: Denver, Atlanta, Seattle, Boston, Detroit, Chicago, Greenville, Winston-Salem, Toledo, and Minneapolis.[31] It was in the NACW that the lives of most of the first generation of prominent black women institution builders intersected. As a highly visible member of the organization, Hunter became well acquainted with the work of Mary McLeod Bethune, Charlotte Hawkins Brown, and Nannie H. Burroughs.

The National Association of Colored Women's Clubs represents the institutionalization of black women's voluntarism and philanthropy. Founded in 1896 by a cadre of well-educated, financially secure black women, among whom were Josephine St. Pierre Ruffin (1842–1924), Mary Church Terrell (1863–1954), Fannie Barrier Williams (1855–1944), Ida Wells Barnett (1862–1931), Mary B. Talbert (1862–1923), Janie Porter Barrett (1865–1948), and Mary Murray Washington (1865–1925), the NACW became a powerful advocate of self-improvement and racial uplift. The broad inclusive vision of these indomitable clubwomen mandated an end to all racial and gender discrimination. Black educator, and former slave Anna Julia Cooper (1858–1964) best "crystalize[d] the sentiment" and articulated the ideology of these pioneer black voluntarists when she declared in 1893:

> The colored woman feels that woman's cause is one and universal; . . . is sacred and inviolable; [and] not till race, color, sex, and condition are seen as the accidents, and not the substance of life, not till the universal title of humanity of life, liberty, and the pursuit of happiness is conceded to be inalienable to all; not till then is woman's lesson taught and woman's cause won—not the white woman's, not the black woman's, not the red woman's, but the cause of every man and of every woman who has writhed silently under a mighty wrong. Woman's wrongs are thus indissolubly

linked with all undefended woe, and the acquirement of her "rights" will mean the final triumph of all right over might, the supremacy of the moral forces of reason, and justice, and love in the government of the nations of earth.[32]

The initial orientation and objectives of the early black women's clubs focused on raising the cultural, intellectual, and educational status of black women and on creating a positive image of their sexuality. The founders of such pioneering clubs as the Woman's Era Club (Boston, 1892), the Colored Women's League (Washington, D.C., 1892), and the Woman's Loyal Union (Brooklyn, 1892) employed identical strategies and rhetoric to achieve their objectives. They asked, usually to no avail, local white employers to hire black women. They raised funds for scholarships and established kindergartens and other childcare facilities, organized clinics and demonstrations for mothers and housewives. Moreover, they sponsored musicals, literary events, and artistic exhibitions. And in the early 1920s the black clubwomen worked assiduously to encourage black women to register and become politically involved.[33]

Hunter's philanthropic activities, like those of the first generation of black clubwomen, were well grounded in a tradition of what may appear to be contradictory impulses. On the one hand, they were fighting to reclaim the bodies and souls of thousands of blacks, men and women and children, adrift in the Northern urban wilderness. Yet their work can also be seen as a pragmatic accommodation to racial segregation. Hunter, with the aid of white beneficence, proved quite adept at inverting and taking advantage of white racial attitudes and customs. She successfully developed an important social service agency, and carved out a sizable private physical space as well, for black working girls and women without appearing to challenge the racial status quo in Cleveland.

In terms of approach, values, and objectives, Hunter differed little from Booker T. Washington, "the wizard of Tuskegee," at one end of the spectrum and the ardent nationalist, Marcus Garvey of Harlem, at the other end of the continuum. Hunter's leadership style suggests that whenever black women entered the public arena and engaged in the process of institution building, they employed the same strategies as did black male leaders, further indicating the blurred spheres within the black community. In this context, a racist and oppressive social order, as had been the case in slavery, transformed all black efforts to survive and advance into acts of passive resistance.

Beginning in 1929, Hunter and Nannie Burroughs launched what would become, especially for Hunter, a life affirming friendship. Their interests, personalities, ages, backgrounds, and work converged to form a bond from which they each drew inspiration and increased determination to persevere, even when chronically strapped with unending fund-raising drives to sustain their respective enterprises. A half continent separated them. Their letters, however, spanned the decades and reflected the deepening relationship. Hunter idolized Burroughs. The mere act of writing, frequently unanswered, letters provided Hunter an important outlet through which she could share her fears, anxiety, successes, and plans for the future. In public, Hunter maintained an imperturbable image of a strong, competent, fearless, resourceful black woman. Perhaps she was able to sustain this public image because she knew that in the privacy of her study or propped up in bed at night, she could write about and share her inner self with a woman whom she trusted to understand.

The Hunter-Burroughs correspondence is a rare mirror onto some of the personal costs extracted when black women devoted entire lives to social reform, and to voluntary and philanthropic work to mitigate the impact of racism in their communities. After visiting with Burroughs, Hunter returned to Cleveland and wrote in 1929, "It was so nice to see you and to know your real sweet self. Surely we will continue to cultivate a lasting friendship. I want to be your devoted sister in kindred thought and love. You are so deserving and so capable. Your work is unique and remarkable; to me it fulfills a need that is not even attempted by other educators. I shall not be happy until I have made a definite contribution in a tangible way to your school."[34]

For Hunter, perhaps more so than for Burroughs, the friendship provided an emotional anchor and became an important vehicle for the release of pent-up frustration and depression. Alone during the 1937 Christmas holidays, Hunter wrote, "Somehow, I just felt that you were going to surprise me with a visit. This, more than any other Christmas I have felt so lonely. With all I have to do, yet I am positively blue for the want of a friend to open my heart to—I have so much buried within that the valves are about to burst." She ended resolutely, "I suppose this is the price we pay for leadership. Somehow, those who dream alike must dwell so far apart in the physical world." A few months later, in March of 1938, a happier Hunter wrote, "You don't know how much you mean to me. I am certainly fortunate to have you for my friend." Each woman annually gave private contributions, and willingly lectured on behalf of the other's institution. Following a visit in 1946, Hunter confessed to Burroughs, "I've been re-inspired and lifted high as a result of my only too brief visit with you. If I had a million dollars I would want to give it to you. Old girl the job you are doing is masterful and unique." In the same letter Hunter mused, "Just think of the girls you have saved from miserable wretched lives to become useful fine citizens. I love you for the high and noble example you have given to all of us. I sincerely hope to always number you as my first and genuine friend."[35]

Hunter and Burroughs not only respected and cared for each other, they were also concerned about their sister-founders of schools for black women, Mary McLeod Bethune and Charlotte Hawkins Brown. This respect was born of the understanding of the degree to which they frequently sacrificed themselves, putting the needs of black girls and women before their own. In December of 1942, in a moment of exhaustion, Hunter confided to her friend, "Somehow I wish that you, Mary Bethune and myself could give up raising money and could devote all of our strengths and spiritual life to the building of God's kingdom. This money getting business destroys so much of one's real self, that we cannot do our best, feeling that we need money all of the time." Fortunately Hunter's exhaustion and depression seldom lasted, for the incessant demands on her time and pocketbook continued. She rhetorically queried Burroughs, "I wonder if people call on you as often as they call on me. Last year [1944] by receipts for income tax—I gave away over $800." She hastened to add that she was "Thankful that I had it to give," and concluded, "I will not forget the great work you are doing there for our girls. I speak of you every time I talk in public."[36]

At the thirty-fifth anniversary of the Phillis Wheatley Association, Hunter presided over a triumphant celebration. She informed Burroughs that "when it was all over I was just about ready to give up the ghost. Was so tired and exhausted." She thanked her friend for her "fine cooperation and generous gift," and reported, "The party was a great success. Two hundred thirty odd persons in attendance and to date $13,546.93 in cash."[37]

By the 1950s, Burroughs, Hunter, and Bethune were winding down their public careers. Soon sickness and death would deplete their ranks. Bethune was the first to succumb. Suffering from bronchial pneumonia, Hunter wrote Burroughs, in the wake of Bethune's death, "Somehow I really loved Mary McLeod Bethune but my deepest admiration has always been centered on Nannie H. Burroughs. You have always impressed me as a true leader with understanding of the human problems of life."[38] Earlier, in fact, the indomitable Burroughs had chided her friend to forego such despair:

> I hope you will not allow yourself to feel as your letter seems to indicate. I urge you to be of good cheer and deepest gratitude to God because He has permitted you to accomplish miracles in the field of Social Science and Human Welfare. . . . You have built a colossal monument that will stand as long as America stands. I know that you are not well but I urge you to be of good cheer. You are no old race horse and cut out that pity stuff—if you do not I shall put you down as an ingrate—what more can God do for you or for any of us for that matter.[39]

The reassuring words must have been what she needed to hear, for a few months later, in August 1955, the retired but still active Hunter announced a final victory, "We reached the goal of $50,000. and sent two girls to college this fall." On her seventy-fourth birthday she reflected on the meaning of their lives, "Of course, you will realize that both you and me have worked too hard and entirely too long. The wonder of it all; we have made a contribution to America that no one else would for the type of young women we've tried to serve."[40]

It is noteworthy that although these women engaged in essentially the same kind of mission—creating institutions to save young black girls—a spirit of mutual cooperation and support pervades these letters. It would be difficult to locate or even to imagine similar correspondence between black male institution builders during this period.

At the time of her death, at the age of seventy-seven, the woman who had come to Cleveland with $1.75 in her pocket, and who entitled her 1940 autobiography *A Nickel and A Prayer*, left an estate of

$409,711.72. In attempting to explain Hunter's holdings, certainly a substantial sum for any person to have accumulated at that time, her attorney declared, "Miss Hunter was a stickler for savings. She held onto every penny and did some shrewd investing. Her salary was only $3,000 for many years (like all other Welfare Federation Workers). But she received excellent free advice on investing from a bank official at Cleveland Trust Co."[41]

Future research may well uncover the specific details of how Hunter accumulated this remarkable sum. This is no simple "rags to riches" story, nor is Hunter a Horatio Alger in blackface and petticoat. The social construction of racism and gender roles in America lends to Hunter's life a more troubling complexity. Although I have not examined the estate records of Nannie H. Burroughs, Charlotte Hawkins Brown, or Mary McLeod Bethune, it is reasonable to speculate that none of them died poverty-stricken. Actually, it is not their relative wealth or capital accumulation that needs explanation. After all, they were daughters of former slaves, they each possessed strong religious convictions, and each had reached maturity in a climate in which the conservative economic ideologies of Booker T. Washington held sway, especially among the ambitious black educated elite. Moreover, their own desires to save money were undoubtedly fired by living through the Great Depression.

More germane to our concerns are the reasons why they were so wedded to the work of helping black girls and women. To what extent were these women affected by the larger society's negative views and stereotypes of black women? At a time when black men were deprived of a meaningful public voice and presence, and few of them could find adequate permanent employment owing to structural inequalities and violence, the sexual exploitation and economic oppression of black women continued. In an 1895 speech delivered before the first national conference of Afro-American women, Josephine St. Pierre Ruffin declared, "if an estimate of the colored women of America is called for, the inevitable reply glibly given is, 'For the most part ignorant and immoral,' some exceptions of course, but these don't count."[42]

Negative images, racial stereotypes, and biased perceptions serve specific functions in a capitalistic patriarchal society. There existed a direct correlation between the low status Afro-Americans occupied in

American society and the derogatory images held of them in the white mind. Prejorative images not only highlight real or imagined differences between ethnic groups, races, and sexes, they also serve as critical indices of social worth, political significance, and economic power. The first postslavery generation of black women activists and club organizers well understood the power of images to determine the treatment of black girls and women by the larger society.

Fannie Barrier Williams of Chicago had commented on the apparent obsession some black women exhibited over the allegations of moral laxity. In an 1893 speech, she proclaimed that "because the morality of our home life has been commented upon so disparagingly and meanly . . . we are placed in the unfortunate position of being defenders of our name."[43] One of the most objectionable stereotypes was the label of prostitute. As Williams and Ruffin intimated, accusations of immorality and the labeling of all black women as prostitutes impeded the development of positive identities and contained even more devastating larger social implications. Such accusations and labels, of course, obscured and attracted attention away from the economic discrimination and lack of good jobs, which made their lives so wretched and forced many of them into prostitution in order to survive. Furthermore, negative images and stereotypes camouflaged the repeated sexual abuse of black women in all regions of the country. As a consequence, rape of black women, when reported, was seldom investigated by police officials, who found it more convenient to attribute blame for such attacks to the victim's "inherent wantonness." Moreover, as historian Rosen has demonstrated, correctional facilities across the country reported an overrepresentation of black women, proving that they were more often arrested for alledged prostitution than were white women.[44]

As long as the larger society viewed black women as whores and prostitutes, they remained vulnerable and powerless. Derogatory images hampered even the work of elite black women who struggled to improve the overall status of blacks in America. In their minds true racial advancement depended upon the extent to which black women themselves could demolish and erase these negative images. Williams's remarks are again illustrative of the deep determination of black women to reclaim themselves and their reputations. She declared, "This moral regeneration of a whole race of women is no idle sentiment—it is a serious business; and everywhere there is witnessed a feverish anxiety to be free from the mean suspicions that have so long underestimated the character strength of our women."[45]

Thus Hunter, Burroughs, Bethune, and Brown, being major representatives of a generation of postslavery black women philanthropists, charitable organizers, and institution builders, carried onward the mission of self-reclamation. These descendants of slaves were active agents for social change throughout the first half of the twentieth century. In their speeches, and writings, and fund-raising drives, these leaders rallied thousands of community women and engaged them in the battle to reclaim and save their defenseless and impoverished black sisters. It matters not a little that several of these schools and homes prepared black girls and young women for skilled service in the domestic sector. Hunter was quite correct when she observed as late as 1957 that no one else would or had paid much, if indeed any, attention to the needs of the thousands of "young women we've tried to serve." Burroughs echoed these sentiments but with a slightly different focus. "We make our girls believe in themselves and in their power to do anything that anybody can do, be it ever so difficult. . . . 'We specialize in the wholly impossible.'"[46]

The philanthropic work of black women contains a palpable undertone of muted defiance of the racial and gender inequalities pervading virtually every aspect of American society. Couched in the rhetoric of religious piousness, their efforts to do good deeds on behalf of black people, to save black women from lives of poverty and induced prostitution, appear on the surface to reflect a conservative embrace of American moral values and of the status quo. Yet each black girl and boy saved from the streets, educated to be productive and self-respecting citizens, restored to good health, and trained for a skilled job represented a resounding blow to the edifice of Jim Crow, patriarchy, and white privilege. Those so reclaimed were able to return to the black community and become additional agents in the struggle for social change and liberation.

NOTES

1   Cynthia Neverdon-Morton, *Afro-American Women of the South and the Advancement of the Race, 1895–1925* (Knoxville: University of Tennessee

Press, 1988); Darlene Clark Hine and Patrick Biddleman, eds., *Black Women in the Middle West Project, Comprehensive Resource Guide— Illinois and Indiana* (Indianapolis: Indiana Historical Bureau, 1985); Deborah Gray White, "Mining the Forgotten: Manuscript Sources for Black Women's History," *Journal of American History* 74 (1987), 237–242.

2 Darlene Clark Hine, "Lifting the Veil, Shattering the Silence: Black Women's History in Slavery and Freedom," in *The State of Afro-American History: Past, Present, and Future*, ed. Hine (Baton Rouge: Louisiana State University Press, 1986), 224–249, Hine, *When the Truth is Told: A History of Black Women's Culture and Community in Indiana, 1875–1950* (Indianapolis: National Council of Negro Women, Indianapolis Section, 1981).

3 Joanne J. Meyerowitz, *Women Adrift: Independent Wage Earners in Chicago, 1880–1930* (Chicago: University of Chicago Press, 1988), xvii– xxiii; Gerda Lerner, "Community Work of Black Club Women," *The Journal of Negro History* 59 (1974), 158–67; Maude T. Jenkins, "The History of the Black Women's Club Movement in America" (Ph.D. diss., Teacher's College, Columbia University, 1984); Lynda Faye Dickson, "The Early Club Movement Among Black Women in Denver, 1890–1925" (Ph.D. diss., University of Colorado, 1982).

4 Hallie Q. Brown, *Homespun Heroines and Other Women of Distinction* (Cleveland: Aldine, 1926; reprint ed. New York: Oxford University Press, The Schombrug Library of Nineteenth-Century Black Women Writers, 1988), introduction by Randall Burkett, xxxii; Mrs. N. F. Mossell, *The Work of the Afro-American Woman* (1894); reprint ed. New York: Oxford University Press, The Schomburg Library of Nineteenth-Century Black Women Writers, 1988), introduction by Joanne Braxton, 104–114; Hine, "The Pursuit of Professional Equality: Meharry Medical College, 1921– 1938, A Case Study," in *New Perspectives on Black Educational History*, ed. James D. Anderson and V. P. Franklin (Boston: G. K. Hall, 1978), 173– 192.

5 Elizabeth Lindsay Davis, *Lifting As They Climb* (N.p., National Association of Colored Women's Clubs, ca. 1933), 315–321; Susan Lynn Smith, "The Black Women's Club Movement: Self-Improvement and Sisterhood, 1890–1915" (M. A. Thesis, University of Wisconsin–Madison 1986).

6 *Indianapolis Star*, August 1, 1909.

7 Ibid.

8 Ibid.; Davis, *Lifting As They Climb*, 13; "Fannie Barrier Williams," in *Black Women in Nineteenth-Century American Life: Their Thoughts, Their Words, Their Feelings*, ed. Bert Loewenberg and Ruth Bogin (University Park: Pennsylvania State University Press, 1976), 263–279.

9   Hine, *When the Truth is Told*, 49–66.

10   D. Augustus Straker, "Manhood and Womanhood Development," *The Colored American Magazine* (1901), 312–313; Paula Giddings, *When and Where I Enter: The Impact of Black Women on Race and Sex in America* (New York: William Morrow, 1984), 135–152; Karen J. Blair, *The Clubwoman as Feminist: True Womanhood Redefined, 1868–1914* (New York: Holmes and Meier, 1980), 117–119.

11   Hine, "Lifting the Veil," 239. See also Sadie Iola Daniel, *Women Builders* (Washington, D.C.: Associated Publishers, 1931; revised and enlarged, 1970), 79–110, quoted on 86; Bernice Reagon, "Bethune, Mary Jane McLeod," in *Dictionary of American Negro Biography*, ed. Rayford W. Logan and Michael R. Winston (New York: W. W. Norton, 1982), 41–43.

12   Daniel, *Women Builders*, 137–167, Brown quoted on 161; see also Elvena Tillman, "Brown, Charlotte Hawkins," in *Dictionary of American Negro Biography*, 65–67.

13   Tillman, "Brown, Charlotte Hawkins," in *Dictionary of American Biography*, 65–67.

14   Daniel, *Women Builders*, 111–136. See also Evelyn Brooks Barnett, "Nannie Burroughs and the Education of Black Women," in *The Afro-American Woman: Struggles and Images* (Port Washington, N.Y.: Kennikat Press, 1978), 97–108; Barnett, "Burroughs, Nannie Helen," in *Dictionary of American Negro Biography*, 81–82.

15   "Nannie H. Burroughs," *National Cyclopedia of the Colored Race* (1919), 89.

16   Ibid.; Daniel, *Women Builders*, 122.

17   Daniel, *Women Builders*, 168–191; John Bennett, "S.C. Negro Woman's Life is Welfare Drama," *The Charleston News and Courier*, November 24, 1940; Jane Edna Hunter, *A Nickle and a Prayer* (Cleveland: Elli Kani, 1940), 63–65, 70–71; Adrienne Lash Jones, "Jane Edna Hunter: A Case Study of Black Leadership, 1910–1950" (Ph.D. diss., Case Western Reserve University, 1983).

18   Jones, "Jane Edna Hunter."

19   Ibid.; Hine, *Black Women in White: Racial Conflict and Cooperation in the Nursing Profession, 1890–1950* (Bloomington: Indiana University Press, 1989), Chapter 3.

20   Biographical information located in the Jane Hunter Papers, Box 1, Folder 1, Western Reserve Historical Society, Cleveland, Ohio.

21   David M. Katzman, *Seven Days A Week: Women and Domestic Service in Industrializing America* (New York: Oxford University Press, 1978), 77–79; Alice Kessler-Harris, *Out to Work: A History of Wage Earning Women in the United States* (New York: Oxford University Press, 1982), 237–238;

Jacqueline Jones, *Labor of Love, Labor of Sorrow: Black Women, Work, and the Family from Slavery to the Present* (New York: Basic Books, 1985), 128, 153–156, 164, 168.

22   Meyerowitz, *Women Adrift*, 36.

23   Katzman, *Seven Days A Week*, 78–79; Kessler-Harris, *Out to Work*, 237–238.

24   Hunter, *A Nickel and A Prayer*, 88. See also Daniel, *Women Builders*, 176–177. Hunter, "My Experiences in Race Relations" (1948). Copy of the speech found in Jane Hunter Papers, Box 1, Folder 9.

25   Hunter, *A Nickel and A Prayer*, 88.

26   *The Charleston News and Courier*, November 24, 1940. Initially the home was named The Working Girls Home Association of Cleveland but was changed to the Phillis Wheatley Home on October 31, 1912. Hunter, as the secretary of the Phillis Wheatley Association, described its purpose as "establishing a home of good repute where good honest, upright working girls can have pure and pleasant surroundings where they can be taught the art of housekeeping technics (*sic*) of hygiene, importance of loyalty, the beauty in neatness and dispatch." The Phillis Wheatley Associaton Manuscript Collection, Box 1 Bound Volume, Minutes of Board of Trustees, 1914–1943, Western Reserve Historical Society.

27   Ruth Rosen, *The Lost Sisterhood: Prostitution in America, 1900–1918* (Baltimore: Johns Hopkins University Press, 1982), 147.

28   Hunter, *A Nickel and A Prayer*, 68. See also Rosen, *Lost Sisterhood*, 80–81.

29   Hunter, *A Nickel and A Prayer*, 93–94, 99–100; Kenneth L. Kusmer, *A Ghetto Takes Shape: Black Cleveland, 1870–1930* (Urbana: University of Illinois Press, 1976), 150–151; Phillis Wheatley Association booklet (1918) found in Papers of Lethia C. Fleming (1876–1963), Box 1, Folder 3, Western Reserve Historical Society. Again the purpose of the home was described: "Special attention is given to training in the domestic arts. . . . It is intended to lay special emphasis on this feature of the work, thus qualifying the less educated girl for domestic service, for which the more recently arrived southern girls are very much in demand."

30   Kusmer, *A Ghetto Takes Shape*, 49; Hunter, *A Nickel and A Prayer*, 90–91.

31   Jenkins, "History of the Black Women's Club Movement," 80–83; Hunter, *A Nickel and A Prayer*, 101. It is interesting to note that in 1930 Hunter and the Phillis Wheatley Association alledgedly rejected an offer of $25,000 from the Rosenwald Fund because of its proviso that the Association had to become a branch of the Young Women's Christian Association. Jane Hunter Papers, Box 1 Folder 7. In her autobiography, Hunter explained that she rejected any merger with the YWCA because, "only as an independent organization could we win a full measure of justice for

colored girls" (*A Nickel and A Prayer*, 110). Of course, by this point, Hunter more likely objected to any dimunition of her personal control and autonomy at the helm of the Phillis Wheatley Home.

32   Louise Daniel Hutchinson, *Anna J. Cooper: A Voice from the South* (Washington, D.C.: Smithsonian Institution Press, 1981), 88; see also "Anna Julia Cooper," in *Black Women in Nineteenth-Century American Life*, 317–331.

33   Willie Mae Coleman, "Keeping the Faith and Disturbing the Peace: Black Women, From Anti-Slavery to Women's Suffrage" (Ph.D. diss. University of California–Irvine, 1982); Rosalyn Terborg-Penn, "Afro-Americans in the Struggle for Woman Suffrage" (Ph.D. diss. Howard University, 1977); Davis, *Lifting As They Climb*, 321–324.

34   Jane Edna Hunter to Nannie H. Burroughs, November 2, 1929. Nannie H. Burroughs Manuscript Collection, Container 13. Manuscript Division, Library of Congress, Washington, D.C. Writing in *The Washington Eagle* (March 9, 1928), Burroughs lavished praise on Hunter. "The new Phillis Wheatley home is the greatest social and economic welfare achievement among women of our day. Jane Hunter has given to her women and girls a business and social institution that takes high rank among the best in the world. . . . The fact of the matter is that Jane Hunter has given us the biggest and best hotel for Negro women in the whole world. . . ." Burroughs Papers, Speeches and Writings File, Container 46.

35   Hunter to Burroughs, December 24, 1937, March 15, 1938, August 6, 1946. Burroughs Papers, Container 13. Again, on December 24, 1940, as she had written on the same date in 1937, Hunter confided, "How much I wish that we could spend this Christmas together in person. Distance cannot make a difference between two sincere friends. . . . Between you and me there is no such thing as distance dear. For I am always there and you are always here in my heart." Burroughs Papers, Container 13.

36   Hunter to Burroughs, December 22, 1942, May 11, 1945. Burroughs Papers, Container 13. Hunter was not alone in expressing frustration with the fund-raising work. On December 29, 1934, Mary McLeod Bethune wrote to Burroughs, "I can never tell you how terrible I feel in not being able to comply with your letter of yesterday. I have tried my utmost to secure the money to send you. My back has been up against a wall for several weeks. I just cant (*sic*) get a dime from any source. I came into the holidays without money to send cards to my friends and my teachers unpaid for two months. My bills are hanging over me for the daily running and everything that would call for money is before me. I went to the bank; I tried personal friends. There is no letting loose at this time. I know just the situation there and how heavy the load is for you but I am

helpless at this moment. If any light comes, any development which will enable me to assist, you will hear from me. You know I would not fail you if it was humanly possible for me to do otherwise. Hold on to everything the best that you can. Light MUST come." Burroughs Papers, Container 13. On May 1, 1941, Bethune shared with Burroughs, "I am very happy to inclose (*sic*) my check for $25 to help you in your cause. I wish it could be $25,000 so that I might relieve you of your anxiety for real money to carry forward your work." Burroughs Papers, Container 13.

37   Hunter to Burroughs, May 16, 1946. Burroughs Papers, Container 13.

38   Hunter to Burroughs, July 7, 1955. Burroughs Papers, Container 13.

39   Burroughs to Hunter, April 1, 1955. Burroughs Papers, Container 38.

40   Hunter to Burroughs, August 16, 1955, February 3, 1957. Burroughs Papers, Container 13.

41   Folder containing undated newspaper press clippings of Hunter's death. Burroughs Papers, Container 13.

42   Josephine St. Pierre Ruffin, quoted in Davis, *Lifting As They Climb*, 13.

43   "Fannie Barrier Williams," in *Black Women in Nineteenth-Century American Life*, 263–279; quote on 270.

44   Rosen, *Lost Sisterhood*, 80.

45   "Fannie Barrier Williams," in *Black Women in Nineteenth-Century American Life*, 263–279.

46   Hunter to Burroughs, February 3, 1957. Burroughs Papers, Container 13.

Who Funded Hull House?

Our image of Hull House finances features Jane Addams's success as a fund-raiser among wealthy Chicagoans. "She was able to obtain gifts of money and service from the well-to-do and social elite in Chicago in part because she was one of them," Allen Davis wrote in *American Heroine*.[1] Her nephew, James Weber Linn, who lived with her at Hull House, said that Addams's reliance on wealthy benefactors meant "the books simply *had* to balance."

> Hull House was not the sort of institution that could afford deficits. Down on the South Side of Chicago William Rainey Harper was about to depend largely on deficits to urge the new University of Chicago forward to greater and greater things in education, but Hull House was different. It was personal, and it was an experiment contrary to the business attitude of the city; therefore it had very definitely to prove itself practical in finance.[2]

Thus our picture of Addams as a fund-raiser conveys the impression that she had little room to maneuver; the requirements of her wealthy patrons and the exigencies of Hull House expenses channeled her vision.

Yet this view contradicts our larger appreciation of Addams as a reformer who transcended practical limitations, including those imposed by fund raising. Her most important achievements—from the founding of Hull House to her labors on behalf of international peace—derived more from the spirit of risk-taking idealism than the restraints of sober realism. What then? Was her fund raising so divorced from her vision of life's possibilities? Or have we misconstrued her financial arrangements? Might a closer look give us a different picture of Addams?

This essay examines the gendered components of Addams's fund raising—especially the process by which she constructed financial networks that blurred the boundaries between her personal and professional lives. Because Addams could pick and choose among funding agents, she chose support that gave her the freest possible hand. Ultimately this support sustained her emotionally as well as financially.

The microfilm edition of *The Jane Addams Papers* gives us convenient access to the Hull House account books, which provide a detailed view of Addams's fund raising and the financial foundation of her world-renowned settlement.[3] There we can find new meaning in familiar facts. Yes, Addams did rely heavily on Chicago's elite, but most of her funding came from three key sources—at first she drew from her own inheritance; then in the mid-1890s Mary Rozet Smith, who became her life partner, began to pay her bills, and soon thereafter her close friend, Louise deKoven Bowen, provided for the settlement's needs. Far more than we might otherwise think, Addams was able to act on impulse, confident that, through her own resources and this support network, she could find the means to match her imagination.

HULL HOUSE financial records reveal one astonishing fact that needs to be incorporated into our historical understanding of this remarkable institution and its talented cofounder—Jane Addams put a great deal of her own money into the settlement during its early years. With the death of her father in 1881 she had inherited an estate worth between $50,000 and $60,000—a sizable sum at a time when skilled artisans earned less than $1,000 a year.[4] This inheritance freed her from the need to marry. It also made it possible for her to consider the fullest possible range of options open to young women who were unfettered by financial constraints. Between 1881 and 1889, when she founded Hull House with Ellen Gates Starr, Addams explored those options. Medical school and travel in Europe sharpened her understanding of her alternatives. In East London, Samuel and Henrietta Barnett's experiment of Toynbee Hall appealed to her as something she could imitate. She might have estimated that her own annual income equaled Barnett's pay as an Anglican clergyman, and, with a more modest physical structure than his, she could cover her own institution's operating costs. Scholars have noted but not explained Addams's dominance in her partnership with Ellen Gates Starr. Starr, a teacher whose family could support her for only one year at Rockford Semi-nary (where the two women met), routinely deferred to Addams's leadership. In part this may have been due to Addams's ability to pay their bills.[5]

And pay she did. During the settlement's first four years Addams contributed a total of $14,684 to its operations—a small fortune that must have included some capital as well as earnings. Addams came to terms with this in October 1893, when she tallied the settlement's receipts and expenditures during its first four years, gravely noting the amounts "Pd by Jane Addams" and "Loaned by Jane Addams." Her calculations showed that she had paid a very significant proportion of the settlement's expenses between 1889 and 1893.[6] (See Table 1.) While the Hull House budget more than doubled during these four years, from $8,634 to $20,871, Jane Addams's proportion steadily fell from 58 percent to 19 percent. Yet in monetary terms, except for the large outlays associated with the founding year, her absolute costs increased.

What categories of expenses was Addams funding? Many of the set-tlement's projects paid their own way. The Summer School produced small profits. Donations and income received for the nursery covered its costs exactly. "Relief" expenses rose rapidly, but donations covered that increase. So, too, income balanced expenses for the kindergarten,

TABLE 1   Jane Addams's Financial Contributions to Hull House

YEAR	RECEIVED	PAID BY JA	LOANED BY JA	TOTAL EXPENSES	PERCENT PD AND LOANED BY JA
89–90	$3,617	$5,017		$8,634	58
90–91	6,758	2,365	$351	9,474	29
91–92	9,723	2,417	603	12,743	24
92–93	16,940	3,738	193	20,871	19

NOTE: Figures have been rounded to the nearest whole number.

the Christmas fund, the gymnasium club and equipment, painting classes, the diet kitchen, cooking classes, entertainment, the Jane Club (a residence home for working women), and the "sociological account," a new and mysterious entry introduced in 1892–93. (This might refer to the social surveys Florence Kelley was conducting in the neighborhood with the aid of other residents, which in 1895 were compiled into path-breaking maps published in *Hull House Maps and Papers.*)[7] (See Table 2.)

Where were the deficits Addams paid for herself? Understandably, during the first year, expenses for "house furniture" and "general repairs" exceeded by almost $4,000 the amounts raised for those categories. Addams brought much of the settlement's furnishings from her Cedarville home, and her proprietary interest in the new furnishings may have made it hard for her to request money for them. So she covered those expenses herself. Helen Culver, the owner of Hull House, provided free rent between 1889 and 1893, but repairs and maintenance were costly. When Addams had difficulty raising money to pay for needed repairs on the house because donors assumed that to be the landlady's responsibility, she also met that expense herself.[8]

Apart from these costs, the single largest deficits in the settlement's first years were outlays for the residents' room and board. Those losses amounted to more than $1,000 annually. Apparently Addams found it too difficult to ask residents to cover their expenses. Florence Kelley exemplified the problem. She arrived at Hull House between Christmas and New Year's Eve, 1891, but her first rent payment was recorded in September 1892. Meanwhile, Jane Addams raised money for her salary as Director of the Hull House Labor Bureau.[9] Though, like Addams, a daughter of the upper-middle class, Kelley was genuinely penniless, since all the money she could borrow from her family went to maintaining her three children and to paying for the costs involved in opposing her estranged husband's claim to custody. Other residents might have been able to pay more, but perhaps Addams felt unable to charge different rates depending on the resident's ability to pay, or to ask some to cover more than their own expenses. After Hull House added a "men's settlement" across the street in 1892–93, the problem intensified. Expenses for that group came to $400 more than Addams received in board payments, and another unsupported expense of $997 went for repairs.[10]

TABLE 2   Annual Income and Expenditures in Hull House Accounts, 1889–1893

	1889–90			1890–91			1891–92			1892–93		
	IN.	EXP.	BALANCE	IN.	EXP.	BALANCE	IN.	EXP.	BALANCE	IN.	EXP.	BALANCE
General Repairs	1,568	3,702	-2,134	255	521	-266	1,895	2,215	-319	3,261	3,244	+17
Ten Account	960	853	+107	1,022	1,337	-315	169	169	0	101	101	0
Miscellaneous	592	592	0									
Creche	80	80	0	1,054	1,054	0	1,826	1,826	0	2,131	2,131	0
Miss Culver	360	240	+120	1,080	960	+120	480	480	0	—	—	
House Furniture		1,861	-1,861		592	-592		582	-582		349	-349
Residents' Board and House Expenses	58	1,080	-1,022	234	1,390	-1,156	738	1,971	-1,233	1,780	2,843	-1,064
Crech Repairs				767	767	0						
Relief				469	493	-24	597	665	-68	1,616	1,549	+67
Library				235	235	0						
Art Exhibition				235	235	0	20	20	0			
Kitchen Garden				35	35	0						
Sewing Classes				20	20	0						
Picnic Fund				56	56	0						
College Extension				158	145	+13	252	248	+4	[437]a	632	-195
Diet Kitchen				100	78	+22	574	574	0	75	75	0
Gymnasium				30	42	-12	356	356	0	1,215	1,215	0
Entertainment				22	22	0	153	153	0	175	175	0

Account									
Summer School	987	884				+103			
Christmas			659	601	+58	278	278	0	
Painting Classes			70	70	0	168	168	0	
Kindergarten			456	456	0				
Jane Club			799	944	−145	1,495	1,495	0	
Labor Bureau			350	420	−70	738	738	0	
Stamps and Bank			50	50	0	30	30	0	
Men's Settlement				300		705	−405		
Men's Settlement Repairs						997	−997		
Cooking Classes				71		71	0		
Playground				947		1,677	−730		
Sociological Account				122		122	0		
HH Kitchen Fund				2,000		2,000	0		
TOTAL	3,617	8,407	6,758	8,866	9,723	12,077	2,417	16,940	20,594
Total Pd by JA[b]	5,017		2,365						3,758

Note: Table 2 has been arranged to convey as much as possible of the original documents, particularly the years in which individual accounts were added. Figures in the income, expenditures, and totals categories come from the originals. The totals paid by Jane Addams each year are the sums of the negative figures on the balance column; the few surplus categories did not enter into her calculations. The "Balance" column has been added to facilitate the location of deficits. Jane Addams's nomenclature and abbreviations have been retained. Figures have been rounded to the nearest dollar.

a This figure, missing from the original, has been calculated by subtraction.
b This excludes her loans.

But this pattern of mounting deficit did not deter Addams from taking financial risks. In 1892–93 in addition to the expenses associated with the residents and the men's settlement, she committed $1,677 to the construction of a playground while receiving only $947 in donations toward that end. Furthermore, she undertook building projects that substantially increased the settlement's space. In 1890–91 she raised and spent $4,000 on the Butler Art Gallery. In 1892–93 she received and spent $18,965 on the construction of other Hull House additions. (These building expenditures were not included in her annual accounts.)[11] Quite apart from these professional obligations, Addams had also assumed personal responsibility for the children of her sister, Mary Linn, who died in 1894, especially for her nephew, Stanley.[12] Yet, for them, if not for herself, her current course of action was fraught with danger.

Thus the moment in October 1893, when Jane Addams sat down with her accounts and calculated the amount she had paid of the settlement's costs between 1889 and 1893, must have been sobering indeed. If she continued to spend at a similar rate, she would eventually consume all her assets and become dependent on the charity of her donors. Assuming she did not want to cut expenses or eliminate newly acquired commitments, such as that of the playground, she could avoid this dependency in two ways—substantially increase the financial obligation of residents, and/or locate new sources of funding. Since the first option would have deprived the settlement of talented figures like Florence Kelley, Addams probably did not seriously consider it. Instead, in the fall of 1893, she created the House Committee, which assumed responsibility for the collection of adequate funds to cover the residents' expenses.[13] More importantly, she also found new sources of funding in close personal relationships with two women.

WHAT ADDAMS NEEDED were donors willing to contribute without regard to the money's use. This had been the purpose of the settlement's first fund-raising efforts—the "Ten Account" for general expenses, which quickly grew beyond the ten initial contributors, but remained the settlement's most essential source of income.[14] Here such routine maintenance costs as "repairing roof," "furnace coal,"

"gas bill," "cleaning," "telephone," "plumbing," "plastering," "service" (meal-time assistants), and "carpentry repairs" were enumer-
ated. Income in that account grew from $960 in 1889–90 to $3,261 in
1892–93.[15] In the summer of 1893, the largest single contributor to the
Ten Account was Addams herself. Her contribution of $508.23 on May
31 covered bills for carpentry and other improvements on the "serving
pantry."[16]

Yet in this account's columns we see the beginning of the end of Addams's need to carry the burden of the settlement's general expenses
alone. On May 31, 1893, Mary R. Smith also made a large contribution
to the Ten Account—$328 for paving and for building a wall in the
yard. Smith's donation was unusual in two ways. Its size was much
larger than the twelve other contributions listed with it between April
and July, which included one for $20, four for $25, five for $50, and one
for $100.[17] And its specific amount shows that, like Addams's, it cov-
ered a specific expense. Thus Mary Smith's gift had more in common
with Addams's own than with those of other Hull House benefactors.
Smith's contribution to the Ten Account in May 1893 represented the
beginnings of a sea change in Addams's financial burden.

Jane Addams's solution to her deficit problems lay in two close
friendships that began in 1891–92 and deepened the next year. The
first was with Mary Rozet Smith. The unmarried daughter of a wealthy
Chicago paper manufacturer, Smith began in 1893 to displace Addams
as the settlement's chief funder. Historians have analyzed the personal side of Addams's relationship with Smith, but they have not ade-
quately understood its material side. We do not have to be cynics to see
that Mary Rozet Smith was the right woman at the right moment for
Jane Addams—financially as well as personally.

More than ten years younger than Addams, Smith was barely
twenty when she first visited Hull House in 1891—"tall, shy, fair, and
eager,' in James Linn's words.[18] She was one of a dozen wealthy young
Chicago women who donated their time to the Hull House experiment. Four years later Addams acknowledged in a love poem the instrumental motives that governed her first encounters with Mary.

> One day I came into Hull House,
>   (No spirit whispered who was there)
> And in the kindergarten room

There sat upon a childish chair
A girl, both tall and fair to see,
   (To look at her gives one a thrill).
But all I thought was, would she be
   Best fitted to lead club, or drill?
You see, I had forgotten Love,
   And only thought of Hull House then.
That is the way with women folks
   When they attempt the things of men;
They grow intense, and love the thing
   Which they so tenderly do rear,
And think that nothing lies beyond
   Which claims from them a smile or tear.
Like mothers, who work long and late
   To rear their children fittingly,
Follow them only with their eyes,
   And love them almost pityingly.
So I was blind and deaf those years
   To all save one absorbing care,
And did not guess what now I know—
   Delivering love was sitting there![19]

Mary Smith became, in James Linn's words, "the highest and clearest note in the music of Jane Addams's personal life."[20] Occurring gradually between 1891 and 1895, when this poem was written, Addams's lifelong commitment to Smith evolved alongside her gratitude for Smith's sharing of her financial responsibilities.

Addams's alliance with Smith began as an amalgam of business and pleasure, and so it remained. Her first extant letter to Smith, dated July 4, 1892, set lasting patterns for sharing her financial thinking. After thanking Smith for a check, for example, Addams noted, "The Summer School finances are going beautifully since we have forty girls."[21] Mary Smith took the initiative in writing Addams that summer. As Addams wrote her in mid-July, referring to Smith's work in the Hull House nursery, "I am very grateful to my sweet nurse for all her good letters, and am ashamed to have appeared so unresponsive."[22]

By far the most notable component of Addams's subsequent letters to Smith was their abundant references to financial planning. More than a donor, Mary became an essential fiscal confidant. "We have secured, you know, one of Miss Culver's cottages. . . . Miss C. does the plumbing, we do the carpenter work, Miss C. furnishes the paper and we put it on," Addams observed in a typical note in 1893.[23] By then she had come to rely on Mary as an alter ego in her plans for the settlement's expansion. "The vision of a lounge sufficiently ample" for the nursery children "flashed upon me," Addams wrote that year. "A great many more things would flash if you were here to help talk about it."[24] Not surprisingly, by 1894 Addams expressed concern about the prominence of finances in their relationship. "It grieves me a little lest our friendship (wh.[ich] is really a very dear thing to me) should be jarred by all these money transactions." But the desire to share her financial planning with Mary was too strong to resist, and she continued:

> I had a long and solemn talk with all the residents last evening, I hope we are going to be more intimate and mutually responsible on the financial side. I am never going to let things get so bad again before I lay it before folks for help and suggestions. It is too bad to let it accumulate to $888.00—it is shocking. Mr. Kohlsaat sent a hundred dollars this morning with a charming letter. I think that by the end of the week we will be quite "out"—I am grateful to all of them but I am more than that to you.[25]

By then her gratitude to Mary was spiritual as well as material. Insofar as her feelings had material roots, they were nourished by Mary's willingness to fund whatever Addams needed. "The check came this afternoon," an 1894 letter began: "It gives me a lump in my throat to think of the round thousand dollars you have put into the prosaic bakery and the more prosaic debt when there are so many more interesting things you might have done and wanted to do."[26] A typical letter in 1895 read: "Your letter with the news of the generous check came to hand this morning. I cannot tell you how relieved and grateful I am, and what a difference it will make in the running order of things for all the next months."[27] Hull House had many donors, but only one Mary Smith. To her Addams felt free to express her financial anxieties as well as her financial need.

James Weber Linn, who provided us with important insights into the Addams-Smith relationship, emphasized the financial themes in the music of their life together. "It was [Smith's] constant overcoming of deficits here and there, small but apparently insurmountable, that literally kept the work going, or at any rate kept Jane Addams from black discouragement," he wrote. Addams was an executive, but she was no financier, and she made mistakes sometimes in her "estimates." Linn noted that in Addams's letters to Smith in the 1890s,

> the strain of this financial struggle constantly emerges, no less exhausting because in the end it was successful. In scores and scores of these letters Jane Addams refers to the necessity of raising money somehow, even to the struggle to pay her own personal expenses in such instances as when she had turned over her own farm rent, or sold a bond, to keep something going which had been started at the House, which was costing more than Jane had hoped, yet which nobody could bear to give up. Sometimes the references are gloomy, more often they are whimsical, but they are constant. Mary Smith's letters in reply are not preserved: but it is easy to see with what equal constancy she responded.[28]

Addams's relationship with Mary was rooted in Mary's ability to help her survive her torrent of obligations at Hull House. First, and most fundamentally, those obligations were financial.

Between 1906, when gifts began to be systematically recorded, and 1934, when she died, Mary Smith contributed $116,395 to the settlement, an average of $4,157 annually, most of which came in small allotments ranging from $30 to $300.[29] Her correspondence with Addams before 1906 suggests that her annual donations reached about the same scale between 1893 and 1906. Addams's deep and enduring relationship with Smith demonstrated that theirs was indeed a "delivering love," but their alliance also shows that love can embrace many kinds of shared concerns.

FOR BETTER OR FOR WORSE, however, Mary Smith could not and did not fund the settlement's phenomenal growth between 1895 and 1907. She lent financial elasticity and security to Addams's life and labor, but others provided more financial muscle.

Who were these others? Hull House records give us an incomplete account of financial donations, but they show quite clearly that promi-

nent Chicago businessmen made minimal donations. Cyrus H. Mc-
Cormick, Jr., son of the inventor of the reaper that bore his name and
head of a giant manufacturing firm, exemplified the tendency of
Chicago's richest businessmen to grant the settlement very limited
support. In 1892 McCormick gave Hull House $100, and made no fur-
ther donations until 1898, when he gave $50. Thereafter he contrib-
uted $100 almost every year for a grand total of $1,500 by 1914.[30]

In 1909, Louise deKoven Bowen, indefatigable treasurer of the Hull
House Association beginning in 1907, sized McCormick up as an un-
dersubscriber, and asked him to increase his "subscription" "because
we are running here at great expense in keeping up all these large
buildings and the Boys Club itself with its 1800 members is costing between $6000.00 and $7000.00 a year to run. We must look to the large
givers and rich men of Chicago to help us out. If you can do any more
for us we shall be most grateful."[31] McCormick's reply was disappoint-
ing. He wished he could give more, "but if you knew my docket of gifts,
I am sure you would feel that it was strained to the utmost, and I could
not feel in justice to other interests that are just as important to me as
Hull House, that I could increase my contribution."[32] McCormick and
others like him knew that Hull House championed striking workers
and nurtured trade unions, especially among women. This partially
accounts for their lukewarm support.[33]

Julius Rosenwald, president of Sears Roebuck, increased his annual donation from $100 to $1,000 in response to Louise Bowen's encouragement in 1908, but he refused to give more. Though a member
of the finance committee of Hull House Association Board in the
1920s, he nevertheless managed to resist or deflect importunings like
that from Allen Pond, fellow board member and association secretary,
in June 1923:

> Mrs. Bowen telephones me that Hull House has some $3800 in un-
> paid bills mostly for large items such as coal and boiler room re-
> pairs, and some $700.00 additional for insurance premiums. . . . I
> am wondering whether you do not know some one who might
> check into it. . . . I understand that Miss Addams and Miss Smith
> are not expected back until the first of September and I suppose
> that the summer will as usual be a lean season and that we shall go
> from bad to worse unless we put our hands on some additional
> funds.[34]

Although Addams and Smith left Chicago each summer, deficits followed them unless others solved the problem. After the creation of the House Committee in 1893, and the Hull House Association and a board of trustees in 1895, others were more systematically placed to help.

Hull House records show that a multitude of individuals supported the settlement through relatively small donations. These ranged from $0.25 to $1,000, with many in the $10 to $100 range. Psychologically this support was crucial, for it bonded the settlement to a wide variety of Chicago constituencies. Yet the vast majority of Hull House costs were paid by a few large donors. Lucy Knight, a fund-raiser herself who is writing about Addams, estimates that the pattern of giving to the 1893 Relief Fund was typical of most fund raising—four-fifths of the contributions came from five people, one-fifth from the remaining forty.[35]

Certainly this pattern prevailed among the donors of Hull House buildings, most of which were paid for by the individuals after whom they were named: the Butler Art Gallery constructed in 1892; the Smith Building, donated by Mary Smith's father, Charles Mather Smith, in 1895, which housed children's activities; Bowen Hall, constructed by Louse deKoven Bowen in 1904 to house the Hull House Women's Club; and the Mary Crane Nursery, which completed the thirteen-building complex in 1907.[36]

This building boom was facilitated by Helen Culver, niece and beneficiary of the man who built Hull House in 1856 and owned the land around it. In 1906 Culver donated to Hull House the land on which it stood and some adjacent lots, worth a total of $76,800. In 1920 Culver gave Hull House its largest single gift—a $250,000 endowment, one-quarter of the income of which was to be reinvested until the total amounted to $300,000.[37] Jane Addams had solicited this final donation from her aging benefactor. Fearing perhaps that this most difficult of donors might prove even more elusive after death than in life, she asked Helen Culver to deed then what she planned to give through her will later. Contributing around $400 annually for rent for many years, giving valuable land in 1906, and a very large donation in 1920, Culver made Addams work for what she got, but she gave what the settlement could not do without—space.

While Culver and other large donors were important, their support was sporadic. With the exception of Mary Smith, they added resources on special occasions, but did not assume an ongoing responsibility for the settlement's welfare. Only one other benefactor—Louise deKoven Bowen—shared Jane Addams's and Mary Rozet Smith's day-to-day, year-in-and-year-out concern for Hull House financing. With Bowen's friendship and support came the largest steady supply of resources available to the settlement. Without a doubt she was the power behind Addams's throne. Over a period of thirty-four years, between 1895 and 1928, Bowen contributed a total of $542,282, averaging $15,049 annually.[38] No other donor came close to her record; compared even to Mary Smith she looms very large indeed.

Like Mary Smith, Bowen was one of many wealthy women who found meaningful activity at Hull House in the early 1890s. When Bowen entered Hull House for the first time in the winter of 1891–92, she was a thirty-two-year-old mother of three. Spotting her as a capable ally, Addams invited her to take charge of the Hull House Women's Club. Bowen replied that she had intended to ask Addams "if I could not do more to help," but "I expect another little baby early in the spring and with all that means you can readily understand that I cannot do much else and do not dare bind myself to any regular work." Bowen feared Addams must think her "a very useless member of society," but, enclosed a check for $100, and hoped the time would come "when I may be able to give my work as well as my good wishes to Hull House."[39]

Part of Louise Bowen's money derived from her maternal grandfather, who built a large fortune from real estate that later became the heart of Chicago's Loop. As a child she belonged to one of the very few families in Chicago whose carriage was attended by liveried servants. Raised with a strong sense of social responsibility, after graduating from the prestigious Dearborn Seminary at the age of sixteen, she began a lifelong commitment to improving the lives of others. By the time she joined Hull House in 1896, she had extensive experience with a variety of charitable work that took her regularly into the city's poor neighborhoods.[40]

Bowen's work for Hull House derived from her personal conviction about the importance of Addams's social vision. "I admired her greatly and loved her dearly," Bowen wrote.[41]

> Miss Addams always had a very clear vision and great sense of justice and I can remember my mortification one day, when I said, "I have done everything in the world for that woman and she is not

even grateful." She looked at me quizzically and said, "Is that the reason you helped her, because you wanted gratitude?" She was, however, never condemning but always reassuring and encouraging.[42]

An important part of Jane Addams's genius for constructing social networks of support for herself and Hull House came from her ability to delegate responsibility to others. Bowen's commitment to Hull House began with her acceptance of Addams's second request in 1896–97 that she direct the settlement's Women's Club. "For about seventeen years I filled some official position in the club, many years being president, and I have always felt that any experience I acquired in speaking was entirely due to practice in this club," she later remembered.[43] Just as Louise Bowen gave to Hull House, so it gave to her.

Bowen's affiliation with Hull House has four levels of historical significance. First, during a time of convulsive and bloody conflict between capital and labor, when Addams and her colleagues often sided with labor, Bowen's eminently respectable standing among Chicago's wealthiest families brought a protective mantle to the settlement, and paved the way for other wealthy donors. A figure of enormous rectitude even as a young matron, Bowen's presence belied efforts to characterize the settlement as a hotbed of radicalism. As she wrote in her autobiography, *Growing Up with a City*,

> [Jane Addams] was having hard work financing Hull-House. Many people felt she was too much in sympathy with the laboring people and some business men listened to exaggerated tales of what they heard went on at the House and refused to help, but there were others who, because of their contact with the House and of their knowledge of the unselfish and devoted work which was done by the residents and especially by Miss Addams, felt that there was nothing else in the city which was such a power for good, not only to the people of the neighborhood, but to the whole community.[44]

Bowen's affiliation lent credibility to Addams's claims that Hull House aired all sides of "the social question."

Second, Bowen's affiliation with Hull House gives us a revealing glimpse into the cross-class alliances in women's political culture in Chicago. Bowen and Addams were part of a larger process whereby women were combining, often across class lines, to devise new solutions to social problems. For example, Ellen Henrotin, wife of a prominent banker who headed the Chicago Stock Exchange, had, since the 1870s, oriented the Chicago Woman's Club toward a program of social activism, particularly on questions about working women.[45] Thus Bowen had important role models.

Third, Bowen served as the settlement's single largest financial contributor—the person without whom Hull House could not have become what it did. Linn described her as "a tower of financial strength."[46] By 1895 Louise Bowen had begun to augment Mary Smith's role as a general provider for otherwise unmet Hull House needs. "I have made Herculean efforts to bring up the nursery account but as yet no one has subscribed by the month," Addams wrote Smith in January 1895. "Mrs. Bowen gave $100.00 which paid up the coal bills ($50) and paid Mary and Mrs. Hansen to February 1st. . . . So we are quite square and a little ahead in certain instances."[47]

In 1901 Bowen's large contributions began with a donation of $14,000, which was supplemented the next year with $11,749, and in 1904 with $40,900 for the building of Bowen Hall. During the next decade, Louise Bowen gave Hull House a total of $297,777.[48] These contributions launched the great expansion of Hull House, which by 1907 occupied a large city block. They propelled the enterprise to a different scale of endeavor, and provided Jane Addams with the wherewithal to link reality with her imagination.

Fourth, Bowen's services as an astute financial manager gradually shifted that area of responsibility from Addams's shoulders to her own. Beginning as a Hull House trustee in 1903, she served as treasurer of the Hull House Association from 1907 until after Addams's death. After 1907 it was Bowen rather than Addams who worried about paying the gas bill, who designed fund-raising strategies, who supervised from a financial point of view the implementation of new Hull House programs. Placing her work for Addams in a personal context, she also supplied personal advice. "My dear," she wrote in 1908, "I have made a lot of inquiries in regard to a boarding plan for your niece."[49] When Addams protested that Bowen was giving too much of herself and her resources to the settlement, she replied, "Don't you worry about what I do. I don't do more than I can afford," and she got "lots of satisfaction out of it."[50] Addams's financial mainstay loved her work.

Everyone close to Jane Addams knew that Mary Smith and Louise Bowen occupied a special place in the settlement's panoply of donors. An amusing exchange between Alice Hamilton and Julius Rosenwald revealed how ferociously this place could be defended by Addams's closest associates. Hamilton, a doctor who began living at Hull House in 1897, remained close to Addams after her appointment as a professor of Industrial Toxicology at the Harvard Medical School in 1919, and spent part of each year at Hull House.[51] In the 1920s fund raising was one of Hamilton's ongoing responsibilities. In 1928 after a particularly frustrating run-in with Julius Rosenwald, Hamilton wrote him feelingly: "When we talked together the other day and you told me that you did not wish to be 'the line of least resistance' when it came to helping Hull House out of difficulties, I felt sure that you were not and that our reliance always has been primarily on Mary Smith and Mrs. Bowen." Hamilton obtained evidence from the two patrons, and triumphantly included Mrs. Bowen's "record of 34 years," concluding: "So you see they have done most generously by us and they have always been our first recourse in time of need."[52]

In response, Rosenwald beat a fast retreat. "I was probably unfortunate in my reference in speaking of not wishing to be the 'line of least resistance.' I had never underestimated the great help Mrs. Bowen and Miss Smith have been. . . . I would like the privilege of withdrawing the unfortunate statement.[53] We may be sure that Alice Hamilton was among the few to speak to Julius Rosenwald so boldly and the only one to draw such an apology from him.

HULL HOUSE financial records require us to revise our estimates of how the settlement was funded. Addams's social and political independence was rooted in her financial independence. More than any historical account has heretofore realized, she was her own best benefactor during the settlement's early years. As a result, Addams's personal preferences played an enormously important role in determining what projects prospered and what projects lapsed at Hull House, Not just its presiding genius, she also served as its hardworking fairy godmother. Hull House was her home, her experiment, her place—in a material as well as a spiritual sense.

From that very personal center she reached out to two unusual women who came to share her intimate feeling for the settlement's welfare. One, Mary Rozet Smith, became a companion who shared all aspects of Addams's life. The other, Louise deKoven Bowen, also made the settlement her life's work. No amount of generalized good will from Chicago's wealthy men and women could have done for Addams and Hull House what Smith and Bowen did. Theirs were acts of love for the person as well as for the institution.

For her part, Addams chose well. To this as to so many other features of the settlement's life, she brought a magic touch. At this moment in the history of American awareness of the needs of the urban poor, one woman and her close friends made all the difference. A full consideration of their impact on public policy lies beyond the scope of this essay, but it is appropriate to mention that Addams's substantial impact on her society occurred in a context in which traditions of limited government curtailed the development of other agencies that might have preempted or competed with Hull House's position in the vanguard of social change. The failure of civil service reform meant that the United States did not follow England's example of generating a group of governmental experts capable of analyzing and implementing new social policies. The power of the courts undercut initiatives from the legislative branch of government. Massive immigration from Southern and Eastern Europe divided the working class into a number of competing ethnic groups, confounding the creation of an effective labor party. This context created immense opportunities for women reformers of Jane Addams's generation to forge new approaches to social problems. Addams took advantage of those opportunities—but she did not do so alone. Essential to her success were her two friends, Mary Rozet Smith and Louise deKoven Bowen. Her example suggests that women reformers in the Progressive era did indeed inhabit a separate political culture—one that gave generously of its own resources in the process of remaking the larger political society.

NOTES

This essay was substantially aided by three scholars of Jane Addams's life. Victoria Brown of Grinnell College has shared with me her insightful interpretation of Addams's reliance on female networks. Lucy Knight of Wheaton

College has generously shared her thinking about Hull House funding. I am grateful to them and to Mary Lynn McCree Bryan, editor of the *Jane Addams Papers*, who helped me find my way in the papers, decipher Addams's hand, and analyze her motivation.

1   Allen F. Davis, *American Heroine: The Life and Legend of Jane Addams* (New York: Oxford University Press, 1973), 106.
2   James Weber Linn, *Jane Addams: A Biography* (New York: D. Appleton-Century, 1938), 120.
3   Mary Lynn McCree Bryan, ed., *The Jane Addams Papers, 1860–1960* (University Microfilms International), 82 reels.
4   Davis, *American Heroine*, 31. For artisans' wages, see John Modell, "Patterns of Consumption, Acculturation, and Family Income Strategies in Late Nineteenth-Century American," in *Family and Population in Nineteenth-Century America*, ed. Tamara K. Hareven and Maris Vinovskis (Princeton: Princeton University Press, 1978).
5   See Allen F. Davis, "Ellen Gates Starr," in *Notable American Women*, ed. Edward James, Janet James, and Paul Boyer (Cambridge: Harvard University Press, 1971).
6   Jane Addams Papers, University of Illinois, Chicago, *Jane Addams Papers*, Hull House Association Records, Administration of Hull House, Financial Records, Account Books, Oct. 1891–Oct. 1893, pp. 206–209, Reel no. 74. In calculating the percent contributed by JA, I added together the two categories, "Pd by Jane Addams" and "loaned by Jane Addams." The records give no indication of how or if the loans were repaid.
7   Ibid.
8   JA to Helen Culver, March 7, 1890, 335 So. Halsted St., Addams Papers, Correspondence, Reel 2.
9   Financial records for 1892 show that $738 was raised and expended for this purpose. Most of this was provided by the Chicago Woman's Club.
10   Addams Papers, Account Books, October 1891–October 1893, 206–209. Reel 74.
11   Ibid.
12   Linn, *Jane Addams*, 25.
13   Lucy Knight points out this function of the House Committee in her forthcoming book.
14   Henry Barrett Learned, "Hull House," *Lend a Hand* (May 1893), 330–31. I am grateful to Lucy Knight for calling this article to my attention.
15   Addams Papers, Accounts Books, October 1891–October 1893, 206–209, Reel 74.
16   Ibid.

17   Ibid.
18   Linn, *Jane Addams*, 289–290.
19   Ibid., 290.
20   Ibid., 147.
21   JA to MRS, July 4, 1892, Rockford, Ill., Swarthmore College Peace Collection, Jane Adams Papers, Series 1, *Jane Addams Papers*, Correspondence, 1885 January–1895 December, Reel 2.
22   JA to MRS, July 21, 1892, Rockford, Ill., Swarthmore College Peace Collection, Jane Addams Papers, Series 1, *Jane Addams Papers*, Correspondence, 1885 January–1895 December, Reel 2.
23   JA to MRS [1893], Rockford, Ill., Swarthmore College Peace Collection, Jane Addams Papers, Series 1, *Jane Addams Papers*, Correspondence, 1885 January–1895 December, Reel 2.
24   JA to MRS [1893], Rockford.
25   JA to MRS, Hull House, [1894], Swarthmore College Peace Collection, Jane Addams Papers, Series 1, *Jane Addams Papers*, Correspondence, 1885 January–1895 December, Reel 2.
26   JA to MRS [1894].
27   JA to MRS, Hull House, [1895], Swarthmore College Peace Collection, Jane Addams Papers, Series 1, *Jane Addams Papers*, Correspondence, 1885 January–1895 December, Reel 2.
28   Linn, *Jane Addams*, 148, 192.
29   Records of Mary Rozet Smith's Contributions to Hull House, Swarthmore College Peace Collection: and Hull House Association Records, Administration of Hull House, Financial Records, Contributions and Donations, Individuals, Mary Rozet Smith, *Jane Addams Papers*, Reel 50.
30   Cyrus H. McCormick Papers, State Historical Society of Wisconsin; Hull House Association Records, Administration of Hull House, Financial Records, Contributions and Donations, Individuals, Cyrus H. McCormick, *Jane Addams Papers*, Reel 50.
31   Louise deKoven Bowen to Cyrus H. McCormick, April 30, 1909, 136 Astor Street, Cyrus H. McCormick, Jr. Papers, State Historical Society of Wisconsin; Hull House Association Records, Administration of Hull House, Financial Records, Contributions and Donations, Individuals, Cyrus H. McCormick, *Jane Addams Papers*, Reel 50.
32   Cyrus H. McCormick to Louise deKoven Bowen, May 15, 1909, McCormick Papers; *Jane Addams Papers*, Reel 50.
33   See quote from Louise Bowen below, and n. 43.
34   Allen B. Pond to Julius Rosenwald, June 9, 1923, 64 E. Van Buren St., Julius Rosenwald Papers, University of Chicago Library; Hull House Association Records, Administration of Hull House, Financial Records,

Contributions and Donations, Individuals, Julius Rosenwald, *Jane Addams Papers*, Reel 50.

35   Author's correspondence with Lucy Knight, November 7, 1989.

36   Allen F. Davis and Mary Lynn McCree, eds., *Eighty Years at Hull House* (Chicago: Quadrangle Books, 1969), 22, 67, 151; Linn, *Jane Addams*, 158.

37   Helen Culver to Jane Addams, October 19, 1920, Lake Forest, Ill., Jane Addams Memorial Collection, Hull House Association Records; Hull House Association Records, Administration of Hull House, Financial Records, Contributions and Donations, Individuals, Helen Culver, *Jane Addams Papers*, Reel 50.

38   Julius Rosenwald Papers, University of Chicago Library; Hull House Association Records, Administration of Hull House, Financial Records, Contributions and Donations, Individuals, Louise deKoven Bowen, *Jane Addams Papers*, Reel 50.

39   Louise deKoven Bowen to Jane Addams, October 26, [1892], 136 Astor St., Louise Hadduck deKoven Bowen Papers, Chicago Historical Society, *Jane Addams Papers*, Reel 2. This letter allows us to date Bowen's arrival at Hull House in 1892 because her last child, whose approaching birth in the spring is mentioned in her letter, was born in 1893. Thus her own recollection of joining Hull House after hearing Addams speak on the Pullman strike of 1894 is mistaken. Louise deKoven Bowen, *Growing Up With a City* (New York: Macmillan, 1926), 81–82. James Linn's estimate (*Jane Addams*, 141) of the timing of Bowen's arrival in the fall of 1893 refers to her permanent attachment to the settlement, not her first visit. Unfortunately Addams's letters to Louise Bowen and Bowen's papers generally have not survived. Her papers at the Chicago Historical Society contain only a few scrapbooks.

40   Mary Lynn McCree, "Louise deKoven Bowen" in *Notable American Women*; Bowen, *Growing Up With a City*, 25–29.

41   Bowen, *Growing Up With a City*, 86–87.

42   Ibid., 87–88.

43   Ibid., 83.

44   Ibid., 87.

45   Paul S. Boyer, "Ellen Martin Henrotin," in *Notable American Women*. In 1894 Henrotin began a four year term as president of the National Federation of Women's Clubs, during which time she doubled the number of women's clubs and established twenty new state federations.

46   Linn, *Jane Addams*, 192.

47   JA to MRS, January 15, 1895, Freeport, Ill., Swarthmore College Peace Collection, Jane Addams Papers, Series 1, *Jane Addams Papers*, Correspondence, 1885 January–1895 December, Reel 2.

48 Julius Rosenwald Papers, University of Chicago Library; and Hull House Association Records, Administration of Hull House, Financial Records, Contributions and Donations, Individuals, Louise deKoven Bowen, *Jane Addams Papers*, Reel 50.

49 Louise deKoven Bowen to Jane Addams, October 4, [1908], enclosure in Jane Addams to Sarah Alice Addams Haldeman, [October 1908], Indiana University, Lilly Library, Mrs. S.A. Haldemann Mss.; and Correspondence, *Jane Addams Papers*, Reel 5.

50 Ibid.

51 See Barbara Sicherman, *Alice Hamilton: A Life in Letters* (Cambridge: Harvard University Press, 1984); and Barbara Sicherman, "Alice Hamilton," in *Notable American Women: The Modern Period*, ed. Sicherman et al. (Cambridge: Harvard University Press, 1980).

52 Alice Hamilton to Julius Rosenwald, June 5, 1928, Julius Rosenwald Papers, University of Chicago Library; and Hull House Association Records, Administration of Hull House, Financial Records, Contributions and Donations, Individuals, Louise deKoven Bowen, *Jane Addams Papers*, Reel 50.

53 Julius Rosenwald to Alice Hamilton, June 15, 1928, Julius Rosenwald Papers, University of Chicago Library; and Hull House Association Records, Administration of Hull House, Financial Records, Contributions and Donations, Individuals, Louise deKoven Bowen, *Jane Addams Papers*, Reel 50.

TWO

Women and Philanthropy

Outside the United States

EDITH COUTURIER

"For the Greater Service of God":

Opulent Foundations and Women's

Philanthropy in Colonial Mexico

"For the greater service of God" is the formulaic phrase that introduces documents establishing charitable foundations of such disparate character as convents, dowry funds, schools, hospitals, and churches. This customary introduction reminds us of the deep religious roots of all charities in colonial Mexico. It might also be noted that this same formula was used in dowry contracts and in denunciations to the Inquisition. Charity, marriage, and religious orthodoxy, although deriving from different historical traditions and human needs, came to be part of a structure of belief governing many actions of those with wealth in colonial Mexico. This essay explores the ways in which men and women used their charitable donations to fulfill religious and social obligations. As Kathleen D. McCarthy and Ann Firor Scott point out, men and women have often espoused different causes, embraced different techniques, and achieved different ends through their gifts of money and time. These differences are evident in colonial Mexico as well, albeit in more subtle forms.[1]

From alms to the poor that both the Christian gospel and Catholic doctrine suggested that the wealthy give directly to the needy, to the construction of houses of worship, from the most modest to the most elaborate—all charitable donations possessed a measure of religious motivation. Almsgiving had spiritual meaning for the donor as well as the recipient. Every Catholic had an obligation to dispense charity for his or her salvation, but also as a "tribute to the spiritual significance of the poor."[2]

119

In colonial Mexico, individuals who had enough disposable income to write a will spent a considerable portion of their resources on goals broadly defined as philanthropic. One Spanish viceroy observed that the "substantial fortunes made in mining, agriculture, trade and manufacturing were invested in opulent foundations, and other classes of· pious works."³ He listed contributions to the faithful that facilitated accomplishments as varied as chantries, missionary enterprise and exploration of the frontier, and the construction and maintenance of hospitals, convents, and colleges. He might have included the dowry funds that would permit ethnically Spanish women to marry at an appropriately high level (or often even to marry at all). Donors of these works could be individuals of either sex, married couples, or confraternities. Motivation for these "pious deeds" or "pious works" derived from religious sentiments as varied as the desire to release souls from purgatory, to recognize high status publicly, to express power in both family and society, as well as to relieve the poor. Until the end of the eighteenth century, secular charity through alms to the poor was not differentiated from support to the Church: both of these causes were considered pious deeds or works.⁴

A consideration of the philanthropic history of sixteenth- and seventeenth-century Mexico shows that Spanish laws influenced gifts and the establishment of philanthropies in ways that affected women both as donors and recipients. Certain laws made it possible for women to have influence as donors and for women to be the recipients of charitable gifts. Secular law and scripture agreed in emphasizing that donors desiring to give alms should give preference to a relative.⁵ In most popular varieties of pious deeds performed by Mexicans in the colonial period—namely chantries and dowry funds—donors preferred to assist family members. Patrons of female convents usually reserved the right to select one or more women to receive dowries so they might profess. Donations benefiting relatives might also have strengthened the lineage and have helped "to organize the relationships between generations . . . by ensuring some measure of financial security for one's descendants" as well as for collateral relatives.⁶ In concentrating upon family, donors responded not only to law and tradition, but also to a human need to be remembered after death in the prayers of family members—some of whom had received benefices from their relatives. Church teaching asserted that these prayers helped rescue the donors from purgatory and surely helped to enlarge the sense of familial continuity.

In legislation about charities, Spanish law found equal merit in donations to lay individuals and religious institutions; in fact, the law specified that any donation to an ecclesiastical institution should be considered a principal instrument of charity.[7] Mexicans wrote wills that bequeathed money or property to Masses for the soul of the deceased (thus supporting the Church), to dowries, and to secular charities that provided food and clothing for various categories of unfortunates. Wealthier Mexicans might have established foundations earlier in their lives for education, health, and more spiritual purposes. The confraternities, to which Mexicans of all classes belonged, usually made provision only for the limited care of their own membership. If the confraternity was sufficiently wealthy, it also could establish foundations for spiritual, educational, and charitable purposes that served a broader public. Scholars working in the archives of Mediterranean Catholic countries have discovered the same patterns of philanthropy from the early Renaissance through the eighteenth century, although details differ among places and periods.[8]

Inheritance law provided women with special influence and power in the distribution of funds for philanthropies and in the foundation of institutions that served the social and spiritual goals of the elite. Because daughters, even as single women, could inherit their parents' estates equally with their brothers, they had access to disposable wealth, and they could mortgage their share of family property for chaplaincies or other philanthropic bequests. As widows, women had even greater freedom to distribute their share of the family's wealth. Whether as single women, widows, or nuns, women's contributions differed in small but significant ways from those of men. Elite women were conceded to be more spiritual (rather than intellectual) than men, and their ties to the Church, to their confessors, and even to several members of the clergy were often strong.[9]

A second and perhaps even more significant aspect of women and philanthropy in colonial Mexico is the issue of women as the special recipients of charities. Because women were perceived to be weaker and more in need of protection than men, certain extremely popular philanthropies—such as dowry funds, feminine convents, endowments for widows, the creation of *recogimientos,* or refuges—were

dedicated exclusively to them. Establishing convents or recogimientos gave families the opportunity both to assert their importance
as leading patrons and to provide for some of their own female relatives. Families or donors of more limited means might invest sums
from 3,000 to 6,000 pesos to establish a dowry fund. These were the
counterparts to the chantries that they might establish for their sons,
nephews, or other male relatives. These two donations followed the
customary endowment of Masses as the most ubiquitous philanthropies of colonial Mexico.

Dowry funds provided a modest sum of money for women to either
marry or profess as a nun. These funds helped defray the expenses for
a woman's entry into a convent, or supplied a small sum (usually 300
pesos) to endow a woman who had recently married, and who had
previously won a lottery entitling her to a dowry. Because the costs of
entry into a convent as a nun ranged from 3,000 to 6,000 pesos, a
woman who received one of these funds needed other familial
sources, or money from more than one dowry fund.

In the sample of those foundations that I have examined, the grants
were relatively small sums of money, between 150 and 500 pesos; the
customary grant was 300 pesos. In the eighteenth century, this was almost equivalent to an artisian's annual wage. It could provide enough
money to buy modest furniture such as a chest, chairs, benches,
cushions, statues of saints, and clothing—the usual furnishing of a
small farmer's or an artisan's home. Whether some women received
substantial sums from numerous dowry funds is impossible to know
until a more systematic examination of the hundreds of dowry funds
and their recipients has been carried out. Such an investigation might
reveal that women from cadet branches of elite families enjoyed access to these dowry funds and were able to accumulate substantial
sums of money through participation in various lotteries over a period
of several years. A number of small dowries from these funds could
supplement familial resources.

Dowry funds were both popular and successful. At the end of the
colonial period, in 1810, one confraternity alone, that of Santísimo
Sacramento, had donated nearly a million pesos and had benefited
4,814 orphans; of this total, 3,500 women had either married or
professed.[10]

Dowry funds worked as follows: donors granted money to an eccle-siastical institution, a confraternity, or to a specified list of patrons, fre-quently mixed between lay and clerics, to provide funds for virgins of legitimate birth of pure Christian ancestry (and without Indian or black parents or grandparents) either to enter a convent or to marry.[11] Usually, the foundation document required that the woman be an or-phan, most often meaning that her father had died. Donors, repre-senting the social aims of the community, assumed the paternal role in providing for the future of daughters.[12]

One of the earliest records of these gifts was in 1586 with a donation to the Cathedral of Mexico of five groups of houses to supply income for the dowries of honest and poor virgins, with preference given to the donors' relatives. In 1608, a female donor provided capital for four dowries of 300 pesos each, which were to be distributed on the feast of San José in the Cathedral of Mexico.[13]

A variety of social classes established these dowry funds. For exam-ple, the viceroy, the Marqués de Casafuerte from 1722 to 1734, do-nated 70,000 pesos for dowries of orphans. He named the Jesuits as administrators and patrons of the fund.[14] A parish priest, Francisco Baeza, who died in the city of Puebla in 1644, established a more lim-ited endowment for his female relatives, to be administered by the priest of the church in which the donor had officiated. Some recipients of this fund married artisans and small businessmen, including a master barber, and a man who was both a shoemaker and an owner of a lime kiln.[15]

In 1775, sixteen women received money from various endowments administered by the confraternity of Rosario. Eleven of these women married men who could sign their names (albeit with some difficulty), and all were addressed with the honorifics *Don* and *Doña*. We know only that one of the men was an official in the tobacco tax office. The rest of the women used the dowry grants to defray the costs of entering and maintaining themselves in a convent. In 1767, one nun received the 300 pesos that had been resigned by a lottery winner of 1766, who "was firmly determined to maintain herself without taking state."[16]

For some of the leading citizens of Mexico, officiating at the ceremonies in which these funds were awarded and then distributed was considered an honor, since such events provided living proof of their devotion to the words of Jesus that it is more blessed to give than to receive. During 1775, Pedro Núñez de Villavicencio, who was then in charge of the Mexico City mint, and also an official of Rosario confraternity, verified that all of the rules of one particular dowry endowment had been fulfilled.[17]

It is difficult to determine if endowing women was a more popular charity among men than women. In a selection of twelve foundations for the "marriage of orphans" from Mexico City records, between 1644 and 1768, four of the original donors were women, two of them were couples, and the remaining six were men. In some cases the establishment of dowry funds seems intimately related to the founding and patronage of convents, as donors began by investing money in dowry funds that would eventually be allocated to young women who wished to enter a convent, which would be created in the future.[18] Given men's greater access to money, the large proportion of women seeking to establish dowry funds is significant.

Even in the provinces, many men sought to facilitate marriage financially and to protect women physically and spiritually. The importance of dowry funds for men is illustrated through the example of a donor, a "patriarch" from the rich agricultural and mining region of the Bajío in east central Mexico, who provided the funds for an annual dowry lottery in the town of Lagos on December 8 (the anniversary of the conception of the Virgin) in the local church. All the descendants of the donor's family who could present their baptismal records and were of the appropriate age were eligible to participate. The donor added that if there were no female relatives among descendants of his line, then any poor Spanish girls of the town of Lagos could compete in the lottery. The twenty-one women who applied in 1741 came from ten different nuclear families, most of them related to the donor. One woman was disqualified because she had been given a 200-pesos award the previous year. (Often, dowry funds were written without such restrictions, permitting one girl to win several times.) The women received the money only when they married, which could be two or three years later.[19]

One explanation for the popularity and purpose of these dowry funds comes from a 1751 provincial document, which noted the "lamentable consequence of the excessive number of women over men. Many women remain without marrying. Others marry unequally, lose

their nobility, live abandoned by their relatives, and suffer other unfortunate consequences. . . . There are more nobles than plebeians,
[one sees] poor noble girls working in the humblest occupations in the
fields"[20]

Modern research in census and parish records confirms the accuracy of this eighteenth-century observation. Among the white population in the frontier town of Guadalajara, 39 percent of the Spanish
offspring were born out of wedlock at the end of the seventeenth century. Other research indicates the ubiquity of consensual unions and
illegitimacy among many groups (including the upper class) in
various parts of Mexico.[21] One motivation for dowry funds stemmed
from an attempt to provide economic protection to white women, to
guard their "honor" by preventing unequal unions, and to avoid race
mixtures. Another incentive for establishing these funds was to
strengthen the practice of marriage, with the subsequent degree of security it might provide. The relationship between the promise of a
dowry and the formalization of marriage vows seems to be a clear one.
It was one way in which those with money and influence in the society
sought to assist both their relatives and affect the behavior of those of
marriageable age. Dowry funds, if they worked as they were intended,
supplied a small amount of money to many young women, and perhaps were an earlier version of welfare assistance given to the needy.

Dowry funds could attract the interest of both large and small donors. Those with limited means could make contributions to confraternities, adding to existing funds through a lien on a small
property; such modest patronage deeds would provide as little as 25
pesos a year. The establishment of institutions such as convents or
female refuges, however, required large capital expenditures, beginning at 50,000 pesos. The donors not only had to fund the construction
of residence and chapels, they also had to provide the considerable
operating funds for these buildings. Convents for women, as well as
many other large donations to the regular orders, exemplify the kind
of "opulent foundation" to which the Spanish viceroy referred at the
end of the eighteenth century.

From the middle of the sixteenth century to the early years of the
nineteenth century, married couples without children, women acting
alone, and in a few cases, laymen or ecclesiastics undertook the establishment and the patronage of the more than thirty female convents

established in Mexico. Founding a convent symbolized the achievement of the highest socioeconomic status and affirmed deep religiosity. It also ensured an institutional framework for remembrance in the prayers of the convent church and the right for family members or other favored women to receive dowries from the nunneries' funds.[22] The cost of patronage could be quite high. By the middle of the eighteenth century, one Franciscan provincial judged even 200,000 pesos to be an inadequate sum for the foundation of a convent.[23]

In contrast to the establishment of dowry funds—a pious work that was selected by both men and women in approximately equal numbers—the foundation and continued sponsorship of convents were pious works in which women played an increasingly important role. Between 1600 and the end of the colonial period, widows or single women founded or promoted sixteen out of the thirty convents established in Mexico.[24] One of the earliest founders was the widow, Catalina Peralta, an heir to a substantial fortune in haciendas and flour mills; in 1592 she instituted the Franciscan convent of Santa Isabel, and then entered the convent herself. Even though a professed nun, after her death, she received the same lavish funeral as was held for male patrons of important institutions. As patron, Peralta had retained the right to nominate six nuns who received dowries supplied from the convent's revenues. This right of appointment remained in her family, even after the patronage had passed to an ecclesiastical institution.[25] Patronage and the power it bestowed on a family over many generations are significant aspects of philanthropy: for example, the right retained by Peralta's descendants to appoint novices to the nunnery, even though they no longer had the funds to supply dowries, assisted them in sustaining their elite status in their family.

The tradition of women founding convents continued throughout the colonial period. As late as 1803, the Marquesa de Selva Nevada established a branch of the Carmelite convent in Querétaro. One of the chief architects of colonial Mexico, Manuel Tolsa, designed the neoclassical building, and the archbishop of Mexico accompanied the founders on their trip to Querétaro. Both the marquesa and her daughters entered the convent.[26]

Nuns themselves were active in finding a patron or group of patrons to provide the funds for buildings, church, and operating capital.

For example, the earliest convent established in Mexico City, the Conceptionist, began with a grant of some houses from one of the conquerors and various other gifts; a century later, the buildings were no longer adequate. The nuns found patrons, but their generosity was inadequate. In 1643, therefore, they enlisted the aid of one of the powerful men of seventeenth-century Mexico, Simón de Haro, and his wife Isabel de la Barrera y Escobar, who provided them with the funds for their convent buildings. Another famous patron of the seventeenth century, Alvaro Lorenzana, completed the work begun by the Haro family and left a small legacy for every nun in Mexico City.[27]

In the first Franciscan foundation of Santa Clara in Mexico City, Andrés Arrás Tenorio and his wife, Jeronima de Meneses, acted as family patrons. They were asked by the nuns to resign their patronage unless they agreed to put a certain large amount of money into the treasury of the convent. The couple refused to do this and became embroiled in a legal suit beginning in 1623. This issue was not resolved until 1659, when the clergyman Juan de Ontiveros Barrera, the brother-in-law of Simón de Haro, gave 50,000 pesos to the convent, with the provision that some of the money be spent to provide dowries for nine women. At the cleric's death, his sister, now widowed, became the patron.[28]

The important role played by nuns in finding patrons and negotiating the conditions of patronage is illustrated by the changes in patronage of the convent of Santa María de Gracía between 1659 and 1660. The original patron had not left sufficient money for a church. The nuns signed different agreements over a period of several years to grant the patronage to Juan Navarro Pastrana and his wife, Agustina de Aguilar. The nuns had to agree to change the name of the convent to San José de Gracía and to provide seats near the high altar on the days of the celebration of the Masses (a chair for him, but a platform and cushions for her), and elaborate funerals for each of them. In addition, the new patrons demanded the right to name two women to receive dowries with no additional cost to the donors, and at the expense of the convent. Agustina de Aguilar had the right to visit the nunnery accompanied by two women whenever she wished.[29] It is significant that neither she nor her husband had the right to name the patrons who would succeed them after their death.

Although almost all these convents were established for the daughters of white citizens, Mestiza and Indian women received the benefits

of patronage deeds as well. An interesting example of such a foundation is the one established by Diego Tapia, an Otomí cacique; inspired
by his daughter, he founded the convent of Santa Clara at Querétaro in
1607. Some Spanish families supported the foundation on the assumption that their daughters would also enter the convent. Their expectations proved well founded, for the convent became exclusively
Spanish or white, and the refuge of the Querétaro elite women, as
widows, daughters, aunts, and varieties of extended family constructed "cells" or houses on the extensive convent grounds.[30] With
only one exception, the convents that initially included Indian women
soon became institutions exclusively dedicated to the spiritual and
perhaps material needs of the white, well-to-do population.

A somewhat different outcome attended the founding of the convent of Corpus Christi in Mexico City in 1724. Established by the viceroy, the Marquis de Valero, this convent was dedicated exclusively to
Indian women of noble parentage. The idea evoked criticism when
first proposed in 1719, and these objections delayed the opening of the
convent for five years. Efforts to transform the convent into one that
would serve the Spanish community continued.[31] Corpus Christi was
the only convent in Mexico that followed the strict order of the Franciscan nuns, and at least one potential patron tried to establish a white
counterpart, possibly with a desire to replicate the religious awe that
the community tendered to the Indian nuns.[32]

If convents usually owed their inspiration and patronage to women,
or to women and men acting together, the institutions called recogimientos, or refuges—which ranged from punitive institutions to
places that protected honorable women—were almost always
founded by men acting alone or in groups such as a confraternity.
While both the recogimiento and the convent provided for women to
be confined, the legal difference appears to be that the nuns in the
convent had the right to elect their leaders (hence self-government),
while the male patrons and administrators governed the women in
the recogimientos.[33] Residents of the recogimientos did not follow a
rule or take vows, and they could leave more freely than in the regular
orders. Male patrons supplied the money or buildings for almost all of
the twenty-nine such institutions founded in the colonial period. The
religious or spiritual aspect of these institutions was secondary to
their character as secular refuges for divorced women, or for women

of "good" family who lacked the money to make an appropriate marriage or enter a convent. Some of them served as penal institutions for prostitutes; this idea of the existence of "loose" women or women in need of reform seems to have been more troubling to men than to women.[34] This feature of philanthropy, providing for the confinement of women—for reasons ranging from spiritual to criminal—was clearly a critical social goal.

To educate women had been a small but perhaps significant motive in establishing some of the institutions founded for women before the middle of the eighteenth century. Many of these earlier institutions had become recogimientos, or their income went into the more easily administered dowry funds.[35] Educational and spiritual aims were closely connected in the sixteenth and seventeenth centuries and into the early years of the eighteenth century, but it had proved difficult to maintain and develop the educational aspects of institutions for women.[36]

In the middle of the eighteenth century, a confraternity of wealthy Basque merchants and a professed nun, one of the heirs of the large landholding family of San Miguel de Aguayo from northern Mexico, established two of the "opulent foundations" of colonial Mexico. Although each of them began with different aims, the efforts resulted in the two eighteenth-century educational institutions for women that endured. A comparison of these two institutions is useful: a masculine and collective effort produced a recogimiento, Las Vizcainas; while a professed nun, with the assistance of her family, founded La Enseñanza, a school for the education of poor girls.

Three wealthy members of the confraternity of Aranzazu, an organization of Basque merchants, decided to establish a recogimiento for their relatives, to be called Las Vizcainas, from the Spanish word for Basque women. Later, the list of possible beneficiaries was extended to include all the daughters and widows of confraternity members. These men raised the enormous sum of 600,000 pesos for the construction of the church, the living quarters, and other rooms. The opposition of the archbishop, however, prevented the opening of the recogimiento for more than thirty years: the confraternity had insisted upon its right to appoint all of the priests who would minister to the women in the recogimiento and had taken other actions that ignored the prerogatives of the archbishop, thus incurring his enmity.

Las Vizcainas had numerous places for girls and women who could not afford to pay the daily cost of 10 pesos a day. The initial list of donors of these "places of grace," or free spots, shows that women donated only 9 places, whereas men supplied funds for 130. Because Basque women could contribute to this cause, it is significant that so few chose to do so.[37] Even more than in the case of dowry funds, the large number of male donors underscores the importance of the masculine role in the protection of young girls and widows.

From the very beginning, as was customary in recogimientos or convents that permitted younger girls, the older girls or women taught the younger ones reading and writing. The addition of a large school for girls occurred during the early years of the 1790s. Two men, both high ecclesiastical officials, decided to use 9,000 pesos that had been allotted in an ecclesiastic's testament to "pious deeds" for the establishment of a school on the first floor of Las Vizcainas. A year after the school opened, 147 girls were enrolled as external students—many of them without paying tuition.[38] This transformation of a traditional recogimiento into an educational enterprise owed its conception to two men influenced by Enlightenment ideas. These men and the society that welcomed La Vizcainas also owed an intellectual debt to the arrival in 1752 of the first teaching order, the Order of Mary, whose convent of La Enseñanza was dedicated to the education of Mexican women.[39]

The guiding spirit behind the foundation of the convent of La Ensenañza, María Ignacia Azlor, had been educated by her Navarrese mother, from who she might have heard about the teaching Order of Mary. Established in seventeenth-century France by a niece of Montaigne, this order had several branches in northern Spain. Azlor had insisted upon professing in Spain, despite the opposition of Mexican authorities, and she single-mindedly pursued her intention to enter the Order of Mary. Her second purpose was to introduce the order into Mexico so that an organized group of nuns dedicated to education would exist in that region.[40]

From its very inception, one mission of the convent of La Enseñanza was to provide education for poor girls: "For lack of education many poor women are lost because they are unable to do the work of men (for whose instruction many different orders are dedicated . . .). [They] have no recourse but to sustain themselves by the labor of their hands. Ignorant of the skills appropriate to their sex, . . . [women] often beg and usurp the alms of the crippled, who need it most."[41] Her object was perhaps to convince the authorities that establishing a school for girls would alleviate certain social problems. Her main concern was for the predicament of poor girls, who lacked the skills to earn a living, although she hoped that the order would educate women of the upper social categories as well. The founding document states that the purpose is to "raise, teach and educate girls in Christian doctrine, the rudiments of our Holy Catholic Faith, as in the feminine skills of sewing, embroidery, reading, writing and arithmetic and other needs of their own sex."[42]

Because LaEnsenañza did not have the power of a large and wealthy confraternity to support it and had depended initially upon the resources of a family experiencing economic difficulties, the convent was underfinanced. In fact, the same archbishop who had prevented the opening of Las Vizcainas for more than thirty years also opposed this project on the grounds that the family had not provided enough money. Family members sold commodities as distinct and conspicuous as jewelry and cattle, and a brother-in-law willed the convent 50,000 pesos. By soliciting contributions from other members of the community to assist in opening the convent, the nuns finally raised enough money to validate their royal license and to build and open this educational institution for women in Mexico. Like many other convents, this educational enterprise depended upon a collective effort.[43]

The convent's fiscal problems, especially those related to providing pensions for poor girls, continued to trouble the administration. Most of the money given as dowries to those nuns who entered the convent of La Enseñanza was invested in twenty-five houses, for which the school received rent. Because these funds were insufficient to support both the convent and to finance scholarships, financial assistance was sought from members of the convent community as well as lay people. This fund-raising effort was not totally successful.

In an examination of the pious works directed to the school, Pilar Foz y Foz notes that the nuns in the convent preferred to will money for Masses and the dowries of future postulants, rather than for scholarships for poor girls. The more secular purposes that were becoming increasingly popular by the end of the eighteenth century did not induce the nuns, even those associated with La Enseñanza, to leave money for scholarships rather than prayers. Male clergymen who contributed to the institution provided some funds for scholarships, but they also donated more for the traditional pious deeds such as Masses and chantries and nothing for the general expenses of the convent. Almost 80 percent of the money contributed in various ways by lay donors between 1754 and 1820 was destined for Masses or other aspects of the liturgy. The general public showed very little interest in supporting scholarships.[44]

This indicates that smaller donors still adhered closely to the charities dedicated to the remembrance of their own souls and those of their families. Perhaps concern about the hereafter and a desire to be remembered by the living continued to govern the charitable impulse of the bulk of the moderate and small donors to institutions of the female orders. Despite the success of Madre Azlor in establishing a teaching order in Mexico, the tendency of donors to favor religious over educational aims threatened the mission of La Ensenanza.

Women contributed substantially to the ordinary and customary charities of the colony of Mexico. Until quantitative studies of wills are conducted, however, we cannot know how women's wills differed from those of men. We still need to explore the contributions of men and women to the regular male orders.[45] An attempt to study the differences in charitable giving in testaments runs into the difficulties of determining the influences of confessors on the direction of their gifts.[46] Substantial donations for the financing of Jesuit missions in Baja California and California, carried out by women, seemed clearly the result of personal contacts between Jesuit friars and donors.[47]

Women participated less actively in the establishment of hospitals than they did in the foundation of convents. They do not appear as individual donors of these institutions, but as members of partnerships with their husbands. Of the twenty-five hospitals founded in the seventeenth century, twenty-one were initiated by confraternities and guilds.[48] The religious orders dedicated to the foundation and administration of hospitals established other hospitals, as did communities. It was already becoming difficult by the mid-seventeenth century for one unassisted family to establish a hospital. Women did contribute land and funds to hospitals, but the conception and organization of major fund-raising for hospitals seem to have attracted them less than other projects. Perhaps this was due to the fact that the construction and maintenance of hospitals were required by secular law and thus fell more directly into the realm of official politics connected with the expenditure of a specific tax revenue. Women's relative lack of interest in this aspect of philanthropy may be explained by their being less influential in this realm than in other areas. Praying for the ill or fulfilling pious deeds might have seemed more pertinent than institutional establishments.

Direct relief of the poor through alms may have been the most important aspect of charity. These contributions leave no records in the archives. Contemporary chroniclers of some of the disastrous epidemics that punctuated the history of colonial Mexico make oblique references to private acts of charity and to the work of women in caring for the sick. One chronicler notes that these "honest matrons brought their servants to the homes of the afflicted, prepared cocoa, made them sweat, changed their clothes, and gave them all kinds of other aid."[49] In the community hospitals that were so much a part of the "cultural landscape" of Mexico, women cared for the sick and supplied meals. In at least one town, women wove cotton into clothing for hospital inmates.[50] It is possible that in future investigations more women will emerge as important providers of care for the sick, in institutional settings as well as in private acts of charity.

Women's access to wealth through inheritance law and custom, their distinct role as moral guardians of society, and their position as the special objects of charity governed their activities in philanthropy. A commitment to the protection of ethnically Spanish women, the religious principles of society, and the existence of female communities in convents and recogimientos inspired support both for women and the institutions designed to benefit them. The need to sustain women became increasingly critical at the end of the colonial period, as the numbers of urban women living alone, either widowed or never married, reached high proportions.[51]

A secular and provincial counterpart to María Ignacia Azlor, who established the Order of Mary for the education of girls, can be found in the person of a Querétaro widow, María Josefa Vergara Hernández. She also illustrates the beginnings of an individual female donor's comprehensive plan to ameliorate social distress by establishing in the provincial city of Querétaro almost all of the beneficent institutions that existed in other parts of Mexico. She named the City Council of Querétaro as the executor of her will, thus imposing upon the municipal authorities the obligation to establish schools for the education of girls, shelters for the poor, a Monte de Piedad (an official pawnbroking establishment), and provisional hospitals for the care of the sick during epidemics.[52] As a sign of at least one woman's attitude toward the traditional recogimiento, it is useful to note that the testator prohibited the introduction of criminals into any of the organizations for women that she founded.

The organization of women by other women for social activism occurs after the events described in this essay. It is tied to women's philanthropy by the emphasis on women as both in special need of charity and women as wealthy providers. Connections between spiritual life, the special needs of women, and women as dispensers of charity emerge in the first centuries of Mexican history. Women as actors on the scene before Independence appear in relation to traditional charities. In the nineteenth century, women acquire a far more public role.[53] In order to discover women as performers on a more public stage in the years before 1900, we need to investigate further the history of a broadly defined philanthropic movement.[54]

In comparing the donations of men and women, we might conclude that male donors acted as the agents of a society that both aimed to protect white, Christian women of legitimate parentage, and viewed marriage and entry into a convent as sacramental acts by carrying out those bequests and donations that conformed to that society's principles. Those men with money and a philanthropic bent might have viewed Spanish women as the ideal instruments for carrying out the religious purposes of the society.

Women who chose between spiritual charities and those directed toward the relief of a social or economic problems tended to favor the spiritual. Even those professed nuns who had elected to enter the teaching Order of Mary still provided more generously in their testaments for Masses than for scholarships. Wealthy women's greater interest in spiritual causes rather than in direct aid to the needy is also indicated by their sponsorship of convents rather than hospitals. These contributions sustained communities of women.[55]

These are preliminary conclusions; a number of research avenues remain to be explored. An assessment of a large number of wills might reveal differences between men's and women's charitable provision, whether for family members or for the unrelated poor. An investigation of epidemics and the response they elicited may tell us more about women's activities in the direct relief of the afflicted. We do know that men, when acting alone, preferred to support recogimientos rather than convents, a choice that probably reflected their paternalistic view of women. Women in a recogimiento did not have the right of self-government, while women in a convent had the right to vote and elect their own spiritual and political leaders, as well as to determine patronage. Women donors were more attracted to convents and displayed less interest in establishing recogimientos. I can only conclude that when given an opportunity to establish an "opulent foundation," either alone or in company with their husbands, women selected the convent, and not the recogimiento or hospital. The convent was not only dedicated especially "to the greater service of God," but it also enhanced the power of women. And perhaps women appreciated that.

NOTES

1   Benjamin Kohl, Comments on the AHA session on Business Social Response in Three Cultures (December 1986). An earlier and more general version of this paper was presented at this session, organized by Paul Abraham. In addition to the comments of Benjamin Kohl, I have benefited from suggestions made by Asunción Lavrin, Linda Martz, Dauril Alden, and Jane Shumate.

2   William J. Callahan, "The Problem of Confinement: An Aspect of Poor Relief in Eighteenth Century Spain," *Hispanic American Historical Review* (hereafter *HAHR*) 51 (1971), 2. Religious manuals referred to those in need of alms as "men of Christ . . . who represent the Lord and were made poor in this world for our [the faithful] benefit," quoted in Callahan. The Gospel of Mark instructs the faithful by reminding them that "Whosoever shall give you a drink of water in my name, because you belong to Christ, verily I say unto you, he shall not lose his reward" (Mark 9:41).

3   Juan Vicente Güemes Pacheco de Padilla, Conde de Revillagigedo, *Instrucción reservada que el Conde de Revillagigedo dió a su succesor en el mando . . .* (Mexico: Imprenta de C. A. Guiol, 1831), 33. Doris Ladd, in her dissertation "The Mexican Nobility at Independence" (Ph.D. diss., Stanford University, 1971) first noted this statement.

4   In Mexico, until the middle of the eighteenth century (or even later), do-
     nors made no distinction between "charitable" gifts and "pious" deeds.
     The failure to make this distinction characterized religious gift giving in
     many other countries in late-medieval and early-modern Europe. Ann
     K. Warren, *Anchorites and their Patrons in Medieval England* (Berkeley:
     University of California Press, 1985), 193. Dauril Alden suggested a num-
     ber of useful sources on English donors.

5   *Patrida 1,* Título 23, Ley 8, in *Las siete partidas del Rey D. Alfonso el
     Sabio, cotejadas con varios codices antiguos,* Vol. 1 (Madrid: La Real Aca-
     demia de la Historia, 1807), 492, advises those with resources "to give to
     their poor relatives, rather than to others, not so that the relatives would
     become rich, but so that they can live without having any reason to do
     evil. It is more valuable that they be aided by their relatives, so that they
     do not shamefully seek alms from strangers." Among other biblical ref-
     erences, see 1 Timothy 5:8, which admonishes, "But if any provide not
     for his own, and especially for those of his own house, he hath denied the
     faith, and is worse than an infidel."

6   Robert Wheaton "Affinity and Descent in Seventeenth-Century Bor-
     deaux," in *Family and Sexuality in French History*, ed. Robert Wheaton
     and Tamara K. Hareven (Philadelphia: University of Pennsylvania Press,
     1980), 130.

7   An unpublished paper by Teófilo Ruíz brought these laws to my atten-
     tion. "From Love to Ritual: Feeding and Clothing the Poor in late Medi-
     eval Castile." Paper given at the Davis Center Seminar, Princeton
     University February 14, 1986.

8   Luisa Ciammitti, "Dowry as Life Annuity: The Bologna Case, 1550–
     1650." Davis Center Seminar, Princeton University, March 14, 1986. Ste-
     ven Epstein, *Wills and Wealth in Medieval Genoa: 1150–1250* (Cam-
     bridge: Cambridge University Press, 1984), 136–200.

9   Asunción Lavrin, "In Search of the Colonial Woman in Mexico" in *Latin
     American Women: Historical Perspectives*, ed. Asunción Lavrin (West-
     port, Ct.: Greenwood Press, 1978), 26, and Lavrin, "Values and Meaning
     of Monastic Life for Nuns in Colonial Mexico," *The Catholic Historical
     Review* 58 (1972), 367–368.

10   Asunción Lavrin, "Mundos en contraste: cofradías rurales y urbanas en
     México a fines del siglo XVIII," in *La Iglesia en la economia de América
     Latina,* Colección Biblioteca de INAH, Serie Historia (Mexico: Instituto
     Nacional de Antropologia y Historia, 1986), 235.

11   It is important to remember that according to the Laws of Toro, which
     governed family relations in New Spain, legally all women and men
     were supposed to "take state," that is, to become nuns or clerics or to

marry. In practice, by the end of the colonial period, the majority of the population probably did neither.

12   Spanish society expressed a special concern for women, especially young marriageable girls, in the distribution of public charity. Linda Martz, *Poverty and Wealth in Hapsburg Spain, The Example of Toledo*, Cambridge Iberian and Latin American Studies (Cambridge: Cambridge University Press, 1983), 202–204. It should also be noted that parents and other relatives established chantries, which were funds for the celebration of memorial Masses, for their sons and nephews. Globally, the amount of money dedicated to chantries reached much higher levels and was more widespread. For the establishment of sixteenth-century chantries, see John Frederick Schwaller, *The Origins of Church Wealth in Mexico* (Albuquerque: University of New Mexico Press, 1986); for the status of these chantry funds in the beginning of the nineteenth century, see Michael Costeloe, *Church Wealth in Mexico: A Study of the Juzgado de Capellanías in the Archbishopric of Mexico, 1800–1856* (Cambridge: Cambridge University Press, 1967).

13   "Razón de los aniversarios capellanías y obras pías," Genaro Garcia Collection, University of Texas, Section of García Grenados. Document 1153, fols. 225–226, 234–236.

14   James Denson Riley, *Hacendados Jesuitas en México, 1685–1767* (Mexico: SepSetentas, 1976), 27.

15   Archivo General de la Nación (hereafter AGN), Bienes Nacionales, Legajo 1926, expedientes 1, 3, 4, 5, 6. This legacy caused considerable dispute, as the donor had assigned the patronage to the parish priest of the church in which he had officiated. The will provided that if there were no female relatives, the income should be used for candles for the church or other expenses. Despite the frequent contentions over this bequest, until the middle of the nineteenth century, there were still applications from those who wished to be considered the donors' relatives.

16   Archivo General de Notarías de Mexico (hereafter ANM), Diego Jacinto de León, fol. 361r.

17   Ibid. fols. 54v–55v; 175v–176v; 202r–202v; 313v–r; 360r–361v; 366v–367r; 381r–382r; 397v–r; 415v; 428v–430r; 443r–v; 527r–527v.

18   It is frequently difficult to determine the original donor and to clarify the patronage history of these funds. Often, intentions were changed as the patrons succeeded each other. (AGN, Bienes Nacionales, Legajo 564, exps. 2, 6, 8; Legajo 64, exp. 5; Legajo 448, exps. 1, 6; Legajo 675, exp. 8; Legajo 868, exp. 1; Legajo 1265, exp. 8; Legajo 1634, exps. 1, 2,3; Legajo 1823, exp. 3; Legajo 1843, exp. 1; Legajo 1923, exp. 3; Legajo 1926, exps. 1–17. I am indebted to Asunción Lavrin for calling these foundations to

my attention and lending me her notes on several of them. See also AGN, Obras Pias, Vol. 1.

19   J. León Helguera, "El Sorteo de las Huerfanas," *Colmena Universitaria* 5(1978), 39–46.

20   Quoted from a 1751 plea by the local curate, Licenciado Diego José Cervantes, in an argument for the establishment of a nunnery. Published in Angel Dávila Garibi, *Colección de documentos inéditos*, quoted in Helguera, "El Sorteo," 41. The close connection between dowry funds and the establishment of nunneries is argued here by Helguera.

21   Thomas Calvo, "Concubinato y mestizaje en el medio urbano: El caso de Guadalajara en el siglo xvii," *Revista de Indias* 44 (1984), 203–212. For a description of other issues in marriage and race mixing, see Robert McCaa, "Calidad, Clase, and Marriage in Colonial Mexico: The Case of Parral, 1788–90," *HAHR* 51 (1984), 477–501. See also Asunción Lavrin, ed., *Sexuality and Marriage in Colonial Latin America* (Lincoln: University of Nebraska Press, 1989), which stresses the importance of consensual unions.

22   Asunción Lavrin, "Female Religious," in *Cities and Society in Colonial Latin America*, ed. Louisa Hoberman and Susan Socolow (Albuquerque: University of New Mexico Press, 1986), 169.

23   Edith Couturier, "The Philanthropic Activities of Pedro Romero de Terreros: First Count of Regla," *The Americas* 32 (1975), 18. Because the government required licenses for the foundations, permission to establish these institutions frequently could be delayed for years and sometimes denied completely. Personal animosities, religious rivalries among the regular orders, and disagreement with the purposes of the convent could mean delay or even denial of permission. See the later discussion of the establishment of La Enseñanza and La Vizcaínas.

24   Lavrin, "Female Religious, 169–170.

25   Josefina Muriel, *Conventos de Monjas en la Nueva España* (Mexico: Editorial Santiago, 1946), 189–91. José F. de la Peña, *Oligarquía y propiedad en Nueva España, 1550–1624* (Mexico: Fondo de Cultura Económica, 1983), 94.

26   Muriel, *Conventos de Monjas*, 390–392. Josefina Muriel y Alicia Grovet, *Fundaciones neoclásicas. La Marquesa de Selva Nevada y sus conventos y sus arquitectos* (Mexico: UNAM, Instituto de Investigaciones Históricas, 1969), 35–48. Lavrin, "Female Religious," 169. D. A. Brading, "Tridentine Catholicism and Enlightened Despotism in Bourbon Mexico," *Journal of Latin American Studies* (1983), 1. Constance H. Berman, "Women as Donors and Patrons to Southern French Monasteries in the Twelfth and Thirteenth Centuries," in *The Worlds of Medieval Women: Creativity, In-*

fluence and Imagination, ed. Constance Bermen, Charles Connell, and Judith Rice Rothschild (Morgantown: West Virginia University Press, 1985), 53, 57, 60. Berman makes the point that many female patrons requested the establishment of houses for religious women.

27 Muriel, *Conventos de Monjas*, 27–32, 150–152. Santiago Ramírez Aparicio, *Los Conventos suprimidos de México* (Mexico: Miguel Angel Porrua, (fascimile edition of an 1861 book); Costeloe (*Church Wealth*, 46) refers to A. Toro as the source for the will of Lorenzana. Among other contributions, Lorenzana assigned 800,000 pesos for various church benefactions, including money for La Encarnación convent, and 20,000 pesos for Masses, as well as substantial contributions to the Jesuits.

28 Muriel, *Conventos de Monjas*, 150–151.

29 AGN, Bienes Nacionales, Legajo 675, exp. 8.

30 Ann Miriam Gallagher, "The Indian Nuns of Mexico City's *Monasterio* of Corpus Christi, 1724–1821," in *Latin American Women*, ed. Lavrin, 167. See also Gallagher, "The Family Background of the Nuns of Two *Monasterios* in Colonial Mexico: Santa Clara, Querétaro and Corpus Christi, Mexico (1724–1822)" (Ph.D. diss., The Catholic University of America, 1972).

31 Gallagher, "Indian Nuns," 152–153.

32 Ibid., 165–166. Couturier, "Philanthropic Activities," 18–19.

33 Gonzalo Obregón, Jr., *El Real Colegio de San Ignacio de México (Las Vizcaínas)* (Mexico: El Colegio de México, 1949), 79.

34 I am indebted to Asunción Lavrin for pointing out the differences in the patronage of convents and recogimientos. See also Lavrin "Female Religious," 188–189. Asunción Lavrin, "Women in Convents," in *Liberating Women's History*, ed. Berenice Carroll (Urbana: University of Illinois Press, 1976), 255, 272. These dangers included unequal marriages as well as illicit sexual relations and abuse by men.

35 Obregón, *El Real Colegio*, 14–35. One of the earliest confraternities, which had as its mission the education of Mestiza women, had been called Ntra. Sra. de la Caridad. With its change in name to Santisimo Sacramento, its educational functions disappeared and the confraternity raised money for dowry funds.

36 Ibid., 30–34, and Pilar Foz y Foz, *La Revolución pedagógica en Nueva España (1754–1820)*, 2 vols. (Madrid: Instituto Gonzalo Fernández de Oviedo, 1981), 1:200–204.

37 The founding document for the Vizcaínas recogimiento is in ANM, Juan Francisco Benítez Trigueras. On April 18, 1733, fifteen members of the confraternity of Aránzazu took "political and economic measures for the foundation of a house for girls, daughters and widows of Basques," fols.

118r–119r (Obregón, *El. Real Colegio*, 44–70 [the list of donors is on 86]). Some of the information on the quarrel with the Church can be found in *Archivo de Instituto Nacional de Antropologia e Historia (AINAH)*, Colección Antigua, 337/297, fols. 180–212.

38   Obregón, *El Real Colegio*, 92–99.

39   Foz y Foz, *La Revolución pedagógica*, 1:254–255.

40   Ibid., 67–172.

41   "Memorial de la R. M. María Ignacia de Azlor . . . solicitando de nuevo licencia para fundar" Archivo General de Indias, Mexico 724, as cited in Foz y Foz, *La Revolutión pedagógica*, 2:68–70.

42   AGN, Templos y Conventos, Vol. 2, from a copy at the Bancroft Library. I owe information about this first foundation in Puebla to Asunción Lavrin. The application was made in 1754, and in 1761 the license was refused.

43   Foz y Foz, *La Revolutión pedagógica*, 1:156–196; Lavrin, "Female Religious," 169.

44   Foz y Foz, *La Revolutión pedagógica*, 1:455–457, 486, 493–500. Fourteen out of fifteen donors were women. There were nine anonymous grants, which accounted for half of the money dedicated to educational purposes. It might be interesting to compare the amounts of the donations with those of other convents and to determine the numbers of donations that might have originated from family members of nuns in La Enseñanza.

45   A particularly interesting and detailed account of patronage in the foundation of a church and monastery for the discalced Carmelite monks in San Luis Potosí in the eighteenth century is to be found in Alfonso Martínez Rosales, *El Gran teatro de un pequeño mundo: El Carmen de San Luis Potosi, 1732–1859* (Mexico: El Colegio de México y Universidad Autónoma de San Luis Potosí, 1985), 19–33.

46   Even after the passage of anticlerical laws in the mid-nineteenth century, women continued to give property and donate to various ecclesiastical institutions. Personal communication from Guadalupe Jiménez Codinach, January 12, 1988.

47   Francisco Javier Clavijero, *Historia de la Antigua Baja California* (Mexico: Porrua, 1970), refers to the Condesa de Montezuma, the Condesa de Gálvez, the viceroy's wife from Mexico City, and a Peninsular noblewomen, María de Borja, Duquesa de Gandia, as contributors to the missions (98, 114, 206, 228). The only non-noble woman in the list is a Da. Josefa de Argüelles y Miranda (222).

48   Josefina Muriel, *Hospitales de Nueva España* (Mexico: Publicaciones del Instituto de Historia, No. 62, 1960), 2:274.

49   Cayetano de Cabrero y Quintero, *Escudo de Armas de México: Escrito . . . para conmemorar el final de la . . . epidemia . . . que asoló a la Nueva España entre 1736–1738,* Edición Facsimilar (Mexico: Instituto Mexicano del Seguro Social, 1981), 232–233.

50   Elinore M. Barrett, "Indian Community Hospitals in Colonial Michoacán," in *Historical Geography of Latin America. Papers in Honor of Robert C. West,* ed. William V. Davidson and James J. Parsons, Geoscience and Man, Vol. 5 (Baton Rouge: Louisiana State University, 1980), 63, 71.

51   Silvia Marina Arrom, *The Women of Mexico City, 1790–1957* (Stanford: Stanford University Press, 1985), 116–119.

52   María Josefa Vergara Hernández, *Testamento.* Documentos de Querétaro (Querétaro: Dirección de Patrimonio Cultural, 1987), 9–35.

53   Edith Couturier, "The Mexican Counts of Regla, 1750–1830," in *Latin American Women,* ed. Lavrin, 143.

54   One nineteenth-century observer, Fanny Calderón de la Barca, a visitor in the 1840s, commended the philanthropic activities of upper-class women in the 1840s. See Frances Calderón de la Barca, *Life in Mexico: The Letters of Fanny Calderón de la Barca with New Material from the Author's Private Journals,* ed. Howard T. Fisher and Marion Hall Fisher (Garden City, N.Y.: Doubleday, 1966), 529–541.

55   The importance of medieval communities of women is emphasized by Jane Tibbetts Schulenburg, "Women's Monastic Communities, 500–1100: Patterns of Expansion and Decline," *Signs: Journal of Women in Culture and Society* (1989), 261–292; see also Mary Martin McLaughlin, "Creating and Recreating Communities of Women: The Case of Corpus Domini, Ferrara, 1406–1452," *Signs* 14(1989), 293–320.

BRENDA MEEHAN-WATERS

From Contemplative Practice to Charitable

Activity: Russian Women's Religious

Communities and the Development

of Charitable Work, 1861–1917

Between 1764 and 1917, over two hundred women's religious communities were formed in Russia. This essay discusses the nature of these communities, the role women played in their formation both as founders and donors, and the marked increase in charitable activity on the part of the communities beginning in the middle of the nineteenth century. This shift, from contemplative practice to charitable activity, is significant within the Russian context, a context notably different from that of America and Western Europe at the same time period in attitudes toward charity, philanthropy, and voluntarism.

Russia in the middle of the nineteenth century was a culture of extremes—between the rich and poor, between the Westernized gentry and intelligentsia and the deeply traditional Russian peasantry, between the autocratic tsar and a society struggling toward political participation and initiative. The middle class and its values of moderation and compromise were relatively undeveloped in Russia. In addition, Russia had experienced neither a Reformation nor a Counter-Reformation. There had, therefore, been no Protestant debunking of monasticism, celibacy, and the contemplative life, and no formation of specialized women's religious orders dedicated to an active apostolate (such as the Ursulines or the Sisters of Charity), which had marked the Catholic Reformation. Only in the second half of the nineteenth century did Russian women's religious communities turn to active work in nursing, teaching, and care of the poor and orphaned. When they did so, the communities were still marked by the Orthodox tradition of entry into monastic life in midlife or widowhood, after fulfilling parental responsibilities toward children. What we see, then, is many mature women undertaking a life of religious discipline and service, a giving of their lives and themselves, in addition to a giving of time and money. To these women, often pious laywomen at midlife, voluntarism may have seemed a halfway measure, while entry into a women's religious community promised a life of total dedication.

In this, there were some parallels to women of the Russian intelligentsia, whom Barbara Engel has characterized as being driven by moral fervor and absolute dedication to their cause. Engel argues that radical Russian women, unlike their male colleagues, were impelled by a religiously based vision of justice and service that made them self-sacrificing almost to the point of martyrdom. Some renounced not only their families of origin and their educational aspirations but also sexuality and personal life. "Their ethical vision and willingness to dispense with other attachments prompted women to an absolutism and intensity of dedication that most male radicals lacked,"[1] and that also set them apart from "their activist sisters to the west."[2]

Russia also differed in its attitude toward charity and the poor. While Protestant societies frequently banned begging, emphasizing the importance of work and fretting over the worthiness of the recipient of charity, Orthodoxy saw in charity a reciprocal relationship, in which the beggar was helped materially and the donor salvifically, through an act of charity.[3] Hence, begging, private almsgiving, and hospitality to pilgrims and strangers remained important religious practices down until the revolution of 1917, although by the end of the century, a growing number of philanthropists were becoming concerned about the effectiveness of private almsgiving.[4]

In addition, the social and political traditions of tsarist Russia had constrained the development of organized private charity and voluntary philanthropic associations. Suspicious of all independent activity and freely associating groups, the government in midcentury evinced a negative attitude toward voluntarism and grass-roots initiative and sought control in all matters. Following the revolution of 1848 in Europe, for example, the government banned the formation of new charitable activities (a ban that remained in effect until 1859) and placed all existing ones under the supervision of the Ministry of the Interior.[5] In the second half of the nineteenth century, in the throes of Westernization, reform, and an increased sense of participatory activity by educated society, many charitable organizations and philanthropic societies were formed, but they always remained under the careful eye of the tsarist government.[6] The opportunity for voluntarism and philanthropic activity was thus more circumscribed for both men and women in Russia than in either Europe or America.

The watchful eye of the tsarist government also extended to the church, and it was the government's regulation of monastic properties, beginning in 1764, that led to the development of the unofficial, autonomous women's religious communities that form the focus of this essay. In that year, the government confiscated monastic property and created a stipendiary clergy.[7] Now that the state had to fund ecclesiastical institutions, it vigorously eliminated "superfluous" clergy, churches, and monasteries, reducing the number by more than half.[8] Smaller monasteries were closed and their monks and nuns, no matter how old or how long in residence, were transferred to larger, funded monasteries in their diocese. In addition, many former residents of dissolved monasteries found themselves without an assigned, stipendiary slot in the new budget. Homeless monks and nuns began appearing in provincial towns and in the streets of Moscow and St. Petersburg, begging for food and shelter. Embarrassed by their appearance in the capital cities, Catherine II issued a strong edict, ordering vagabond clergy to return to the diocese from which they had come.[9] In addition, vigorous measures were taken to conscript superfluous clergy in to the army.[10] Although the government's restriction on the number and location of monasteries and clergy applied to both men and women, women responded in a special way, by forming almost immediately unofficial religious communities called *zhenskie obshchiny;* between 1764 and 1917, 217 of these autonomous women's religious communities were formed.[11]

Although the earliest communities were formed by displaced nuns of suppressed monasteries, in the course of the nineteenth century, pious laywomen (particularly widows) became the typical founders of zhenskie obshchiny.[12] Such women often donated their land, their property, and their capital to create a structure in which religiously inclined women, who were shut out of monastic life by the government's restrictive budget, could live a life of prayer and piety and be supported through the community's collective, usually agricultural, work. The very creation of such a community was, then, an act of philanthropy because it offered support to other women seeking a disciplined way of life and prayer; it was also an act of commitment on the part of the founder, because she typically undertook a religiously based life and acted as mother superior to the new community.

Among the earliest, and one of the most prominent, of the women's communities was Spaso-Borodinskaia, formed by Margarita Mikhailovna Tuchkova, the widow of General Tuchkov, who was killed in the famous battle of Borodino in 1812.[13] Grief-stricken by her loss, Tuchkova vowed to build a church in honor of her husband on the spot where he and so many other brave Russians had fallen. Determined, indefatigable, and well connected, she eventually received permission for the construction of the church, and even a donation of 10,000 rubles from the Tsar. But it was tough going in the beginning, and Tuchkova had to sell property and jewelry to realize her project. During the long years of construction, she traveled back and forth between the construction site and her house in Moscow, where she was supervising the education of her son.[14] While in Borodino, she lived in a small house, described as a hermit's hut, and her reputation for piety and almsgiving drew people to the spot. One day, when traveling through a neighboring village, she came upon a trembling, beaten-up woman who was lying in a cart. Upon inquiry she found that the woman's husband was a notorious drunkard who regularly beat and terrorized his wife and two daughters. She determined to provide protection and shelter for these women and insisted on getting permission from the local authority to remove them from the village. Out of the women's shelter she built for them—a shelter for battered women—gradually grew the Spaso-Borodino women's community.[15] When Tuchkova's son died, she settled at Spaso-Borodino, living a life of prayer, doing charitable work for the neighboring peasants, and counseling the women who had settled there to be under her spiritual direction. In 1818, when there were over forty sisters in the community, it was transformed into an official, communal monastery, and Tuchkova's sizable widow's pension was applied toward its support.[16]

The success of the Spaso-Borodino community inspired other pious women to think of forming religious communities on their estates. Among these was the community of Anosino-Boriso-Glebskaia, founded by Princess Evdokiia Mescherskaia. Born in 1774, she married in 1796 Prince Boris Ivanovich Meshcherskii, who died three months after their wedding, leaving her pregnant with a daughter.[17] She retired to her estate of Anosino to raise her daughter and lead a pious life.[18] During her daughter's youth, she built a stone church at Anosino; in 1821, in honor of her deceased husband, she established an almshouse for homeless women, which formed the basis for a woman's religious community. Of lively intelligence, Evgeniia developed a reputation for wise counsel, despite a noticeable stutter.[19] She was also renowned for the simplicity of her life, and the community she established supported itself through agricultural work. Her granddaughter, who entered the community in 1844 and was the daughter of a senator, followed in her footsteps, leading a simple outdoors life, chopping wood, washing laundry, fixing food for the refectory and even, as Archimandrite Pimen himself witnessed, grooming horses.[20]

The examples given are of aristocratic women, but widows of all social classes participated in this phenomenon, including widows of merchants, artisans, and after the emancipation of the serfs in 1861, wives of peasants.[21] In addition, women and men of all social classes acted as financial supporters of the communities, generous donors, who valued the good works of prayer and service performed by the communities. For example, the Troitskaia Novaia community was established in 1874 by the resources of Varentsova, a local gentry woman who donated a wood house, five outbuildings, 430 *desiatiny* of land (one *desiatina* equals 2.7 acres), and 4,000 rubles for the support of the community and the almshouse for elderly women that was built at the community. A more humble soldier's wife, Irina Lazareva, founded the Spasskaia Zelengorskaia community in the first quarter of the nineteenth century as a shelter for orphans, and the merchant Afanasii Torpov donated 470 desiatiny of land, a watermill, and 10,000 rubles, and pledged to build at his own expense a church, an almshouse, and all the necessary buildings for the construction of a women's religious community in the village of Pososhka.[22]

To date, information has been gathered on the founding donors for 67 of the 113 women's religious communities formed in villages, and for 65 of the 102 formed in towns. In the villages the founding donors included 31 men and 49 women, including gentry, merchants, peasants, tradespeople, and clergy, with the gentry forming the majority; in the towns, the founding donors included 34 men and 38 women, again from a range of social classes, but with the merchants predominating.[23] As the charitable and educational work of women's religious communities increased, local priests or community figures occasionally encouraged the creation of a woman's religious community as a way of organizing a local school, almshouse, or orphanage. Thus in 1866, the parish priest Zosimov, along with tradesman Chebanenko, donated land for the creation of the Tikhvinskaia Ekaterinoslavskaia women's community, which opened a school for girls and an almshouse; in 1877, in the interest of establishing a woman's religious community with a school for Cheremiss girls, the town society of Kozmodem'ianski (Kazan province) ceded a parcel of land, the merchant Zubov gave two houses and 3,000 rubles, and Cheremiss peasants gave 7,700 rubles.[24]

Before turning to an analysis of the good works performed by the communities, the crucial and obvious relationship between philanthropy and financial control should be underscored. Financial philanthropy is an act of power—the power to dispose of property, the power to give, not just to serve. Both the women who founded the communities under study here, and the women who acted as their generous supporters, could only perform these particular acts of philanthropy because they had the power to dispose of property. Unlike most married women in the West in the beginning of the nineteenth century, Russian noble women and merchant women could own property, and their dowries remained firmly under their control.[25] This was essential in the formation of women's religious communities, and for the range of philanthropic activity possible for Russian women.[26]

What were the charitable activities of the women's religious communities, and how did they develop? From the beginning, women's religious communities were associated with the care and shelter of homeless and familyless women. The communities themselves attracted women without families as members, and they frequently ministered to elderly and homeless women; at least thirty-six of the women's religious communities under study began as almshouses.

In the middle of the nineteenth century there is a marked increase in the number of charitable and educational facilities associated with women's religious communities, including orphanages, infirmaries, and schools for young girls. During the reign of Nicholas I, the church, fearful of lagging behind educated society, became increasingly concerned about the education of the clergy and their sons and daughters (the parish clergy in Russia married and formed a hereditary social caste). Special schools for daughters of the clerical estate were opened in several dioceses, including by 1855, twelve under the auspices of convents.[27] One such school was begun sometime before 1852 by women of the Arkadievskaia-Viazemskaia community, a community that had been formed in 1780 by suppressed nuns.[28] Several other women's communities opened schools and orphanages for girls of the clerical estate, and in so doing performed a welfare role for the clerical estate.[29]

But the educational mission of women's religious communities reached well beyond the clerical estate and became a small but integral part of the rapid spread of rural primary schools in nineteenth-century Russia. Over eighty of the women's religious communities ran some form of school for girls, and several included boys in their instruction. The schools sometimes developed out of orphanages, sometimes at the behest of peasant villages or town associations, and sometimes as parish schools or with the encouragement of diocesan authorities.[30] The opening of such a proliferation of schools by women's religious communities was the result of several important social and cultural developments in Russia. Among them were the Great Reforms of the 1850s and 1860s, which stimulated initiative and public action in general, ended serfdom, and created organs of local self-government, the *zemstvos*—which included among their concerns popular education.[31] The Orthodox Church, too, showed an interest in developing primary education through parish schools, beginning with the issuance of the Rules of Village Education in 1836 and becoming more vehement with the Regulations for Church Parish Schools in 1884.[32] More importantly, as Ben Eklof has recently argued, peasants themselves became the main sponsors of primary schools and showed a consistent desire to educate their children.[33] My own research attests that they welcomed—sometimes initiated—the opening of schools by women's religious communities and supported them as generously as they could.

The change to a more active charitable and educational role on the part of women's religious communities marked changes within Orthodoxy itself. A certain defensive posture toward the West, and toward the intellectual and social-service aspects of Catholicism, becomes noticeable in Russian Orthodox circles in the middle of the nineteenth century. At a time when reformers and revolutionaries were drawing attention to the plight of the impoverished peasantry and the growing urban poor, monasticism, with its traditional inward, contemplative emphasis, was criticized as socially irresponsible at best, corrupt at worst.[34] In undertaking a more active role in village and town life, the new women's religious communities were breaking out of the limitations of the traditional monastic life and transforming the religious conscience and practice of Orthodoxy itself. And there is some evidence that in so doing, they looked to the model of women's religious orders in the West, with their emphasis on an active charitable and educational apostolate. This spirit is reflected in a book that appeared in Russia in 1861, entitled *Charitable Women. A Description of Several Women's Charitable Communities of the Roman Church*, which began with the Beguines and then discussed chronologically all Catholic women's religious orders and their particular charitable, teaching, or nursing apostolate.[35] It extolled the charitable activity of "our western sisters" and hoped that the "false principles of Roman teaching" would not prevent Russian women from emulating the good deeds of Western women's religious orders.[36]

Unlike Western women's religious orders, zhenskie obshchiny did not become specialized in their charitable and pastoral activities, often combining care of the poor (almshouses), education of the young (schools), and care of the sick (infirmaries or small hospitals). Thus in 1907, the Otrada i Uteshenie community, on the Muscovite estate of its founder, Countess Orlova-Davydova, consisted of forty-five sisters, who ran an orphan asylum for approximately fifty children, an almshouse for seventy, a parish school for fifty or sixty children, and a hospital with sixty to seventy beds.[37]

In addition to the zhenskie obshchiny, communities of Sisters of

Mercy (*obschiny sester miloserdiia*) developed in Russia in the nineteenth century. The first, the Holy Trinity Community of Sisters of Mercy (Sviato-Troitskaia obshchina sester miloserdiia) was founded in 1844 on the initiative of Grand Duchess Aleksandra Nikolaevna and Princess Tereziia Ol'denburgskaia. According to one authority, its spirit and aims were reminiscent of those of European Catholic orders and had broad goals such as the care of sick and abandoned children, and fallen women.[38] However, the history of Russian Sisters of Mercy is most commonly dated from the Crimean War, from the formation in September 1854 by the Grand Duchess Elena Pavlovna of the Exaltation of the Cross Community of Sisters of Mercy (Krestovozdvizhenskaia obshchina sester miloserdiia), with the purpose of caring for those wounded in battle.[39] The Crimean War marked the introductin of women as nurses in military hospitals in the war zone, and the French Sisters of Mercy led the way. Before Florence Nightingale set out with thirty-eight nurses in later October for the Scutari hospital, a British war correspondent for *The Times*, describing French military hospitals, had written: "Here the French are greatly our superiors. Their medical arrangements are extremely good and they have the help of the Sisters of Charity. . . . These devoted women are excellent nurses." And immediately after, a long letter to *The Times* demanded: "Why have we no Sisters of Charity?"[40]

Russian men and women began asking the same question. According to the memoirs of Ekaterina M. Bakunina, one of the early members and later director of the Russian Sisters of Mercy, she was distraught in the late fall of 1854 to read in the papers first "that French sisters had been sent to the military hospitals and then that Miss Nightingale had gone to English hospitals with ladies and sisters."[41] She wanted to know why Russian women were not doing a similar thing and was delighted to learn of the plans underway in St. Petersburg to send the first contingent of Russian sisters, who began work in Simferopol in December 1854.[42]

While some of the British nurses under Nightingale came from Anglican and Roman Catholic religious orders and others received salaries that were twice those paid in London hospitals, the Russian sisters received no pay and appear to have served from motives of patriotism and altruism.[43] Although the more prominent women, like Bakunina, were from the aristocracy, many were from the lesser nobility, wives or widows of army or navy officers or of minor officials; some were from merchant or lower-urban families, and a few were nuns.[44] Religion suffused the initiation ceremony, and their charter of 1870 specified the goals of the community as care of the sick in medical institutions and "other works of Christian charity."[45]

During the Crimean War, the Sisters of Mercy, who numbered 250 at the battlefront, were supplemented by groups of "Compassionate Widows" (*serdobol'nye vdovy*) from Moscow, St. Petersburg, and Odessa.[46] Compassionate Widows, a special order of widows dating from the early nineteenth century, took a vow of compassion and performed works of charity.[47] In 1821, upon the occasion of a liturgy inducting a group of women into the order, Metropolitan Filaret preached a sermon elaborating a special role for "true widows" or deaconesses (*diakonissi*).[48] Filaret was, I believe, an advocate of the restoration of the order of deaconesses or dedicated widows, the forgotten, ancient order of the early Christian church.[49] In legitimizing the model of the deaconess, Filaret looked to the venerable Orthodox past and the tradition of religous widows, rather than to the Western model of the Lutheran deaconess.[50]

We see, then, competing models of charitable activity for women and a wealth of factors stimulating philanthropic and educational work in Russia in the second half of the nineteenth century. The Great Reforms were themselves an act of Westernization on the part of the government, and they inspired further initiative, reform, and social action.[51] Historians have often contrasted Western-inspired secular philanthropy with Russian-inspired religious charity, but the study of women's religious communities indicates that Western *religious* models, such as the Sisters of Charity and Roman Catholic religious orders, were also important in fostering philanthropic and educational work as Orthodox women sought to move from a contemplative life to an active apostolate, and from almsgiving to organized educational and charitable work.

A STUDY of women's religious communities in prerevolutionary Russia underscores certain particularities of the Russian situation and their relationship to the development of women's charitable activity.

The first is the tradition within Orthodoxy of women's entry into religous life after they had fulfilled family obligations, which gave a life-cycle aspect to Russian women's religious life. Orthodoxy encouraged certain widows to become founders, donors, and mother superiors of religious communities, and others to enter these communities if they were childless, familyless, or homeless. The Russian cultural tradition of extremism (and the relatively late development of middle-class values of moderation) also encouraged a greater tendency to altruism and to total dedication; perhaps it made voluntarism and part-time social service seem unsatisfying to some.

The government's political tradition of suspicion toward initiative, grass-roots organizations, and independent activity long hindered the development of organized private charity and voluntary philanthropic organizations. When philanthropic organizations did begin to flourish in the second half of the nineteenth century, they remained under the surveillance of the government, and men seem to have played a stronger leadership role in them than women.[52]

And yet, as the creation and history of women's religious communities indicate, there were specific legal and geographic factors that enabled Russian women to act autonomously and effectively in the development of certain charitable and philanthropic undertakings. The property and inheritance rights of married women allowed them to dispose of dower property, thereby empowering them to bequeath property to charitable institutions or to create those institutions themselves. And the vastness of the Russian countryside, the under-governed nature of rural areas, and the autonomy of provincial estates enabled women to form unofficial religious communities on their own property, relatively free of the long arm of the central bureaucracy.[53]

As the case of women's religious communities illustrates, the balance sheet for women's charitable and philanthropic activity was mixed in Russia, with some traditions fostering supply, some inhibiting opportunity, and others offering considerable scope for the exercise of will and action. Although the women of the zhenskie obshchiny would not have viewed their activities in terms of claims to power or autonomy, they used the resources and opportunities offered to them to create a life of their own making, a life of altruism, service, and community, a life lived in religious community with other women, and a life increasingly dedicated to the welfare of others.

NOTES

1   Barbara Engel, *Mothers and Daughters: Women of the Intelligentsia in Nineteenth-Century Russia* (Cambridge: Cambridge University Press, 1983), 5.

2   Ibid., 3.

3   Adele Lindenmeyr, "Public Poor Relief and Private Charity in Late Imperial Russia" (Ph.D. diss., Princeton University, 1980), 97–98.

4   Ibid., 141–142; Jo Ann Ruckman, *The Moscow Business Elite. A Social and Cultural Portrait of Two Generations, 1840–1905* (DeKalb: Northern Illinois University Press, 1984), 94–95.

5   Lindenmeyr, "Public Poor Relief," 137–138. For examples of surveillance of women's religious communities, see "Zhenskie obshchiny v nizhegorodskoi gubernii," *Zhurnal ministerstva vnutrennikh del* 19 (1847), 268–285.

6   For the rules governing charitable and other voluntary associations, see Lindenmeyr, "Public Poor Relief," 211–216; for the growth in charitable and philanthropic activities among Moscow merchants in the late nineteenth century, see Ruckman, *Moscow Business Elite*, 73–108. Ruckman notes that because of the relative weakness of middle-class, bourgeois values in Russian culture, Moscow merchants were able to gain respect only by imitating the values of the dominant classes (the nobility and the intelligentsia), which included service to society and cultural development (17–18).

7   *Polnoe sobranie postanovlenii i rasporiazhenii po vedomstvu pravoslavnogo ispovedaniia. Tsarstvovanie imperatritsy Ekateriny Alekseevny,* No. 167, February 28, 1764. Hereafter *PSPR.*

8   V. V. Zverinskii, *Material dlia istoriko-topograficheskogo issledovaniia o pravoslavnykh monastyriakh v rossiiskoi imperii,* 2 vols. (St. Petersburg, 1890), 1: xi.

9   *PSPR,* No. 212, November 12, 1764.

10   Gregory L. Freeze, *The Russian Levites: Parish Clergy in the Eighteenth Century* (Cambridge: Harvard University Press, 1977), 40.

11   This is my compilation, based on data from L. I. Denisov, *Pravoslavnye monastyri rossiiskoi imperii. Polnyi spisok vsekh 1105 nyne sushchestvuiushchikh v 75 guberniakh i oblastiakh Rossii (i 2 inostrannykh gosudarstvakh) muzhiskikh, zhenskikh monastyrei, arkhiereiskikh*

domov i zhenskikh obshchin (Moscow, 1908), and Zverinskii, *Material*,
Vols. 1 and 2.

12   Brenda Meehan-Waters, "Popular Piety, Local Initiative and the Founding of Women's Religious Communities in Russia, 1764–1907," *St. Vla-
dimir's Theological Quarterly* 30 (1986), 130.

13   Pimcn, "Vospominaniia arkhimandrita Pimena, nastoiatelia Niolaev-
skogo monastyria, chto na Ugreshe," *Chteniia v Imperatorskom
obshchestve istorii i drevnostei rossiiskikh pri moskovskom universitete*
(1877), 1: 294–295.

14   E. V. Novosil'tseva (pseud. T. Tolycheva), *Spaso-Borodinskii monastyr' i
ego osnovatel'nitsa, (Posviaschchaetsia vsem pochitalushchim pamiat'
Margarity Mikhailovny Tuchkovoi*, 3rd ed. (Moscow, 1889), 16–18.

15   Ibid., 28–29.

16   Taisiia (monakhinia), *Russ'koe pravoslavnoe zhenskoe monashestvo,
XVIII–XX vekov* (Jordanville: Holy Trinity Monastery, 1985), 38–39;
Novosil'tseva, *Spaso Borodinskii*, 23–24, 30–33.

17   Pimen, "Vospominaniia," 288.

18   "Igumen'ia Evdokiia, osnovatel'nitsa Boriso-Glebo-Anosina obshche-
zhitel'nogo devich'ia monastyria," *Chteniia v Imperatorskom obshchestve istorii i drevnostei rossiiskikh pri moskovskom universitete* (1876), 2:
i–iii.

19   Pimen, "Vospominaniia," 288.

20   Ibid., 288–289.

21   Meehan-Waters, "Popular Piety," 130–135.

22   For Troitskaia Novaia, see Zverinskii, *Material*, 1: 262 and Denisov, *Pravoslavnye monastyri*, 335–336; for Spasskaia Zelengorskaia, see
Zverinskii, *Material*, 1: 249 and Denisov, *Pravoslavnye monastyri*, 542;
for Posochka, see Zverinskii, *Material*, 1: 210 and Denisov, *Pravoslavnye
monastyri*, 642.

23   Meehan-Waters, "Popular Piety," 138–139.

24   For Tikhvinskaia Ekaterinoskavskaia, see Zverinskii, *Material*, 1: 254;
for Kozmodem'ianski, ibid., 271.

25   *Svod zakonov rossiiskoi imperii* (1857), 10:1, arts. 109–118, 180–195,
226, 229, 230, 256–258, 294–295, 397; pt. 6 art. 995. Brenda Meehan-
Waters, "Women, Property and Inheritance in Eighteenth-Century Russia," and William Wagner, "Women and Property and Inheritance Law in
Russia, 1866–1914," papers presented at the American Association for
the Advancement of Slavic Studies National Convention, Asilomar, 1981.

26   In her study of philanthropy in Chicago, Kathleen McCarthy demonstrates the decisive impact on women's philanthropy of a betterment in
their property rights. Following the 1861 passage of the Illinois Married

Women's Property Act, women's philanthropic activity expanded noticeably beyond rendering service in asylums to becoming bountilful patronesses and benefactors. Kathleen McCarthy, *Noblesse Oblige: Charity and Cultural Philanthropy in Chicago, 1849–1929* (Chicago: University of Chicago Press, 1982), 30.

27   Gregory L. Freeze, *The Parish Clergy in Nineteenth-Century Russia. Crisis, Reform, Counter-Reform* (Princeton: Princeton University Press, 1983), 178–179.

28   Denisov, *Pravoslavnye monastyri*, 780.

29   In order of year of founding of the community: Tikhvinskaia-Bogoroditskaia-Kerenskaia (1848), Denisov, *Pravoslavnye monastyri*, 650; Dmitrievskaia-Milosofova-Bogoroditskaia-Kamdomskaia (1849), ibid., 817; Nikolaevskaia-Dal'ne-Davydovskaia (1857), ibid., 558; Kazanskaia (1884), ibid., 187; Bogoroditskaia-Chitinskaia (1886), ibid., 225.

30   For an example of a school that developed out of an orphanage, see Bogoliubskaia-Tishenovskaia: Denisov, *Pravoslavnye monastyri*, 812 and Zverinskii, *Material*, 1: 89–90; for a school founded at the behest of a peasant village and town association, see Troitskaia-Cheremisskaia-Kozmodemiansk: Zverinskii, 1: 271; for an example of a parish school, see Dmitrievskaia-Troekurovskaia: Denisov, *Pravoslavyne monastyri*, 816; for an example of an eparchial school, see Ioanna-Predtecheva-Innokentievskaia-Tomskaia; ibid., 866.

31   Ben Eklof, *Russian Peasant Schools. Officialdom, Village Culture, and Popular Pedagogy, 1861–1914* (Berkeley: University of California Press, 1986), 50–83.

32   Ibid., 29, 155–176.

33   Ibid., 83–88.

34   On the criticism of monasticism, see *Igumeniia Feofaniia* (St. Petersburg, 1868), 30–31.

35   *Blagotvoritel'nye zhenshchiny. Opisanie nekotorykh zhenshikh blagotvoritel'nykh obshchin rimskoi tserkvi* (Tver, 1861).

36   Ibid., 144–145.

37   Denisov, *Pravoslavyne monastyri*, 527.

38   "Sestry i brat'ia miloserdiia," *Entsiklopedicheskii slovar'* 58 (St. Petersburg, 1900), 714.

39   John Shelton Curtiss, "Russian Sisters of Mercy in the Crimea, 1854–1855," *Slavic Review* 35 (1966), 84.

40   Ibid.

41   Ekaterina Bakunina, "Vospominaniia sestry miloserdiia Krestovozdvizhenskoi obshchiny, 1854–1860 gg.," *Vestnik evropy* 190 (1898), 134.

42   Ibid.; Curtiss, "Russian Sisters of Mercy," 100.

43   Martha Vicinus, *Independent Women: Work and Community for Single Women, 1850–1920* (Chicago: University of Chicago Press, 1985); Curtiss, "Russian Sisters of Mercy," 85.

44   Curtiss, "Russian Sisters of Mercy," 85.

45   Bakunina, "Vospominaniia sestry," 137–138; "Krestovozdvizhenskaia obshchina sester miloserdiia v SPB," *Entsiklopedicheskii slovar'* 32 (St. Petersburg, 1895), 650.

46   "Sestry," 714.

47   "Vdova serdobol'naia," *Entsiklopedicheskii slovar'* 5a (St. Petersburg, 1893), 672.

48   Filaret (Drozdov), *Slova i rechi synodal'nogo chlena Filareta, mitropolita moskovskogo* 3 (Moscow, 1845), 193–200.

49   On deaconesses in the early church, see JoAnn McNamara, *A New Song: Celibate Women in the First Three Christian Centuries* (New York: Haworth Press, 1983), 62.

50   On the revival of the order of deaconesses in nineteenth-century England, see Vicinus, *Independent Women*, 46–48, 57–61.

51   For the impact of the Great Reforms on Russian philanthropy and initiative, see Lindenmeyr, "Public Poor Relief," 143–151.

52   Ibid., 173–175.

53   It should be noted, however, that many of the zhenskie obshchiny that began as unofficial religious communities eventually came under the supervision of the ecclesiastical hierarchy and were transformed into official women's monasteries (Meehan-Waters, "Popular Piety," 123).

ALISA KLAUS

Women's Organizations and the Infant Health Movement in France and the United States, 1890–1920

In her autobiography, published in 1939, S. Josephine Baker, head of the New York City Division of Child Hygiene, reviewed her long career in child health. She recalled that in 1924, three years after the passage of the Sheppard-Towner Act for the protection of maternal and infant health, women dominated public child welfare work: all but three of the forty-five state directors of federal child welfare work were women. Fifteen years later, four years after the passage of the Social Security Act of 1935, three-quarters were men. "I am not impugning the capacity of any of these men as individuals," Baker wrote, "when I say that that looks very strange in a line of activity which was invented and developed by women."[1]

Baker was one of a group of professional women reformers including Florence Kelley, Alice Hamilton, Grace and Edith Abbott, and Sophonisba Breckenridge, who, with the institutionalization of Progressive social reforms, rose to official positions of power and influence. These women, for a brief period, participated in the formation of social policy to an unprecedented extent. In no area, perhaps, was their influence greater than in maternal and infant health. Women had a prominent voice in the American Association for the Study and Prevention of Infant Mortality and headed the Committee on Women's and Children's Welfare of the American Medical Association. They directed many municipal and state divisions of child hygiene and, perhaps most important, organized, administered, and staffed the United States Children's Bureau. These professional women saw themselves

157

as the leaders and representatives of a massive grass-roots infant health movement whose rank and file were the hundreds and thousands of members of women's clubs, mothers' congresses, and parent-teacher associations. As a result, public child welfare policy, particularly on the state and national level, reflected the larger goals and interests of this movement of women. The Sheppard-Towner Act for the protection of maternal and infant health was largely the fruit of a decade of political activity on the part of these women.

In Europe women also claimed much of the credit for the development of child welfare institutions. Women's influence in pediatric institutions and in maternal and child welfare policy, however, did not always reflect the extent of their voluntary activity. This was particularly true in France. In contrast to their counterparts in the United States, French women had practically no voice outside their own charitable institutions and little influence on public maternal and child health policy. They virtually never sat on official commissions to investigate maternal and infant health and, if any were present, they never spoke up in debates on infant mortality in the Academy of Medicine. Very few positions in public or private welfare agencies of any kind were open to women, and as late as 1919 a French feminist journalist complained that even women who had founded and administered private institutions and served as the leaders of national social welfare organizations were unable to find paid employment.[2]

The focus of French women's charitable activity suggests that they, like American women, took a particular interest in maternal and child welfare. Why, then, were they unable to participate in the making of public policy? This comparative study of the role of women in a particular area of social welfare suggests that both the political and institutional context and the nature and strength of the feminist movement were important factors in determining the effectiveness of women's efforts in social reform.

In the late nineteenth century, maternal and child health became an important political issue in France, as part of a demographic "crisis" that, according to politicians across the political spectrum, endangered the nation's political and economic security.[3] Laden with political significance, motherhood was not solely a "women's issue" in France. The French movement to prevent infant mortality, led by well-known pediatricians and obstetricians and Radical Republican politicians, often with the support of the government in power, was able to make use of a national public health and welfare bureaucracy developed through centuries of state interventionism—a bureaucracy from which women were systematically excluded. In the United States, on the other hand, only a small group of men—including public health officials and pediatricians and obstetricians in large cities—exhibited much interest in infant health; this was, by and large, an area they were content to leave to women. Furthermore, not only did American political culture prevent the formation of an extensive federal bureaucracy, but the rudimentary nature of public health and welfare institutions outside of metropolitan areas allowed women's voluntary organizations to retain a greater degree of autonomy than in France, and to play a leading role in the formation of policy. Finally, women in the United States were psychologically and organizationally prepared to take advantage of this opportunity in a way that French women were not.

French maternal and infant health programs were part of a larger pronatalist family policy. France was the first European country to face the prospect of a declining rate of population growth. The French fertility rate had begun its decline in the late eighteenth century, and by the end of the nineteenth century, France had the lowest birthrate in the world; deaths actually exceeded births in twenty of the years between 1850 and 1920.[4] France's defeat in the Franco-Prussian War precipitated a flurry of warnings that "depopulation" would result in a national catastrophe if measures were not taken to counteract it. In this context, a consensus emerged in the national legislature in favor of measures to protect maternal and child welfare with the explicit goal of preserving lives for future battlefields. Infant mortality was thus one of the most prominent concerns of the national Commission on Depopulation appointed in 1902.[5] The prestigious Academy of Medicine in Paris took up the issue; on numerous occasions its members heatedly debated the causes of infant mortality and preventive measures.[6] Virtually every author of a work on infant mortality opened with an introductory section on France's declining birthrate and the nation's increasing military vulnerability to Germany.

In the United States, during the same period, the birthrate declined among native-born whites, but this decline was more than offset by immigration and the higher birthrate among immigrants.[7] Because infant mortality was relatively low among the native-born middle class, the declining birthrate did not provide a rationale for maternal and child welfare programs in the United States. Progressive reformers were far more concerned with the changing composition of the population than with its size. They feared the proliferation of the eastern and southern immigrants who crowded the nation's cities; if anything, reducing the urban infant mortality rate would increase the threat of Anglo-Saxon "race suicide."[8]

Not until World War I did the United States Congress consider the issue of infant health, and then only after the loss of young men overseas and the appalling physical condition of army recruits had, briefly, brought home the importance of health and reproduction to the nation. The only men who took an interest in infant health, for the most part, were pediatricians and obstetricians in large cities. These men, concerned to win women over to their techniques and institutions, and with rather blatant professional self-interest, dominated public health and medical institutions in cities like New York, Boston, Philadelphia, and Cleveland; the women of the United States Children's Bureau found their real sphere of action outside of these cities. The bureau's first project was a study of infant mortality in a representative group of small cities.[9] After this, they turned their attention to small towns and rural communities, where public health institutions were undeveloped but women's associations were vital and influential.

Alice Hamilton observed, "The American man gives over to the woman all the things he is profoundly disinterested in, and keeps business and politics to himself."[10] Only such disinterest in child health could have led political leaders in the Progressive era to allow the United States Children's Bureau to be headed and staffed by women, and to allow women to direct state and municipal divisions of child hygiene. To a certain extent, the difference in the political importance of infant health can explain why American women's role in maternal and child welfare policy was so much more visible than that of French women. French women, however, also lacked the political and institutional resources with which to influence public policy.

In nineteenth-century United States, evangelical Protestantism provided the rationale and impetus for women's organizations and political activity.[11] The General Federation of Women's Clubs, the National Congress of Mothers and PTA's, along with the Women's Christian Temperance Union, boasted hundreds of thousands of members by the early twentieth century. These organizations had developed a political program that encompassed all aspects of education and social reforms conducive to a wholesome family life; they supported temperance reform, child labor legislation, public health programs, regulation of drugs, medical inspection of schools, and eugenic legislation.[12] These programs reflected the members' conviction that women's moral superiority, their commitment to children and the family, and their detachment from party politics and business gave them the right to a voice not only in their own homes but in the public sphere.

Religious orders provided professional opportunities for French women in education, nursing, and midwifery into the twentieth century, but Catholic piety was not a vehicle for independent women's political action or social reform. Like American Protestant women, French Catholic women who met to discuss their children's moral education began to address social conditions that affected the economic and moral well-being of women and children. Like women's organizations in the United States, they developed a rationale for women's political participation based on the connection between public and private life. In the context of Republican attacks on the Catholic Church, however, Catholic women's organizations consistently defended religious morality and the institutional power of the Church. The Patriotic League of French Women, founded in 1902 to defend freedom of religion and freedom of education—in other words to counter the state's attack on Catholic education—became the most powerful women's organization in the country, with 400,000 members in 1909.[13] The group's political program was that of the Church. The Jeanne d'Arc Congress, a coalition of women's charitable organizations, adhered strictly to Catholic Church policy; the educational work of all its affiliates was required to conform to Catholic doctrine and all members had to be Catholic.[14]

Insofar as French women sought an independent voice in maternal and infant health policy, they came from the group of feminists who made up the National Council of French Women, a moderate and nonsectarian feminist organization whose leadership was disproportionately Protestant and Jewish and whose political philosophy generally coincided with that of the Radical Republicans.[15] They did not, however, before 1920, develop an approach to maternal and child welfare policy distinct from that of their male colleagues and did not challenge the pronatalist basis of the political debates on the family. Karen Offen has argued that, since nationalism and pronatalism combined to create a political atmosphere that was hostile to feminism, many feminists strategically chose to exploit pronatalism in their own interests rather than challenge it.[16] In addition, their structural relationship to medicine and family policy was very different from that of American women reformers. Even in fields other than maternal and child health, French women were far more often relegated to political invisibility and professional inferiority than their American counterparts.

The importance of autonomous female institutions to female professionals and reformers in the United States is familiar to women's historians and has been well documented; French women, for the most part, lacked such institutions.[17] The effect of this on the professional opportunities available to women in medicine is most striking. In 1900 there were seven thousand female physicians in the United States and only ninety five in France, most of these in Paris. In the United States in the late nineteenth century, women's medical colleges and a few women's hospitals provided clinical training often not available to women anywhere else; they also provided role models, an atmosphere that was emotionally supportive, professional connections, and an opportunity for women to hold teaching and administrative positions.[18] The women's hospitals were pioneers in general public health as well as in maternal and infant care; it was in these fields that female physicians were concentrated; few hospitals offered them training in other specialities.

It was in public maternal and child health, an area of low prestige, that female physicians were able to have their greatest impact, since pediatric and obstetrical research and hospitals were dominated by men. Women who started out in low-status jobs in public health could easily end up in responsible positions. S. Josephine Baker, for example, began her medical career as a tenement inspector in New York City and was one of the physicians assigned to seek out sick infants as part of the city's first campaign to prevent infant mortality in the summer of 1902. When the New York City Council appropriated funds for a

Division of Child Hygiene in 1908, Baker became its first director. She served in that position for more than twenty years and became one of the nation's most respected authorities on child welfare.[19]

Other female physicians achieved national prominence as activists in private organizations and later became public health officials. As director of the Children's Department of the *Woman's Home Companion*, Lydia Allen deVilbiss helped launch the baby health contest movement in 1913. When the Kansas State Board of Health created a Division of Child Hygiene, deVilbiss moved west to serve as its director. Florence Sherbon, Secretary of the American Baby Health Contest Association in 1913, later conducted surveys for the United States Children's Bureau for several years and succeeded deVilbiss in Kansas in 1920.[20]

The prominence of women in public child welfare agencies provided an impetus for the voluntary child welfare work of women and gave women's organizations access to policymaking bodies. Perhaps the most significant public health positions held by women were in the United States Children's Bureau, headed by Julia Lathrop, a former Hull House resident and a close friend of Jane Addams. The physicians hired to do fieldwork, their assistants, and the head of the bureau's medical division were all women. Several were personal friends of women in the social settlement movement and some were members of the General Federation of Women's Clubs. The bureau staff viewed themselves as leaders of the larger women's infant health movement, and women throughout the nation saw the staff as their allies and often wrote for advice on child care or organizing child welfare programs. The bureau staff invariably responded with friendly guidance and inspiration, and appealed to local women's organizations for assistance in carrying out their programs.

Soon after the bureau's creation in 1912, for example, Julia Lathrop went to the Biennial Convention of the General Federation of Women's Clubs and called on local women's clubs to carry out a campaign for birth registration, which many did.[21] The National Baby Week campaign of 1916, a joint effort of the Children's Bureau and the General Federation of Women's Clubs, demonstrated the extent of grass-roots interest in infant health and solidified the relationship between the bureau and the women's movement. The campaign built on the highly popular "Better Baby" movement initiated by the *Woman's*

Home Companion. The "Better Baby" movement centered on the baby health contest, developed by two Iowa clubwomen and modeled on the stock show.[22] The contest was easy for a small club to organize and was a brilliant strategy for reaching rural women, since it could be featured at an agricultural fair, a well-established rural institution.

More than two thousand of the fourteen thousand incorporated communities in the United States reported Baby Week celebrations; the success of the campaign far exceeded the expectations of the national organizers. "I had hoped in the stress of last March," Lathrop wrote after the event was over, "that there would never be another, but it is inevitable."[23] The event put many local women's organizations in touch with the bureau; the participation of the federal government also lent an official importance to the work, which made local organizers more confident and endowed them with greater legitimacy in the eyes of others. This partnership between women's organizations and the Children's Bureau, and in some cases state public health agencies, provided the basis for a wartime infant health campaign and ultimately for the successful campaign for the Sheppard-Towner Act.

The extensive organizational structure and local strength of the National Congress of Mothers and the General Federation of Women's Clubs were clearly the keys to the success of the Baby Weeks. It was the absence of any other significant child health efforts outside of major cities, however, that enabled this alliance between the Children's Bureau and the women's organizations to define the nation's approach to this issue during the 1910s. A large proportion of rural counties had almost no public health or welfare institutions at all. In one Kansas county, for example, the county board of health consisted of a health officer paid $250 a year to inspect stores, restaurants, slaughterhouses, and schools and to control contagious diseases. In a typical year, however, he actually inspected stores, restaurants, and slaughterhouses twice, and visited about six of the sixty-seven schools in the county. In 1916 the only infant health work was initiated by a visiting nurse hired by the social service league of the county seat who arranged a "Baby Day" series in the town and three of the villages, at which local physicians and dentists examined children.[24]

Even in 1918 most villages in Wisconsin had still fewer adequate public health provisions. Each township or village had a local board of health with an officer who might be a farmer or a physician, usually paid $10 a year but sometimes nothing. The main work of this officer was to post and remove quarantine notices and fumigate for severe contagious diseases; some did nothing at all.[25] Female physicians hired by the Children's Bureau to investigate rural child welfare routinely sought the cooperation of local medical societies, but they almost invariably found small-town physicians to be either overtly hostile to their work or so ignorant of child hygiene as to be of little assistance.[26] Members of women's organizations who read about the infant health movement in women's magazines or the publications of the General Federation of Women's Clubs or the National Congress of Mothers could thus turn only to the Children's Bureau or to the state or national leaders of their organizations for guidance.

Leaders of local women's organizations generally reported that their greatest obstacle was indifference. In communities where informal political structures were critical, women's organizations could wield a great deal of power—enough, on occasion, to overcome the opposition of local male leadership. The women of Arena, Wisconsin, demonstrated this when the influential Commercial Club rejected their proposal for Baby Week because they had failed to present it early enough. In a striking display of solidarity, representatives of the local Women's Christian Temperance Union and Reading Club, and the Congregational, Methodist-Episcopal, Baptist, and Lutheran Ladies' Aid Societies met and agreed to go ahead with the program. Faced with a united front of women, the Commercial Club backed down and promised financial support but not time or leadership.[27] It was this kind of alliance on the national level that led to the passage of the Sheppard-Towner Act in 1921.

Political and religious cleavages prevented the formation of such solidarity among French women's organizations; their leadership also lacked access to political and professional power. French women who met American female professionals were impressed with the respect the American women commanded. One Parisian woman who spent time with the American Red Cross in France during World War I was struck by the importance of female physicians in that organization. She felt a shock of surprise upon meeting a woman who was chief physician in a hospital for soldiers with tuberculosis. That a woman should be invested with such a high position in a hospital devoted only to men, she exclaimed, was "so contrary to our customs!" Were French women, she wondered, intellectually and morally so inferior to American women?[28]

In their search for professional and political opportunities, French women faced more rigid and powerful male-dominated health and social welfare institutions than American women. They faced not only a centralized bureaucratic state but also the entrenched power of social welfare institutions under the control of the Catholic Church. A major obstacle to French women entering the medical profession, for example, was the highly structured and exclusive system of exams and competitions for places in medical schools, hospital appointments, and teaching positions. Women who broke down these barriers also aroused violent hostility. The first women to enter medical schools in the United States were excluded from certain laboratories and ostracized by their fellow students, but probably none encountered threats of violence as serious as those faced by Blanche Edwards-Pilliet when she took the exam for the Parisian hospital internship in 1887. Protesters tried to force open the door of the building where she was taking the exam, and some threatened to kidnap her, screaming, "Down with Blanche!" That evening, students burned her in effigy in front of the Hotel de Ville.[29]

Despite this opposition, by 1900 French women had gained the right to compete for hospital internships, and a few women held official appointments as physicians attached to local welfare bureaus and schools for girls, as teachers in nursing schools, and as medical inspectors of children placed out to nurse. They could not, however, compete for medical teaching positions and lacked the financial support and professional networks needed to open clinics and dispensaries, though some women recognized that a woman's hospital or clinic would provide them with important advantages.[30] Like female physicians in the United States, French women physicians were concentrated in maternal and child health, but the physicians who sat on official commissions and on the boards of private institutions—even those founded and administered by women—were male.

Few paid jobs in maternal and child welfare were open to French women at any level. For example, visiting nurses specializing in child hygiene were virtually unknown in France before World War I, though they were the mainstay of infant health institutions in the United States. Nursing remained a predominantly volunteer occupation for a longer time in France than in the United States, partly because nursing had been the domain of nuns and partly because of the obstacles to women's professional activity in general. A lay nursing profession began to develop in the late nineteenth century when physicians, who saw the religious loyalties and moral priorities of nursing nuns as a threat, began to train their own nurses, educated in orthodox scientific medicine and with a clear understanding of their place in the medical hierarchy.[31] Exacerbated by the political contest over the Church's control of hospitals and social welfare institutions, divisions between religious and nonreligious, volunteers and professionals, prevented French nurses from developing a clear sense of their profession.

There were a few paid positions in child welfare open to French women. Beginning in 1899, for example, the city of Paris hired women to visit poor maternity patients and infants placed out to nurse. The competition for these jobs was fierce, however. In 1896 there were eighteen positions for female inspectors in the infant protective services and places for eleven volunteer substitutes. One hundred and twenty women were waiting for a chance at one of these jobs; there had not been an opening in three years and some of the applicants had been waiting for as long as five or six years.[32]

French women did play an important role in maternal and child welfare programs, but almost exclusively as volunteers, with virtually no voice in public policy, and under close state supervision. One of the most important strategies employed by the French government in protecting maternal and child health before 1919 was through financial support of private charities. The government encouraged the voluntary activity of women specifically, hoping that personal contact between wealthy women and poor would prevent some of the pitfalls of an increasingly bureaucratic welfare state. As private agencies increasingly became agents of public policy, however, they found themselves under increasingly strict government regulation.

The history of the Society for Maternal Charity, the oldest private maternal welfare organization, founded by aristocratic women and dating back to 1784, illustrates this process. This agency, which had at least eighty-one branches by the end of the nineteenth century, was designed to prevent the abandonment of legitimate children through aid to poor married women at the time of childbirth. The society aided only women who had been married in a religious ceremony. Until the 1870s the Society for Maternal Charity essentially served, in the words of one historian, as an "official alms-purse"; it received large subsidies and enjoyed royal patronage under the various regimes.[33]

Under the Third Republic, however, the Society for Maternal Charity faced a serious challenge. Run by aristocratic women with moral and religious priorities and patronized by ecclesiastical notables, the society was not popular with anticlerical Republican politicians. In the 1880s and 1890s the government began to place restrictions on its funds, stipulating, for example, that no branch that still had the religious marriage requirement could receive state subsidies. As a result, the number of branches receiving funds decreased, as did the total amount of money they received.[34]

In 1908 the national legislature increased the funds allocated to maternal and child welfare agencies threefold, but at the same time removed any special claim to these funds on the part of the Society for Maternal Charity. Like other organizations—and by this time there were quite a few—maternal charity societies had to compete for funds. Still, the Society for Maternal Charity of Paris received the second largest single grant.[35]

Many of the competing secular organizations had been formed by women with Radical Republican ties and political views. These agencies offered services compatible with the Republican program but not quite appropriate to public welfare or too expensive for the public purse—free meals for nursing mothers, free milk, day care, maternity assistance, and medical care. The women who founded and funded these private institutions saw themselves as responding to a secular ideal of charity, contributing to the defense of their nation, and answering the call of their sisters in distress. Women, proclaimed Olga Veil-Picard, a leader in Parisian women's charitable work, should claim the privilege of forming the army of "auxiliaries for the propagation of infant hygiene."[36]

In part, the increased subsidies were a means of providing maternity benefits, day care, and medical care for which the government was not willing to pay directly. In addition, however, legislators encouraged private charity because wealthy volunteers could, in theory at least, exert the kind of moral influence that fell by the wayside in the transition from private to public assistance. The most important pieces of child health legislation in the late nineteenth and early twentieth centuries incorporated the "lady patron." The Roussel Law, passed in 1874 to provide medical supervision of children placed out to nurse, also provided for the creation of local committees composed of clergy, private welfare officials, and two married women, who were to visit the children's homes regularly. Volunteer female home visitors were an integral part of the law passed in July 1913, which required women to take maternity leaves. In order to receive her compensatory benefits, a woman had to rest and follow certain rules of hygiene. The welfare bureau of each commune was responsible for designating someone to make sure that these conditions were met. The Minister of the Interior specified that this function could be fulfilled by volunteers. Referring to the "natural sympathy and deep instinct, so strong in the hearts of the women of France," he suggested that local, upright and respected women would be ideal.[37]

"Lady patrons" were essential to the policymakers' vision. They were the police of the system, making sure that women actually used their free milk, charitable gifts, and financial assistance in the manner intended. Unlike American visiting nurses, whose authority was a function of their training, French female visitors were deemed qualified to supervise and instruct other women by virtue of their social position. Though ostensibly the personification of the new political theory of social solidarity, they helped to maintain existing class distinctions and deference within a bureaucratic welfare system, through the time-honored aristocratic tradition of charitable visiting.

Thus, while French women mobilized in the interests of maternal and child welfare, their efforts were constrained and co-opted to work within the public system created by male politicians. Divided, like male politicians, by the struggle between the Catholic Church and anticlerical Republicanism, French women failed to develop the solidarity that enabled American women to successfully fight for certain parts of their social program. Excluded from positions of influence and prestige within the medical profession to a greater extent than American women, French women faced an additional obstacle in that infant health, as a factor in "depopulation," was too important to men to allow women a voice.

American women did not aspire to be the Ladies' Auxiliary of the infant health movement. They were not only fund-raisers and providers of services, but activists who believed they had a mission to arouse the general public to take responsibility for protecting children's lives. They discovered that they alone represented the interests of young children and that, where hospitals and medical schools were absent, maternal and infant health institutions were theirs to create, as long as they could persuade the community to grant the resources.

That American women were able to influence public policy so successfully is a tribute to the strength of the women's movement and to autonomous female institutions. Women were able to maintain their position, however, only as long as powerful men remained indifferent. World War I provided justification for federal government activity in new areas of society and also brought child life to the attention of the public to a greater extent than ever before. As a result, the United States Public Health Service, an agency controlled by men, developed its own child health programs for the first time and launched a concerted assault on the domain of the Children's Bureau.[38] With the conservative backlash against Progressive social programs and against feminism, the American Medical Association, as part of its campaign against compulsory insurance, was able to label the Sheppard-Towner Act a Bolshevik plot. Congress, no longer perceiving women as a united powerful political force, failed to renew the program's funding in 1928.[39] Ultimately, the physicians' struggle to nurture and protect their professional interests, and the belief that welfare was a degrading and dangerous institution, were the priorities that would define American maternal and child welfare policy.

NOTES

1   S. Josephine Baker, *Fighting for Life* (New York: Macmillan, 1939), 201.

2   Mme Remember, "Le vote familial et la repopulation," *Féminisme intégral* 7 (1919).

3   Angus McLaren, *Sexuality and Social Order: The Debate over the Fertility of Women and Workers in France, 1770–1920* (New York: Holmes and Meier, 1983), Chapter 11.

4   Joseph J. Spengler, *France Faces Depopulation: Postlude Edition, 1939–1976* (Durham: Duke University Press, 1979), 52.

5   Commission de dépopulation, *Séance du 29 janvier 1902* (Melun: Imprimerie administrative, n.d.), 2; Commission de dépopulation, Sous-

commission de la mortalité, *Séances, 1902–3,* Séance du 17 décembre 1902, 4.

6   *Bulletin de l'Académie de Médecine* 31 (1866–1867); 34 (1869); 35 (1870); 40 (1870); Mathilde Dubesset, Françoise Thébaud, and Catherine Vincent, "Les munitionettes de la Seine," in *1914–1918, L'autre front,* ed. Patrick Fridenson (Paris: Editions Ouvrières, 1977), 202–203.

7   U.S. Bureau of the Census, *Sixteenth Census of the United States: 1940; Differential Fertility 1940 and 1910* (Washington, D.C.: Government Printing Office, 1945), 3–4; George J. Engelmann, "Education not the Cause of Race Decline," *Popular Science Monthly* 63 (1903), 176.

8   While no author publicly argued in favor of allowing infants to die on these grounds, leaders in the movement to prevent infant mortality often did support eugenics as an adjunct to their campaigns. Charles Richmond Henderson, Greetings by the President for 1911, *Transactions of the American Association for the Study and Prevention of Infant Mortality,* 1910, 19; Joseph Neff, "A City's Duty in the Prevention of Infant Mortality," ibid., 154; A. Jacobi, Address, ibid., 44–45.

9   U.S. Department of Labor, Children's Bureau, Infant Mortality Series, Nos. 2, 3, 4, 6, 8, 9 (Washington, D.C.: Government Printing Office, 1914–1919).

10 Barbara Sicherman, *Alice Hamilton: A Life in Letters* (Cambridge: Harvard University Press, 1984), 3.

11 Nancy F. Cott, *The Bonds of Womanhood: Woman's Sphere in New England, 1780–1835* (New Haven: Yale University Press, 1977), 154; Ellen C. DuBois, *Feminism and Suffrage: The Emergence of an Independent Woman's Movement in America, 1848–1869* (Ithaca: Cornell University Press, 1978), 32; Blanche Glassman Hersh, *The Slavery of Sex: Feminist-Abolitionists in America* (Urban: University of Illinois Press, 1978), 2–3.

12 "Resolutions Adopted by the Second International Congress on Child Welfare, National Congress of Mothers," *Child-Welfare Magazine* 5 (1911), 189–195; General Federation of Women's Clubs, *Biennial Convention: Official Report,* 1912, 596–602.

13 Anne-Marie Sohn, "Les Femmes catholiques et la vie publique en France, 1900–1930," in *Stratégies des femmes,* ed. Marie-Claire Pasquier et al. (Amsterdam: Editions Tierce, 1984), 105.

14 Henri Rollet, *L'Action sociale des catholiques en France, 1871–1914* (Paris: Editions Anthropos, 1978), 101.

15 Steven C. Hause with Anne R. Kenney, *Women's Suffrage and Social Politics in the French Third Republic* (Princeton: Princeton University Press, 1984), 36–39.

16 Karen Offen, "Depopulation, Nationalism, and Feminism in Fin-de-Siècle France," *American Historical Review* 89 (1984), 674.

17   Estelle Freedman, "Separatism as Strategy: Female Institution Building and American Feminism, 1870–1930," *Feminist Studies* 5 (1979), 512–529.

18   Mary Roth Walsh, *"Doctors Wanted: No Women Need Apply": Sexual Barriers in the Medical Profession, 1835–1975* (New Haven: Yale University Press, 1977), xvi–xvii; Regina Markell Morantz-Sanchez, *Sympathy and Science: Women Physicians in American Medicine* (New York: Oxford University Press, 1985), 234, 245.

19   Baker tells the story of her career in her autobiography, *Fighting for Life.*

20   The careers of deVilbiss and Sherbon can be traced through their correspondence with the staff of the U.S. Children's Bureau. Record Group 102, National Archives, Washington, D.C.

21   Julia Lathrop, "Children's Bureau," in General Federation of Women's Clubs, *Biennial Convention: Official Report*, 1912, 447–448.

22   See the monthly reports in the *Woman's Home Companion*, March 1913 through December 1914.

23   Julia Lathrop to Frank Spooner Churchill, September 25, 1916, Records of the U.S. Children's Bureau, National Archives, Washington, D.C., 4–14–2–2–6.

24   Elizabeth Moore, *Maternity and Infant Care in a Rural County in Kansas*, U.S. Children's Bureau, Rural Child Welfare Series No. 1 (Washington, D.C.: Government Printing Office, 1917), 20.

25   "The Work of the State Department of Health," memo enclosed in a letter from Hutchcraft to Charles U. Moore, Records of the U.S. Children's Bureau, National Archives, Washington, D.C., January 9, 1918, 4-11-3-2.

26   Arthur B. Emmons to Mrs. Max West, April 25, 1916, Records of the U.S. Children's Bureau, National Archives, Washington, D.C., 4–3–0–4; "A Trip to Lexington, Virginia, May 10 and 11, 1915," Memo, U.S. Children's Bureau, 4–15–0; Mary Bartlett Dixon to Miss Rose, May 22, 1918, U.S. Children's Bureau, 4–12–1; Grace Meigs, Memorandum on visit to Boston, November 15–16, 1917, U.S. Children's Bureau, 4–15–4–3; "Question Corner," *National Organization of Public Health Nursing* (1917), 197.

27   *Baby Week Campaigns*, U.S. Children's Bureau, Miscellaneous Series No. 5 (Washington, D.C.: Government Printing Office, 1917), 35.

28   [Jeanne Forpomès], *Notre oncle d'Amérique: Souvenirs et impressions d'une Parisienne sur les travaux de la Croix-rouge américaine* (Paris: Perris et Cie., 1919), 167–168.

29   Hélène Bory, "Maternité finit par l'emporter," *Le jour*, 1935. Clipping in Bibliotèque Marguerite Durand, Dossier EDW, Paris.

30   *Deuxième congrès international des oeuvres et institutions féminines. Tenu au Palais des congrès de l'Exposition universelle de 1900. Compte*

rendu des travaux (Paris: Imprimerie typographique Charles Blot, 1902), 4: 110, 126, 145.

31   Yvonne Kniebhler, *Cornettes et blouses blanches; les infirmières dans la société française 1880–1920* (Paris: Hachette, 1984), Chapter 1; Jacques Léonard, "Femmes, religion et médecine: les religieuses qui soignent, en France au XIXe siècle," *Annales E.S.C* 32 (1977), 887–907.

32   Madeleine, "Un nouvel emploi pour les femmes," *La fronde*, October 14, 1889; Memo, May 20, 1896, Paris, Préfecture de Police, DB 31.

33   Maurice Melin, *L'Assurance maternelle* (Paris: Librarie de la Société du Recueil Sirey, 1911), 172; Albert de Mun, *La Société de charité maternelle de Moulins* (Paris: Imprimerie Crépin-Leblond, 1912); Paul Delauney, *La Sociéte de charité maternelle du Mans et ses origines* (Le Mans: Imprimerie Monnoyer, 1911); A. Cornereau, "Notice sur la Société de charité maternelle de Dijon," *Mémoires de l'Académie de sciences, arts et belles-lettres de Dijon*, 4th ser., vol. 7 (1899–1900).

34   France, Conseil supérieur de l'assistance publique, "Crèches, sociétés de charité maternelle," Compte-rendu, Fascicule No. 76, 1888.

35   France, Ministre de l'Intérieur, Circular, September 10, 1908, Archives nationales, Paris, Fla 3157; "Rapport sur l'emploi du crédit ouvert au Ministre de l'Intérieur pour subventionner aux oeuvres d'assistance maternelle et de protection du premier age," *Journal officiel*, January 16, 1913, 447–451.

36   Olga J. Veil-Picard, "La puériculture à Porchefontaine." Lecture given at the Croix-blanche—Vie heureuse, January 27, 1913 (n.p., 1913), 2.

37   Ministre de l'Intérieur, Circulaire, *Journal officiel*, August 11, 1913, 1724.

38   Taliaferro Clark, "Report on Conference on Child Conservation at Office of Surgeon-General of the United States Public Health Service," December 2, 1918, Records of the U.S. Children's Bureau, National Archives, Washington, D.C., 4–15–4–3; Rupert Blue to Julia Lathrop, November 22, 1919, U.S. Children's Bureau, 4–12–4; U.S. Congress, House, Committee on Interstate and Foreign Commerce, *Public Protection of Maternity and Infancy: Hearings before the Committee on Interstate and Foreign Commerce*, December 9–21, 1920, 165, 138–139.

39   Molly Ladd-Taylor, "Protecting Mothers and Infants: The Rise and Fall of the Sheppard-Towner Act," paper presented at the Berkshire Conference on the History of Women, June 19–21, 1987, 23; J. Stanley Lemons, *The Woman Citizen: Social Feminism in the 1920s* (Urbana: University of Illinois Press, 1973), 162–163.

Good and Bad Mothers: Lady Philanthropists and London Housewives before the First World War

Colonial metaphors abound in the nineteenth century's construction of the relationship between the British poor and the philanthropists and social workers who lived among them. Dark, exotic, possibly dangerous; yet intriguing and childlike, the "natives" provided, among other things, an arena for middle-class female adventure and self-discovery. By the 1880s the poor of London, the world's largest city, were replacing those of the northern industrial belt as central objects of official scrutiny and philanthropic activity. When Beatrice Potter sought a public identity for herself, she signed on as a rent collector in East London, and there became a part of a group of women who had made similar choices. In the 1890s settlement worker Clara Grant gave up her lifelong ambition to be a missionary in Central Africa in order to live, work, and teach among the East London poor. Marcella, the female protagonist in Mary Ward's mostly rural 1894 novel about conflicting models of philanthropy, seeks peace and wisdom working as a district nurse among London's chaotic Soho poor. Katharine Symonds, in the late 1890s, yearned to work at Toynbee Hall in Whitechapel "but mother was afraid that I should pick up some infectious disease." The compromise was a clerical job at a Charity Organisation Society (cos) office in Whitechapel Road. By the 1900's, though, the school charity bureaucracy and borough health visiting programs were supplanting the cos as places where a young lady could volunteer for some modest adventures.[1]

A less openly articulated imaginative structure—the good

mother/bad mother dichotomy—also shaped the thought and work of philanthropists in their contact with the London poor, especially in the two decades before 1918 when motherhood was a key word in a series of public debates. I am thinking, in very simplified terms, of Melanie Klein's position that infants and toddlers maintain the image of perfection in one parent, usually the mother, by splitting away her bad parts—her anger, her nastiness, her tendency to frustrate infant desires. Splitting creates two separate fantasy mothers, one good, one bad. In practice, the bad mother may become lodged in an imaginary figure, or, as in London's highly sex antagonistic and divided working-class domestic culture where so many men lived on the periphery of family life, the father. As Klein, and somewhat differently, Harry Stack Sullivan, outline the genesis of the good/bad mother split in child development, it is bound to exist in some form in people of all classes and in both sexes, as products of the universal, unavoidable experience of being an infant.[2]

Motherly superintendence of the young and old had long been a pillar of activist women's identity in the worlds of charity and public service. The arguments of both suffragists and nonsuffragists for the local and national franchise, and for female officeholding were routinely expressed in the language of national motherhood. Wherever they were elected, and whatever their political views, women were placed, and placed themselves, in situations where they worked with children. Lady Margaret Sandhurst, one of two (progressive) women elected to the London County Council (LCC) in 1888, whose victory as a woman was eventually successfully challenged by a disgruntled Tory rival, nonetheless plunged headlong into inspecting twenty-three "baby farms" for the LCC. Tory Susan Lawrence, long an activist in child-oriented charities, elected to the LCC (successfully) in 1907, quickly broke with the Conservatives, in good measure over their positions relating to children.[3]

In pointing to the "good mother/bad mother" dichotomy, my aim is to add a new dimension to our readings of the language and gestures of welfare workers and policymakers in the years of the infant welfare movement of the early twentieth century, when officials in several fields were attempting to transform the meaning of motherhood among the majority of the population. Philanthropic contacts between the classes were already complicated enough by habits of thought and speech and differences in access to state power. They would be further compounded, but also enriched, through the half-conscious rivalry between welfare workers and their clients for recognition as good mothers. For the charity givers of the infant welfare years, especially for the numerous women among them, adventure, professional satisfaction, and the exercise of patriotic duty could be confounded by envy and hatred of the working-class mothers who were central to many of their programs: by love of their children, and by rivalry with them (and sometimes with other charitable women as well) for the label of "good mother." While there are many appropriate ways of analyzing the infant welfare movement, the fact that good mothering was manifestly at its center really invites a reading through the participants' spoken and unspoken images of motherhood.

The infant welfare movement was at its height in the years just after the Boer War, with its revelations of the poor physical state of Britain's working-class recruits. In the first two decades of this century, unprecedented private and public resources were channeled in the direction of infants and children in the form of babies' clinics, pure milk depots, home visiting for new mothers, and classes in the domestic arts for girls and women. Scrutiny was directed at the newly urgent problem of the ability of the nation's working-class mothers, who reared Britain's foot soldiers, to bring up healthy children. Motherhood was no longer a natural attribute of women but a *problem* and an achievement. As one of the movement's male activists put it later, in his own history of those years: "The mother was evidently the factor of paramount importance. Evidently, also, the capacity to bring up a baby successfully through the first year of life was not an innate feminine character, with which all women are endowed at birth. . . . It was proved to be a skilled job requiring a technique which, like any other kind of technique, has to be acquired."[4]

In the highly charged language of good mother/bad mother, leaders in the infant welfare movement often spoke as children rather than as parents and located the mothers at one pole or another. Former dockworker John Burns, opening the first National Conference on Infantile Mortality in 1906 in his capacity as president of the Local Government Board, could think of little beside good and bad mothers, and, as one recent commentator put it, "did nothing more than fulmi-

nate against modern women while praising his mother." The explanation for infant mortality figures, high or low, he said, was nothing
more than "good or bad motherhood."[5]

The infant welfare movement has recently attracted a good deal of
thoughtful study. Several feminist "good mother" readings of this
era—by Anna Davin, Carol Dyhouse, and Jane Lewis—have demonstrated the stunning material difficulties of rearing children in urban
poverty, and stress the misanthropy and class hostility of officials who
blamed mothers' own practices for Britain's record high rates of infant
illness and death. A recent study by Deborah Dwork minimizes the
movement's antimaternalism, stressing instead its medical and public
health work. Nikolas Rose's *The Psychological Complex* notes that
Britain's working-class mothers were at the eye of two whirling
storms of professional discourse, one eugenist, the other hygienic.[6]
Whatever the mothers themselves might have been doing, they were
trapped in what Rose describes as a kind of discursive gridlock. The
issue I wish to inject into this discussion is the special way in which
this movement might have been shaped by the fact that it moved in the
heavily mined terrain of motherhood.

It was Major General Sir Frederick Maurice, KCB, who, in a series
of 1902 articles rather hysterically raised the threat of race degenera-
tion, long a theme among eugenicists, locating its main cause in "ignorance on the part of the mothers of the necessary conditions for the
bringing up of healthy children."[7] The figure of the bad mother dominated here: poor, lazy, ignorant, slovenly, and possibly drunken, she
hovered near the surface of all subsequent discussion of infant mortality and "physical deterioration," the subject of a series of government Inter-Departmental Committee hearings in 1903 and 1904. Even
when the practical and more distinctly medical and sanitary problems
of tuberculous milk or poorly designed privies were addressed, the
bad mother was not dispensed with. As Anna Davin points out, though
the committee made fifty-three different recommendations in its final
report in 1904, dealing with such social problems as overcrowding,
sanitation, the milk supply, overwork, food adulteration and the like,
only a few of them were taken up by policymakers in subsequent
years, those that in fact involved instructing women and girls in the
care of infants and children.[8]

Health visitors, sanitary inspectors, and clinic workers began with principles of good mothering that they were taught in training programs. In her series of lectures for health visitors, midwife Emilia Kanthack assumed that the workers would be schooling local mothers in new and unfamiliar principles: the necessity for unsupplemented breastfeeding in the early months; the vital importance of medical advice as a guide to infant care; the evils of pacifiers; the dangers of letting babies share the parent's bed. Ultimately, they wanted to inculcate the proposition that the infant's life was purely its mother's responsibility.[9] The infant welfare workers portrayed the mothers alternately as compliant and grateful for professional help, and as "pitiably ignorant and superstitious." The neighbor, the grandmother, "ignorant old women who have buried 10 out of 14 or 15," as one social worker put it, were rivals for mothers' souls and for their children's bodies with the medico-hygienic (to adapt from Donzelot's vocabulary) personnel, who yearned for women who could "launch out into the experiences of motherhood unchained by superstition and vulgar prejudice.[10] Indeed, there is strong evidence that it was first-time mothers who most often used the new clinics, and who looked to nurses and health visitors for childcare advice. Women who were isolated from neighbors or relatives were most enthusiastic about professional infant welfare services.[11]

The mothers themselves, when they appear in the human encounters generated by the infant welfare movement, were cautious, tight-lipped, and instrumental in their conception of the meaning of charity and welfare programs. They weighed their obligations toward individual children against the claims of their other children, and the demands of childcare against the more pressing need for daily subsistence. When the London Care Committees, groups of volunteer school-based charity workers, dealt with mothers who were charged with carrying out the school doctors' orders for their children, the mothers irritatingly dodged the labels and instructions that were intended for them: "Unable to leave her other children to take [Benjamin] to Treatment Centre," or "inconvenient to leave her stall to take the boy to the hospital," the committees recorded regularly in their minutes.[12]

When they spoke of the value of children's school meals, for instance, the mothers making similar, nearly unconscious, calculations, weighing a child's needs against those of the household as a whole. Rejecting the meals offered by a particularly niggardly committee, an East London woman charged, "I can give them better at home than what you gives them." A Rotherhithe mother commented, in support of the meals: "If you spend a bit less on food there's a bit more for coals and boots: and if your big girl falls out of work you can feed her on what you save on the little ones." While the philanthropists declaimed to each other about school dinners improving children's school performance, table manners, health, and eating habits, or even about the dinners as "human communion," the mothers of London were weighing the "gains" in dinners offered in terms of reduced household expenses against the "losses" in trouble and humiliation.[13]

London's late Victorian and Edwardian working-class culture dignified mothers considerably more than did contemporaneous bourgeois culture. Children's street chants are built of respect and fear of mothers, their main subject. Music-hall songs like "If You Knew my Muvver," often comic, rejoice in the power of mothers in their households and neighborhoods. London mothers had their own ideas about fulfilling this ideal, practical definitions of good and bad mothering that differed profoundly from those of infant welfare workers. The differences were in part over the concrete kinds of care that babies and young children needed—adequate feeding, comfortable clothing, sufficient sleep, etc. The poor mothers thought babies should be plump and worried that breast milk alone would keep them too skinny and vulnerable; they carried their infants constantly, slept with them, and dressed them very warmly in layer after layer—all practices that for the infant welfare workers were tantamount to infanticide. More profoundly disturbing for these workers was the refusal of most working-class women to accept guilt if any of their children died, no matter how much they mourned. If a mother had "done all I could," she did not see blame as relevant, for she saw her own practices and ministrations as severely constrained by her income and living conditions. More elusively still, the poor mothers defined themselves in ways that their middle-class peers had not yet dreamed of—simultaneously as child caretakers, as workers, and as people who belonged to neighborhoods.

The obligation to work for cash that could mean survival was an essential and longstanding part of working-class motherhood, but it conflicted squarely with the newer obligations the middle-class volunteers believed in: to improve children's physical comfort with eye glasses, impetigo treatments, or tonsil surgery; and to cultivate their imaginations by listening to their stories of school experiences and recent adventures. A Bethnal Green woman sitting grimly silent night after night with a dying baby, sewing endlessly, as George Acorn's mother did in a scene her son described in his autobiography, was not suppressing her grief or her love for her infant. Through her work, which would pay a doctor and a pharmacist, the woman demonstrated her love. The work and love were inseparable.[14]

Working-class children surely carried split images of motherhood with them, though to read the autobiographical legacy of Edwardian children, London mothers were all angelically good. Nearly all the autobiographies are posited on the central place in the child's life of the mother's sacrifice; the books are offered as payments, debts of gratitude. The good mothers, as their children reconstruct them, "worked for" their children as the term went, rather than, as we do, ministering to their feelings or becoming their friends. They patched boys' trousers when they might have let them go about in rags, ate bread at their own meals so that their children could have stew, told off teachers who had caned their sons or daughters. It is often fathers who are the repositories of badness, the result of a psychic process whose origins have a great deal to do with the men's selfishness and violence, but perhaps also something to do with mother's own directives to their children.

Implementing the new policies of infant preservation generated thousands of new middle-class jobs, some voluntary, some professional, and most of them for women: health visitors, school meals organizers, school doctors and nurses, clinic workers, district nurses, licensed midwives. By 1910, for example, the London Medical Officer of Health reported that only three of the twenty-nine London boroughs had no health visiting program. In ten very populous boroughs, health visitors were actually getting to 60 percent or more of the homes of newborns with a few days of the births. The North Islington School for Mothers, a mothers' and babies' clinic founded in 1913, listed by the end of the war a staff of three visiting women doctors, five nurses, and thirty-seven volunteers, most of whom did home visiting

among the center's clients.[15] The duties of the London Care Committees expanded in the "deterioration" era, and by the eve of World War I
involved close to ten thousand men and women members.[16]

From the trickle of ladies doing church visiting in the 1840s and the
district nurses and social investigators of the 1880s, middle-class
women had, by the 1900s, become a real presence in the lives of poor
mothers. They came to their homes with leaflets and instructions
when their babies were a few days old, nagged them to get their school
children deloused, questioned them about why Jim or Violet at age
twelve or fourteen was being placed in a dead-end job rather than an
apprenticeship. The ladies helped the women save money for children's winter boots and for summer country holidays, provided nursery schools and after-school play programs for (a few of) their
children, sat up nights with them caring for the sick. These contacts
invited some kinds of intimacy and certainly generated strong emotions on the middle-class side—which were filtered through the good
mother/bad mother split.

Elizabeth Wilson rather unkindly remarks in *Women and the Welfare State* that the story of Victorian social work involves "an army of
surplus middle-class spinsters" whose task it was to teach "their impoverished married sisters how to be better wives and mothers."[17]
Though it is true that the volunteers and professionals were heavily,
though not exclusively, single—remaining daughters rather than becoming mothers—this fact was intensely problematic for them.[18]
Beatrice Potter documented in detail in her diaries her anguish over
the prospect of an offer of marriage from Joseph Chamberlain, a marriage that would have destroyed her career ambitions; throughout her
life she regretted not having children. Martha Vicinus's *Independent
Women*, a book about single women's communities in this period, is
filled with the doubts and misgivings of stalwart women in hard-
earned and rewarding professional positions. Constance Maynard,
head of Westfield College, for example, was tormented by a series of
relationships with her pupils in which her hunger to mother them was
surely as disruptive as her unacknowledged sexual passions. Many
single women activists, like Mary Carpenter in an earlier generation,
eventually adopted children of their own.[19] Biblewomen, most of
whom were working-class residents of the neighborhoods to which

they were assigned, sometimes adopted local children whose homes were being broken up, and so did members of other nursing services.[20]

The matter of their own childbearing was a live one even for the more favored generation of social workers and activists of the 1900s. Clearly their clients were constantly bringing it up. *The Sanitary Officer*, a journal whose readers included health visitors, editorialized in its first year, 1909, that the view that unmarried inspectors could know nothing of babies was "absolute nonsense." As a female sanitary inspector wrote in another issue of the journal, pointed references to their professional training as nurses could help refute the mothers' charges that single women were ignorant of babies: "A reminder that I was a hospital nurse, and have had a great many children under my care, soon puts the matter to right."[21] Nursery pioneer Margaret McMillan, admitting that "no crèche can take the place of home," defended her Deptford nursery as "a school for home makers."[22] Their right to prescribe for children, and their anomalous situation in doing so, were burning issues for many of the ladies who worked with poor women and children.

One solution to the apparent contradiction of spinsters being in charge of the children of the nation was to grant them fictive motherhood. At a 1912 conference, Ethel Bentham, then a volunteer doctor at the Women's Labour League babies clinic in Kensington, somewhat awkwardly assigned her organization the mother's role toward the nation's children, and a sisterly one toward its mothers: "Being, many of us mothers, and the rest of us at least 'maiden aunts,' we know that [medical care] is something . . . that could lift a burden of worry and anxiety from many a woman's life." Caleb Williams Saleeby, a militant eugenist and infant welfare activist, made a case for the maternal superiority of the single women teachers and nurses who were at the center of the infant work. Naming them "foster mothers," and even "Virgin Mothers," Saleeby argued, "Everyone knows maiden aunts who are better, more valuable, completer mothers in every non-physical way than the actual mothers of their nephews and nieces. This is woman's wonderful prerogative, that in virtue of her *psyche*, she can realize herself, and serve others . . . even though she forego physical motherhood."[23]

The life trajectories of upper-class women tended to bring them to the slums when they were young, though the philanthropic agencies were often grossly insensitive to the incongruity of such young women, many of them just out of secondary school, teaching or monitoring mature women with many children. A young settlement worker's first assignment was often as an investigator for the Charity Organisation Society, which meant thoroughly probing a family's affairs through many home visits and lengthy interviews, usually with the woman of the house. In the early years of World War I, a private charity, the Soldiers' and Sailors' Family Association, carried out investigations of mothers' and wives' claims for separation allowances, and the youth and inexperience of the young ladies—many of them schoolgirls—who staffed so many of the offices led them to make many cruel mistakes, a recurring theme in Sylvia Pankhurst's accounts of the war's injustices on the home front. At least one labor organization complained abut the youth of the social workers at well.[24] Indeed, Mary Brinton's mother, from the prominent and socially active Liberal Rendel family, refused to let her own seventeen-year-old daughter do any home visiting for the Saffron Hill Elementary School Care Committee, of which Mary became secretary in 1908. For a girl so young to make home visits to "mature mothers of families . . . and possibly question them" was to Mrs. Brinton simply "impertinent."[25]

For the welfare workers the temptation to be the good mother, a foil to the poor and bad mothers of London, was hard to resist entirely. The rhetoric of the infant welfare movement invited this response by defining working-class care of infants as a problem, and the bulk of the new workers in inner London neighborhoods were indeed there to monitor the mothers. The Notification of Births Act of 1907 (which local governments were permitted but not required to enact) was adopted in twenty of the twenty-nine boroughs that made up Greater London. Its explicit purpose was to enable local health officials to locate newborn babies and to superintend the care they were getting. As one worker representing the St. Pancras Mothers' and Infants' Society gleefully put it in 1908: "Directly a baby was heard of [we] pounced down upon it."[26]

A special object of the welfare workers' solicitude was the "ex-baby," the small child, usually between one and two years old, who had just acquired a new younger sibling. These children were casualties of the closely spaced births that still dominated inner London. Sometimes newly weaned, ex-babies were, it was speculated, subject to wasting and other nutritional disorders.[27] Normal working-class mothering in London involved close confinement of two- and three-year-olds, whose high spirits, curiosity, and mobility were ill-suited to the close quarters, steep stairs, hot grates, kettles of water, etc. that were part of ordinary working homes. During much of the day, toddlers were often stuck into highchairs, or just tied into ordinary seats, waiting in frustration for older siblings to return from school to take them out. Middle-class educators, especially progressive women with a knowledge of Montessori principles, were deeply attracted to the friendly, chatty cockney children and obviously thought they were getting bad mothering, though, on the political level, many of these women were staunch defenders of the mothers' "goodness." Honnor Morten in the 1890s, Muriel Wragge and Margaret McMillan in the 1900s, and many anonymous others asserted that the mothers were far too hard on their toddlers: too ready to punish with violence, too demanding of quiet and order.[28]

Clearly the presence of toddlers overloaded the frail domestic systems of London mothers. The London Board schools were forced to fill this large gap in resources. The schools officially accepted children as young as three, unofficially even younger than that; children five and under comprised a tenth of the London elementary school population in 1904.[29] School officials well knew that the childcare gap, which flooded schools with babies, had been created by compulsory education itself, which removed the toddlers' normal playmates and babysitters from their homes every day. Nursery education in the London Board schools began when thousands of mothers sent their three- and four-year-olds to school at the start of compulsory schooling in 1871; older children could be found carrying smaller children into their own classrooms.

Nursery schools and crèches made similar efforts to fill the childcare gap. The Women's Freedom League's settlement in Nine Elms, south of the Thames, addressed the ex-baby directly when in 1916 it founded a guest house for children as young as two years old. The workers' description of their program very characteristically mingles a reproach to the mothers with the recognition of a need and the offer of a service.

> The Guest House for children was started by the Settlement to supply a want that seemed to have been hitherto overlooked—a home where mothers could send what have been called the "dowager babies" to be cared for while they themselves were laid up during the advent of a new baby, or in hospital for an operation. The workers here watched the results in our street, where new babies arrive with alarming frequency, and their elders, often only just able to crawl, spend their time on the doorstep, eating frequent unvaried meals of bread-and-margarine, or taking adventurous walks in the gutter.[30]

In the writings of Margaret McMillan, a crusader for municipally funded school meals and clinics, the tension between a political "good mother" position—a powerful commitment to defending the rights and meeting the needs of working-class mothers and children—is undercut by her identification with the children at her Deptford school in their many clashes with their mothers, clashes she was rather proud of stimulating. McMillan saw herself as an ally of the imagination and physical freedom of her young charges as they struggled with the confinement their mothers thought natural for them and needed from them. In a moving fictionalized sketch of an encounter between a boy and his harassed, overworked mother, McMillan described the boy's long and painful efforts to get his mother to share his excitement at seeing the stars for the first time after sleeping outdoors at the school. A similar boy, Jack, a six-year-old pupil at the Deptford nursery, had become (in another account by McMillan) quite a problem for his mother, a "delicate" woman who took in sewing for the income. Before Jack started at the school, the child had sat "quiet as a mouse" near his mother all day, winding spools or putting pins into a cushion. But after some months under McMillan's care, Jack became so noisy and spirited that his mother threatened to take him away. "He used to sit still for hours but now he has that much life in him that I can't abide him in the room," was the mother's view.[31] McMillan clearly imagined herself as the children's good mother, who would bring out the spontaneity, joy, and energy stifled by their own mothers. Yet she fully recognized the forces that kept these mothers "bad," and maintained such warm relations with most of them that the bulk of her fund raising was actually done among the poor households in the streets surrounding the school.

The regular requirement of most crèches and nursery schools (of which there were only fifty-five in the city in 1904) that children must bathe and/or wear a special uniform was quite correctly interpreted by mothers as a vote of no confidence in their standards of dress and cleanliness. Even Sylvia Pankhurst's wartime Norman Road Babies' House followed this convention. The chairman of the National Society of Day Nurseries was aware that "the usual bath upon admission" with its "implied neglect of cleanliness on the part of the parent" told against the crèches with the local mothers.[32]

Clothing the children was a way in which nursery staffs laid claim to them, muting their working-class identity, their existence as other people's daughters and sons. At McMillan's school, the children were given colorful tunic-style smocked uniforms, suggesting rural laborers of an earlier era. The teachers were always saddened, McMillan reported, at the end of each day when the children put on their own clothes and were transformed from gay wood folk into grubby slum children. McMillan was convinced, too, that the school's month-long summer holiday, when the children were out of her care so long, did their health and morale enormous harm. The workers at the Nine Elms guest house felt the same wrenching loss when their children returned to their homes on the streets surrounding the huge West Thames Gas Board Works. "The sad part for the Settlement workers," wrote one of them, "comes at the end, when the neat, pretty clothes are taken off and the babies dressed up again in their poor little Cinderella garments, minus, sometimes, so many tapes, buttons, and hooks and eyes, and always either much too warm or not half warm enough." The settlement workers did take pride in the fact that while they had charge of the children they got better care than when at home; the "open windows day and night, nightly baths, wholesome and regular meals, and a long sleep at night" left the children fitter and healthier, they were certain. One of the young guests was quoted in *The Vote,* the Women's Freedom League newspaper, proclaiming that the guest house, with its attractive toys and plentiful food, was "like Heaven."[33] This Nine Elms child was not the only slum youngster to be seduced by the sweetness of young settlement workers, school teachers, or hospital nurses whose offers of friendship were often accompanied by snowy linen and steaming cups of cocoa.[34]

The infant welfare years were thus, among other things, a battle for the love of little children and for the right to be called a good mother. Many of the women most caught up in this competition—McMillan, Anna Martin, Clara Grant—were, however, in public, determined and effective advocates for the poor mothers of the country.

Disenfranchised, sorely overworked, poorly educated, active in national politics only at widely separated points, the actual London mothers had almost no public voice during the years when they were constant objects of discussion, speculation, and policymaking. For the middle-class feminists who worked among them, women who did have links to major national political parties and organizations, giving the poor a voice with which to defend themselves against the "bad mother" charges was a solemn obligation and, as Bonnie Smith suggests, a central element in their feminism.[35]

During the late 1880s, when Annie Besant was an advocate for London working women, the motto of the newspaper she edited, *The Link*, was a quotation from Victor Hugo: "The people are silence. I will be the advocate of this silence. I will speak for the dumb. I will speak of the small to the great and of the feeble to the strong. . . . I will be the Word of the People."[36] Hugo's remarkable formulation really does mute the poor, whose silence is axiomatic here; any public murmurs they might utter are drowned out in the speaker's booming self-importance. The mothers' advocates of early-twentieth-century Britain not only listened and tried to reproduce the words of poor women, but also used other rhetorical gestures in their own writings with which to give them space. Though the authorial voice was surely the one that prevailed (the women themselves have to be classed as "informants," in the anthropologists' sense), the *mixture* of voices is quite new in turn-of-the-century writings, and so is the mixture of modes—the scientific ideas of the professional women about budgets and nutrition, the shopping and family and street stories of the mothers. The infant welfare movement not only involved coercing mothers, it also gave them new dignity and political importance. As Smith insists, women and ladies all over Europe were talking together in these years, often about newly politicized topics: birth control, husbands' violence or drinking, maternity provisions. Some pairs became friends, like Frances Orchard, who first applied to the COS in 1908 when she was thirty, married to a painter, and a mother of three children, and who grew old with her case workers, remaining in the active file through 1946.[37] In London, settlement workers or health visitors and their clients could be coworkers for women's suffrage; they marched together in the 1905 unemployment demonstrations; they could be found in some of the local Women's Cooperative Guild chapters.[38]

While many of the writings of the early-twentieth-century feminist generation take the stance of witnesses of working-class life, their gaze is warm and sympathetic, in comparison with the cool, critical appraisals of such earlier observers as Beatrice Potter and Helen Dendy. In *Round About a Pound a Week,* an account of a Fabian Women's Group project (from 1909 to 1913) with Lambeth mothers and infants living on subsistence incomes, the view is in fact from the *inside* of the working woman's house. In her account of the project, Maud Pember Reeves makes herself and her ladies at several points the outsiders intruding into the mothers' space: "A weekly caller becomes the abashed object of intense interest on the part of everybody in the street, from the curious glances of the greengrocer's lady at the corner to the appraising stare of the fat little baker who always manages to be on his doorstep across the road. And everywhere along the street is the visitor conscious of eyes which disappear from behind veiled windows."[39] The book's political statement is that the Lambeth women were indeed very good mothers: given their poor cooking facilities, overcrowded and decayed housing, large families, and small cash reserves, they were nothing less than national heroes. When outsiders criticized working-class wives for improvidence, for a penchant for fried or grilled foods over nutritious dishes like oatmeal, or for their efforts to get free school dinners for their children, it was simply because they did not know what it was like inside the working-class woman's world. Oatmeal, for example, Pember Reeves spelled out very carefully (for the "oatmeal question" was another hot issue between social workers and mothers), might be nutritious and cheap, but it is disgusting if you have to climb several flights of stairs to get water for washing the pot for cooking it and so skip that step; or if you lack fuel for the long cooking oatmeal requires; or if you cannot—as was usually the case—afford the milk and sugar that always appear on the breakfast tables of the rich. The proof that the women were good mothers was to be found in just such concrete investigations.

The Women's Cooperative Guild, an organization of working-class women with many middle-class leaders, was still more—and more self-consciously—determined to make poor women audible subjects in national debates, and its three now widely read collections on divorce (1911), maternity (1915), and the lives of poor women in general (1931) were the result. *Maternity: Letters from Working Women* was an attempt to intervene in formulating national policy on state provision of care for childbirth and infants by injecting into the discussions the actual experiences and opinions of the women in question, women whose views were solicited through a questionnaire circulated among Coop Guild members. This book was a part of the campaign that led to the passage of the 1918 Maternity and Child Welfare Act. The guild's testimony before the Royal Commission on Divorce in 1911 was also largely made up of a survey of the views of officers of the organization's many local chapters.[40]

Other feminist writings of this era show the same determination to speak for—and to let speak—working-class women's goodness as mothers: Emmeline Pethick's accounts of her life as a West London settlement worker years before she took up the suffrage cause; Margaret McMillan's pleas for school clinics, meals, and public nursery provision; the wartime work of Sylvia Pankhurst, who had perfected the old feminist propaganda technique of introducing delegations of live, speaking, working-class women, often in their everyday clothes, to members of the cabinet.[41]

Anna Martin, a suffragist and social worker with the Nonconformist Bermondsey Settlement in Rotherhithe from 1899 until her death in 1937, was a particularly passionate defender of London's working-class mothers, "the staunchest champion that working women ever had," her friend Emmeline Pethick-Lawrence wrote the year after her death. Martin was a prolific writer of articles and pamphlets, each one representing the views and interests of the Rotherhithe married women who were her special charge at the settlement. One of her very first pieces of writing is a short 1910 description of "The Women's Socials at Beatrice House," the women's branch of the settlement, in its annual report. These socials were not ordinary mothers' meetings, Martin insisted, whose usual purpose was to preach to women:

The members of Beatrice House lend no support to the present-day theory that the average workman's wife spends most of her spare time in the public-house, and can neither sew, cook, wash, nor bring up her baby. On the contrary, their hard self-sacrificing lives and amazing powers of endurance, are only equalled by the skill and ingenuity with which they contrive to keep their families, on about half the weekly sum per head found necessary in the Poor Law schools for each child's food and clothing.[42]

Martin's own political ideas are spirited amalgam of radical liberalism, feminism, and socialism. Her major rhetorical strategy is to fill her texts with Rotherhithe women speaking on the issues that concerned them: school lunches, drink, husbands' money, education for the handicapped, a rise in the legal school-leaving age. Martin was enraged, for example, in 1915 at local provisions in some English towns making pubs partly off-limits to women and wrote two articles in a prominent journal, *The Nineteenth Century and After,* "from the point of view of one whose knowledge of the subject [of women's drinking] comes from many years' close intercourse with poor working-women living in a London waterside district." The women were given space to defend themselves against constantly reiterated charges that mothers' drinking was a major cause of infant mortality. Within a few paragraphs, Martin was quoting at length from "Mrs. G.," who explained in half a page that by 11:00 A.M., after five hours of domestic work, she was ready for lunch and a glass of beer. The neighborhood standard of moderation, half a pint or a pint a day, Martin establishes by reproducing a discussion between three local women. Alcoholism, Martin concludes in her own more sociological voice, is overwhelmingly a male, not a female problem; drink is not what keeps women from rearing healthy children, but the fact that their husbands give them so little of their wages, while the state does nothing to intervene.[43]

Martin, as a mothers' advocate, was very critical of most of the policy generated by the infant welfare movement, posited as it was on the assumption that mothers would be better if scrutinized more closely and regulated more tightly. Her tirades against it stress the legislating role of a male-controlled state, which, with the consent of organized male workers, attempts to solve national problems of health and welfare by heaping ever more burdens on the backs of disenfranchised working-class women with few resources for defending themselves.

> In London and other large towns children are ordered up to the hospitals in droves to have their spectacles fitted, their teeth out, and their tonsils cut. . . . Grave legislators debate the material of which baby's nightwear should be composed, and endeavour to lay down the principles which should regulate its sleeping arrangements. Local authorities decide the hours at which Annie may earn twopence by cleaning steps or Johnnie add to the family income by lathering chins. School doctors take a hand in the administration of the family finances, and virtually decree that Mrs. Smith shall spend less on bread and boots and more on Adeline's adenoids.[44]

After a decade or so of work with Rotherhithe mothers, Martin had come to fuse her identity with theirs as few social workers could. Or, perhaps, having been adopted into a neighborhood accustomed to taking in wanderers, she was simultaneously taking on the conventional working-class child's "good mother" position.

Do psychic categories like good mother/bad mother make social structures like class irrelevant in assessing the relationship between philanthropists and recipients? I don't think so. First of all, I can see a great many ways in which motherhood in general was entwined with class divisions in the infant welfare movement years. On the broadest level, it is possible to view, in this period, the mother as an intensely powerful symbol of the working classes. It was, after all, mothers, or more precisely the way they created security inside poverty by binding their children tightly to them, who seemed to keep children in their working-class jobs and neighborhoods. Attributing either goodness or evil to mothers is not a statement of fact but a position; in the infant welfare era it was a political position as well. John Burns, a dockworker who rose in the world to wear politician's top hat, might praise his own mother, but Britain's working-class mothers in general were careless sluts, he did not tire of saying. Working-class male leaders like Thomas Bell or Will Crooks, who by their own lights, at least, stayed faithful to the labor movement, were not only true to their own mothers in their autobiographies of class ascent but to all the working-class mothers of Britain. A chapter or at least a paragraph honoring "mother," and sometimes motherhood in general, was obligatory in biographies and autobiographies of the generations of working-class males who became public figures in the twentieth century via trade unions or the Labour party.[45]

Two fascinating autobiographical statements by upwardly mobile young people, Kathleen Woodward's fictionalized *Jipping Street* and George Acorn's *One of the Multitude*, both revolve around bad mothers. Woodward's is the story of a girl yearning to get away from a cold, tough mother whom she admires but cannot love. Acorn's repetitive insistence on his right to leave his one-room dwelling (with its six children and sullen, violent parents) as a young working man in his twenties tells us, too, that only a bad mother gave one the right to leave home.[46] In the slightly loosening class structure of the first three decades of the twentieth century, "white weddings"—expensive and more elaborately ritualized than the quick, simple ceremonies earlier couples had chosen—became more popular among workers.[47] Were these dramatic ceremonies, marking the separation of the young couple from their parents, a way of letting young people leave even good mothers?

The good mother/bad mother dichotomy gave the infant welfare movement some of its characteristic political and administrative shape. The middle classes' sheer ignorance of life among the workers invited fantasies of drunken, superstitious crones among the legislators, medical officers, and journalists who dominated the debates of this era. Class barriers served up bad mothers of the working classes as obvious mirror images to the policymakers' own sentimentalized mothers. Accordingly, it was morally and psychologically possible to take the mean-spirited stance that dominated the legislation of this era aimed at mothers: far more resources, both public and private, were devoted to regulating, correcting, and policing working-class mothers than toward offering them food, clothing, medical services, housing, or cash. The Children Act of 1908 is, for example, an astonishing omnibus piece of legislation based on the proposition that parenting among the workers is just a step away from neglect; it criminalized a number of standard working-class childcare practices. School Care Committees and health visiting schemes put more energy and personnel into harassing mothers than into helping them get food and clothing for their children.

As for the women who carried out the more intimate work of the movement, visiting real mothers in their own homes, attending them at clinics, or caring for their children in crèches and classes, their own positions between good and bad mother must have been most complicated. Dreams of reconciliation with and reformation of bad mothers; fantasies of finding the perfect mother, a golden thread hidden in the coarse working-class weave; the illusion of supplanting the client mothers, becoming the nation's maternal ideal—all of these must have mingled with the more prosaic pleasure of finding decently paid professional jobs and sometimes helping prople.

NOTES

The research on which this paper is based was done with the help of the Shelby Cullom Davis Center for Historical Studies at Princeton University, of which I was a fellow in the spring of 1986; and Ramapo College, which granted me a sabbatical leave in 1985 as well as funds for research and travel in subsequent years. Though I did not follow all of the leads she offered, I also want to thank Elaine Showalter for her instructive comments on an earlier version of this paper offered at the Berkshire Conference of Women Historians in June 1987.

1   Clara Grant, *Farthing Bundles* (London: Fern Street Settlement, [1930], 72; Mrs. Humphrey Ward, *Marcella* (1894), reprint ed. (New York: Viking Penguin, 1985); Dame Katharine Furse (born 1875), *Hearts and Pomegranates. The Story of Fifty-Five Years 1875 to 1920* (London: Peter Davies, 1940), 156. The author was a daughter of the scholar John Addington Symonds. She worked at two different cos offices during the nineties, the first in Buckingham Road and obviously less interesting because of its West London location.

2   Melanie Klein, *Envy and Gratitude* (London: Tavistock, 1957). For a brief discussion of Klein and one author's readings of its implications for both private and public behavior, see Dorothy Dinnerstein, *The Mermaid and the Minotaur. Sexual Arrangements and Human Malaise* (New York: Harper Colophon Books, 1977), 95–100. A much fuller discussion of

Klein is Phyllis Grosskruth's *Melanie Klein. Her World and her Work* (Cambridge: Harvard University Press, 1987).

3   F. K. Prochaska, *Women and Philanthropy in Nineteenth-Century England* (Oxford: Clarendon Press, 1980); Jo Manton, *Mary Carpenter and the Children of the Streets* (London: Heinemann, 1976). Patricia Hollis, *Ladies Elect. Women in English Local Government 1865–1914* (Oxford: Clarendon Press, 1987), tells this story of women in local government in wonderful detail. On Lady Sandhurst's election to the LCC along with Jane Cobden, see 307–317; on Susan Lawrence, see 415.

4   G. F. McCleary, *The Early History of the Infant Welfare Movement* (London: H. K. Lewis, 1933), 35.

5   Deborah Dwork, *War is Good for Babies and Other Young Children. A History of the Infant and Child Welfare Movement in England 1898–1918* (London: Tavistock, 1987), 114.

6   Anna Davin, "Imperialism and Motherhood," *History Workshop* 5 (1978), 6–66; Carol Dyhouse, "Working-Class Mothers and Infant Mortality in England, 1895–1914," *Journal of Social History* 12 (1978), 248–267. Jane Lewis, *The Politics of Motherhood* (London: Hutchinson, 1982), deals with the same issues for the period between the wars. Nikolas Rose, *The Psychological Complex. Psychology, Politics and Society in England 1869–1939* (London: Routledge, 1985).

7   Quoted in Davin, "Imperialism and Motherhood," 15; see also Rose, *Psychological Complex*, Chapter 6; Bentley B. Gilbert. *The Evolution of National Insurance in Britain. The Origins of the Welfare State* (London: Michael Joseph, 1966), 81–101, and Dwork, *War is Good for Babies*, especially Chapters 1 and 2.

8   Davin, "Imperialism and Motherhood," 27.

9   Emilia Kanthack, *The Preservation of Infant Life. A Guide for Health Visitors* (London: H. K. Lewis, 1907). See Evelyn Bunting et al., *A School for Mothers* (London: Horace Marshall & Son, 1907), 38–39, for a proud account of a Marylebone clinic's success with a "rather 'low' working girl," a faithful clinic patient who tried to follow its instructions carefully, and was seen "sobbing over her baby's loss of weight."

10   Kanthack, *Preservaton*, 4; Helen M. Blagg, *Statistical Analysis of Infant Mortality and its Causes in the U.K.* (London: P. S. King, 1910), 15. S.B.A., "A School for Mothers," *Toynbee Record* (January 1908), 54.

11   The statement about first-time mothers is based on my unpublished study, "Transforming Motherhood," which cites patient records and the accounts of health workers. The Women's Cooperative Guild's members who contributed to its *Maternity* collection recount their trials in childbirth and difficulties in getting advice on sex and gestation, and see

the latter as functions of having moved away from their mothers and sisters, or of having lost them through death (Margaret Llewelyn Davies, ed., *Maternity. Letters from Working Women* [1915], reprint ed. [New York: W. W. Norton, 1978]).

12   Minutes of Children's Care Committees: St. Matthews (N.) School, January 28, 1916; and Popham Road school, April 22, 1910, both in Greater London Record Office (EO/WEL/2/vols. 17 and 6).

13   Rev. Henry Iselin, "The Story of a Children's Care Committee," *Economic Review* 22 (1912), 43; Anna Martin, *The Married Working Woman. A Study* (National Union of Women's Suffrage Societies, 1911), 31.

14   George Acorn (pseud.), *One of the Multitude. Autobiography of an Inhabitant of Bethnal Green* (London: William Heinemann, 1911), Chapter 5. The women seem to have absorbed relatively little of the official language of motherhood. Indeed, it is quite likely that mothers themselves of any class and time have had great difficulty fitting their own experiences into formal categories. Recent attempts to interview women who are in the process of mothering small children suggest the confused and contradictory ways in which the women try to mesh their hopes, pleasures, and worries with a language ill-suited to these purposes. See, for example, Helena Lopata, *Occupation Housewife* (New York: Oxford University Press, 1971); Mary Georgina Boulton, *On Being a Mother. A Study of Women with Pre-School Children* (London: Tavistock, 1983); Hilary Graham and Lorna McKee, *The First Months of Motherhood* (London: Health Education Council Monograph Series, No. 3, 1983); Andrea Boroff Eagon, *The Newly Born Mother: Stages of her Growth* (Boston: Little, Brown, 1985).

15   Janet Campbell, *Report on the Physical Welfare of Mothers and Children: England and Wales,* 4 vols. (Liverpool: Carnegie UK Trust, 1917), 2: 86–90.

16   An 1884 survey of London school managers found enormous variations in the committees' sexual composition. Women listing themselves as "ladies" were only 11 percent of the total in Southwark, but were almost half of the Marylebone members. My own crude calculations, based on constantly shifting membership lists of a few London committees in the 1900s and 1910s, suggest that the proportion of women (some of whom were teachers, settlement workers, and lay church workers; not all were full-time "ladies") had risen somewhat by then. The managers of the Curtain Road School, EC2, consisted of nine men and eight women in 1909; at the Wood Close School, E2, there were four women and only two men; the Bay Street School in Central Hackney had, in 1908, a committee of five men and two women (Greater London Record Office,

EO/WEL/2/vols. 2, 10, and 15). The 1884 survey of school managers is described in Peter Gordon's *The Victorian School Manager. A Study in the Management of Education 1800–1902* (London: Woburn Press, 1974), 161–164.

17   Elizabeth Wilson, *Women and the Welfare State* (London: Tavistock, 1977), 43.

18   I do not wish to imply here that parenthood automatically transforms the emotional lives of adults. Psychologist Jessica Benjamin has suggested that since the acquisition of symbolic though is the central achievement of early childhood, when people are thinking symbolically (that is, telling stories, or writing them) they do it *as children,* no matter what their age or status in relation to parenthood (Comment, Columbia University Seminar on Women and Society, January 21, 1987).

19   Martha Vicinus, *Independent Women: Work and Community for Single Women, 1850–1920* (Chicago: University of Chicago Press, 1985), 195, 43–44.

20   On the Biblewomen, see *The Missing Link* and its successor journals, the newsletters of Ellen Ranyard's Bible and Domestic Female Mission. For a description of a group of nurses temporarily adopting two motherless babies in succession, see Edith E. G. May, *True Tales of a District* (London: W. Knott, 1908).

21   *The Sanitary Officer* (August 1909) 51; June 1910, 253; see also October 1909, 95.

22   Margaret McMillan, *Infant Mortality* (London: Independent Labour Party, n.d. [1907?]), 14.

23   Women's Labour League of Central London, *The Needs of Little Children. Report of a Conference on the Care of Babies and Young Children* (London, 1912), 22; C. W. Saleeby, *Woman and Womanhood* (New York: Mitchell Kennedy, 1911), 164; quoted in Davin, "Imperialism and Motherhood," 51.

24   Vicinus, *Independent Women*, 226; E. Sylvia Pankhurst, *The Home Front. A Mirror to Life in England during the World War* (London: Hutchinson, 1932), 25, 46, 252. *The Sanitary Officer* (October 1909), 97. See also Margaret Loane, *From Their Point of View* (London: Edward Arnold, 1908), 128.

25   Mary Stocks, *My Commonplace Book* (London: Peter Davies, 1970), 58.

26   *Report of the Proceedings of the National Conference on Infantile Mortality* (London: P. S. King, 1908), 69.

27   Bunting, *School for Mothers*, 6 and passim; Maud Pember Reeves, *Round About a Pound a Week* (1913), reprint ed. (London: Virago, 1979), Chapter 13; [Florence] Petty et al., *The Pudding Lady. A New Departure in Social Work* (London: Stead's Publishing House, [1910]), 2.

28   Honnor Morten and H. F. Gethen, *Tales of the Children's Ward* (London: Sampson Low, 1894); Muriel Wragge, "News of the Woolwich Mission Kindergarten," *Child Life* 10 (1901), 100.

29   Nanette Whitbread, *The Evolution of the Nursery-Infant School* (London: Routledge, 1972), 66, Table 3; 68, Table 4; David Rubinstein, *School Attendance in London 1870–1904: A Social History* (Hull: University of Hull Occasional Papers in Social and Economic History, No. 1 [1969]), 11.

30   *The Vote*, August 4, 1916, 1127.

31   Margaret McMillan, "Guy and the Stars" in *The Nursery School* (London: Dent, 1919); see also 185 of this same work.

32   Anna Davin, *Little Women. Nineteenth-Century Girlhood in London*, Chapter 8 (London: Routledge, forthcoming); F. S. Toogood, M.D., "The Role of the Creche or Day Nursery," in *Infancy*, ed. Theophilus N. Kelynack (London: Robert Culley, 1910), 84.

33   McMillan, *Nursery School*, Chapter 6 and 286–287; *The Vote*, August 4, 1916, 1127.

34   See, among many such accounts, Alice Linton, whose *Not Expecting Miracles* (London: Centerprise, 1982) includes an account of a long stay at Great Ormond Street Children's Hospital where she got much finer food and bedding than she had at home, but was also befriended by some sweet nurses, one of whom even took her out to see a Christmas pantomine. Also see Acorn, *One of the Multitude*, for the story of a Bethnal Green schoolboy's encounters with a teacher living at Toynbee Hall.

35   Bonnie Smith, "Writing Women's Work," unpublished paper, University of Rochester, June 1987.

36   Quoted in Annie Besant, *An Autobiography* (Philadelphia: Henry Artemus, n.d. [1893]), 331.

37   Smith, "Writing Women's Work." Frances Orchard is a fictionalized name for a cos case from St. Pancras North (A/FWA/TH/B2/2, Family Welfare Association Papers, Greater London Record Office; used with kind permission of the fwa).

38   The unemployment agitation, centered in East London but involving other districts too, was directed against the newly passed and extremely ineffectual Unemployed Workmen Act. There were separate women's meetings and marches as well as mass events during the months of October and November 1905. Clara Grant was extremely active in these events, along with Dora Montefiore, Charlotte Despard, and several other settlement house women and women local government officials. (Chronicled in the *East London Observer*, the *Daily News*, *Justice*, and the *Daily Chronicle*.)

39   Pember Reeves, *Round About a Pound*, 4; see also (on 16) the author's very empathic grasp of the housewives' discomfort in her presence.

40   Margaret Llewelyn Davies, *Maternity, Letters from Working Women* (1915); reprint ed. (New York: W. W. Norton, 1978); Women's Cooperative Guild, *Working Women and Divorce* (London: David Nutt, 1911). This has been reprinted recently by Garland Publishing Company (New York, 1980).

41   Emmeline Pethick-Lawrence, *My Part in a Changing World* (London: Victor Golancz, 1938), Chapters 6 and 7. In the agitation around the Mines Regulation Amendment Act of 1887 outlawing women's pit head work in mines, and regulating also the weight of the hammers used by women nailmakers and chainmakers, Louisa, Lady Goldsmid and Millicent Fawcett sponsored a deputation of Cradley Heath chainmakers to the Home Secretary (see Ray Strachey, *"The Cause."A Short History of the Women's Movement in Great Britain* [1928], reprint ed. [Port Washington, N.Y.: Kennikat Press, 1969], 236–237.

42   Pethick-Lawrence, *Changing World*, 346; Bermondsey Settlement, *Eighteenth Annual Report* (1910), 14, Southwark Local History Library.

43   Anna Martin, "Working Women and Drink," Part 1, *The Nineteenth Century and After* 78 (1915), 1378–1379.

44   Anna Martin, "The Mother and Social Reform," *The Nineteenth Century and After* 73 (1913), 1061–1062.

45   Thomas Bell was a founder of the Communist party of Great Britain. His autobiography, recounting his childhood in Glasgow, is *Pioneering Days* (London: Lawrence & Wishart, 1941). George Haw, *From Workhouse to Westminister. The Life Story of Will Crooks, M.P.* (London: Cassell, 1911).

46   Kathleen Woodward, *Jipping Street. Childhood in a London Slum* (London: Harper, 1928); Acorn, *One of the Multitude.*

47   John Gillis, *For Better, For Worse, British Marriages, 1600 to the Present* (New York: Oxford University Press, 1985), Chapter 10.

ABOUT THE AUTHORS

KATHLEEN D. MCCARTHY received her Ph.D. from the University of Chicago, after which she worked as a Visiting Research Fellow with the Rockefeller Foundation, and at the National Endowment for the Humanities and the Metropolitan Life Foundation. In 1986, she became the Director of the Center for the Study of Philanthropy at the Graduate School of the City University of New York, where she is also an Associate Professor of History. She is the author of *Noblesse Oblige: Charity and Cultural Philanthropy in Chicago, 1849–1929*, and many articles on local, national, and international philanthropy. Dr. McCarthy is currently completing a book on women and American cultural philanthropy.

ANNE FIROR SCOTT holds degrees from Northwestern University and Harvard. After completing her graduate studies, Dr. Scott worked for the League of Women Voters before returning to academia in 1958. She has taught at Haverford College, the University of North Carolina, Stanford University, the University of Washington, Johns Hopkins, Harvard University, and Duke University, where she currently holds the W. K. Boyd Chair in History. Her books include *The Southern Lady* (1970), *One Half the People* (with Andrew M. Scott, 1975), and *Making the Invisible Woman Visible* (1984). She is presently finishing a book on women's voluntary associations and their part in shaping American society.

NANCY A. HEWITT received her degrees from Smith College and the University of Pennsylvania. She is an Associate Professor of History at the University of South Florida in Tampa, and is the author of *Women's Activism and Social Change* (1984) and editor of *Women, Families, and Communities: Readings in American History* (1989). She is currently completing a study of women, work, and politics among Tampa's Latin, Black, and Anglo women in the years 1885 to 1945. Dr. Hewitt is also American Editor for *Gender & History*, published by Basil Blackwell, Ltd.

199

DARLENE CLARK HINE received her Ph.D. from Kent State University and has served on the faculties of South Carolina State College, Purdue University, and was Visiting Distinguished Professor of History at Arizona State University in Tempe. Dr. Hine is presently John Hannah Professor of History at Michigan State University. She is the author of numerous books and articles including *Black Victory: The Rise and Fall of the White Primary in Texas* and *Black Women in White: Racial Conflict and Cooperation in the Nursing Profession, 1890–1950*, and is coeditor of *Eyes On The Prize, History of the Civil Rights Era, A Reader*, published by Viking Press.

KATHRYN KISH SKLAR holds degrees from Radcliffe College and the University of Michigan. She has served on the faculties of the University of Michigan, as well as UCLA, and the State University of New York, Binghamton, where she is presently Distinguished Professor. Dr. Sklar is the author and editor of numerous articles and books including *Catharine Beecher, A Study in American Domesticity*, which won the Berkshire Prize and was nominated for a National Book Award. She has received many major fellowships and grants, including a Guggenheim Fellowship, and has lectured widely in the United States and Europe. Dr. Sklar is presently completing two new books, *Doing the Nation's Work: Florence Kelley and Women's Political Culture, 1830–1930*, and *The Political History of American Women, 1607–1987*.

EDITH COUTURIER received her doctorate from Columbia University and is currently an administrator in the Division of Fellowships and Seminars at the National Endowment for the Humanities. She has published articles in the *Hispanic American Historical Review*, the *Journal of Family History*, and *Americas*. Dr. Couturier is currently completing a book entitled *Philanthropy, Women and Patronage in New Spain: 1600–1810*.

BRENDA MEEHAN-WATERS earned her Ph.D. from the University of Rochester, where she is Professor of History. Dr. Meehan-Waters has held numerous national appointments including Senior Fellow at the Kennan Institute for Advanced Russian Studies at the Wilson Center, and two International Research and Exchange Board Fellowships for research in the Soviet Union. She is the author of *Autocracy and Aris-*

tocracy: The Russian Service Elite of 1730, as well as many articles on Russian history. She currently holds a National Humanities Center Fellowship.

ALISA KLAUS received her B.A. from Yale University and her Ph.D. from the University of Pennsylvania. She has taught at Fort Lewis College in Colorado and is currently Visiting Assistant Professor at the University of California, Santa Cruz. She is the author of the forthcoming book, *Every Child a Lion: The Origins of Infant Health Policy in the United States and France, 1890–1920*.

ELLEN ROSS holds degrees from Columbia University and the University of Chicago. She is presently Associate Professor at Ramapo College in New Jersey. Dr. Ross lectures widely and is the author of *Queen of the Earth: Wives and Mothers in Working Class London, 1870–1918*. She is currently completing her forthcoming book, *Women's Social Explorers in Darkest London*.